We Ate All the Pies

How football swallowed Britain whole

John Nicholson

biteback ˇˇ
ˆˆˆ
SPORT

First published in Great Britain in 2010 by
Biteback Publishing Ltd
Heal House
375 Kennington Lane
London
SE11 5QY

ISBN 978-1-84954-067-4

10 9 8 7 6 5 4 3 2 1

A CIP catalogue record for this book is available from the British Library.

Set in Georgia and Bell Gothic
Printed and bound in Great Britain by CPI Cox & Wyman, Reading, RG1 8EX

We are grateful for permission to reproduce lyrics from the following songs:
'Jackson Kent Blues'
Words and music by Steve Miller; pub. des. ... administered by
P&P Songs Limited
'Gangrene'
Words and music by Todd Rundgren ... © Warner-Chappell ... merline
Publishing Corp. (BMI), Rodger Powell pub. des. (BMI), John Wilcox pub. des.
(BMI), Kasim Sulton pub. des, (BMI) ... all rights
administered by Warner Chappell North America Ltd

Contents

Acknowledgements

Thanks to Winty, Nick, Pete and Tim at Football365 for all their help and support over the years.

Cheers to Robert for the pie memories and to Kev for all the Teesside recollections and for over 30 years of rock 'n' roll.

Thanks also to Andy for info on Scottish drinking – a matter close to all our hearts – and to Alan for his encouragement throughout this project.

Finally, thanks to Humf for his help in getting this off the ground and to Dawn for telling me to bloody well get on with it and make us some money.

Introduction

IT was 30 July 1966 when, as a five-year-old boy, I realised the power of football for the first time. England were in the process of winning the Jules Rimet Trophy live on our 12-inch black-and-white television but outside our house in Hull, our next-door neighbours, the Coates, were cutting their grass, and ignoring Bobby Moore's triumph.

My mother peered out and tutted, 'Look at them, doing that, on a day like this. There's something wrong with them.'

Dad nodded sagely. 'It's unpatriotic if you ask me, cutting your grass while England's playing in a World Cup Final,' he said, peering over his glasses at the action out on their front lawn.

'You're right, Eric,' she said, unusually agreeing with him. 'It wouldn't surprise me if they were German, on the quiet.'

'Aye, probably changed his accent or something,' said Dad, his paranoia increasing, 'or he might be Scottish!!'

Mam frowned and wagged her finger at me. 'Don't you go speaking to them, our John. We don't want you talking to people like that. Isn't that right, Eric?'

'Aye. You never know with people like that, could be up to all sorts,' said Dad, ominously, as Nobby Stiles kicked Wolfgang Overath, maybe as revenge for the Luftwaffe bombing his chippy.

Previously, these neighbours had been blameless in my parents eyes, certainly not regarded as odd, possible enemies of the state, Germans or, worse still, Scottish, but because they were not in the least bit interested in watching England playing football, they were now some kind of outlaws.

Even at the time I thought this was a bit odd. You don't *have* to like football. Not wanting to watch England kick a ball around doesn't mean you want to assassinate the Queen, establish a fourth Reich or even wear a kilt.

But football is not a normal sport, it is a cultural phenomenon around which all manner of attitudes, beliefs, hopes and desires are wrapped and, even as a boy, as I witnessed it being used by my parents as a stick to beat the neighbours with, I realised it was something very special and it began to affect me from that day onwards.

Football. Football. Football. You love football. I love football. The world loves football. Why the hell are we all so obsessed with football?

When you stop to think about it, it's astonishing how much it preoccupies so many millions of us virtually every day of our lives. It's not a recent, media-driven phenomenon, it's always been like this. Huge crowds of people have watched the game since its inception over 140 years ago.

It can't just be twenty-two people with varying degrees of talent kicking a ball around a rectangle of grass that makes it so compelling. It must be something else; something that pulls us in and holds us captivated.

So what is this football dark matter? That's what *We Ate All the Pies* is all about. I wanted to know how and why football has managed to consume my life so completely and why it's done the same thing for millions of people for over a century.

Along with rock 'n' roll, it was the enduring, profound influence in my formative years.

It's been a major part of, not just my life, but of me. It made me who I am.

Football isn't just the game on the pitch; while that is at the core of it, there is a huge cultural vortex that swirls around those ninety minutes. For me, and I'm sure for many people, the various cultural activities that surround the game, like planets orbiting a sun, are every bit as enjoyable as the on-pitch action, often much more so.

It's easy to forget just how huge football is in the UK. Go anywhere in Britain and you'll find a football team. Put a very big duffle coat on and go right up in the north of Scotland; there you'll find Wick Academy who are the most northerly football club in the

UK, located on a latitude line north of Moscow and stuck right on the Caithness peninsula. And this is no modern dalliance; it was formed in 1893 and currently plays in the Highland League, a collection of clubs based in wonderful, remote, small towns north of the Grampians.

Then fly over 890 miles south to the other end of the land to Mousehole FC (pronounced Mowzle), a tiny club south of Penzance in the deep south west who play at Trungle Parc and compete in the South West Peninsula League. It's at the bottom of the football league pyramid but they don't just have a first team but a reserve team as well!

Go anywhere in the UK and you'll find a football ground of one size or another; from Tow Law on the bleakest, windswept moors of County Durham to bucolic Newport on the Isle of Wight. At times it's almost invisible because we take a set of goals, a pitch and some sort of stand so for granted.

The amount of clubs that form the complete English football pyramid alone is enormous for a relatively small country. After the four top leagues there are another seven steps from the Blue Square Premier League right down to local leagues such as the Northern Alliance League or the West Sussex Football League.

There are a total of ninety-one different leagues and 1,600 different clubs and all of them are in theory capable of rising to the Premier League via promotion. Who knows, maybe Stobswood Welfare from the Northern Alliance second division could, in a mere twelve or thirteen years, winning their league each year, be playing Chelsea in the Premier League, if Chelsea and the Premier League still exist in twelve or thirteen years, which is by no means certain.

Add to that the leagues in Scotland, Wales and Northern Ireland and it's surprising there's room for anything else in the UK except football pitches.

But it's not just the actual playing of football that comprises the culture of the game; there are just so many football-related activities in this country that are important in moulding and shaping our lives. Whether it's a pint and pie before a game, whether it's slobbing out on the sofa watching six hours of games and punditry or whether it's collecting memorabilia and buying shirts, it's all a massive part of the football fan's life.

Then there's going to the games. Millions do it every week at all levels of the game. Football is so popular in England that the Championship – the second tier – is the fourth best attended in Europe. Overall attendance figures are only a few million less than in the peak post-war years, when football was virtually the only affordable working-class entertainment and there was no health and safety legislation stopping you cramming 83,000 people into creaking old wooden stands designed to hold no more than 40,000. Having your internal organs crushed on an iron crash barrier was a rite of passage back then.

On top of the high, high attendance figures are the millions watching on TV too. Indeed, the highest viewed programme in the history of British television isn't, as you might assume, an episode of *EastEnders* or *Coronation Street*, not a Morecambe and Wise Christmas special or the relentlessly mawkish coverage of Diana's funeral. No, it is the 1966 World Cup Final. Some 32.3 million people watched that on just 15 million TV sets. Sixth on that list is the Chelsea vs Leeds 1970 FA Cup replay at 28.49 million. By God, we like watching football on TV in this country.

The game is so endemic in our lives that we probably don't even realise it most of the time. For example, if you're a serious football fan, the chances are that whatever the time of day it is when you read this, you have already thought quite a bit about football, especially if your club has got a game in the next day or two.

You may well have checked your club's website, looked at TV listings for tonight's games, read match reviews, interviews or predictions in a newspaper or on the internet. Maybe you've played a football game on your computer games console or perhaps you've tweaked your fantasy football team or picked up a football magazine at the station for the train journey into work or maybe you've filled in your pools coupon. You may have posted a comment on a football-based blog or message board or are about to play for your local pub team or just have a kick-around in the park. And all of this before you even meet your mates at work or down the pub and spend several hours agreeing, arguing and laughing about all manner of football matters.

How do I know this? Don't worry, it's not because I'm following you around, it's just because we all do it. All football fans concern themselves with some aspect of the culture of football practically every day of their lives, and not just briefly. It is the very fabric of our existence, the framework around which we build each new day. And all because of that ninety-minute game between twenty-two men in polyester clothing.

Go anywhere in the world and someone will be kicking a ball around. From the rubbish heaps of Rio to the back gardens of people called Dave from Billingham, there'll be people hoofing something spherical and inflated, be it a ball, a small fat child or one of those hamsters the herdsmen of the Mongolian steppes make air-tight, put a hot stone inside, inflate and cook from the inside out. They make a great, edible football.

And where someone is kicking a ball around several more people will be talking about it being kicked around, because football is massive not just due to its high participation levels but because many more people love to talk about it, think about it, name their children after its players and tattoo strikers' names across their shoulders.

This phenomenon has always fascinated me, so in *We Ate All the Pies* I'll look at what we love, why we love it and how it makes us who we are through my own experience of football over the past forty-eight years. I'll try to pick it all apart and see how we got to where we are today and why the game endures as Britain's big love.

There are plenty of doom-mongers out there who will tell you the game is going to hell in a handcart, though how you get a game into a handcart and what the hell a handcart is anyway is never fully explained. Why are they reserved purely for taking things into hell? Does nobody do anything positive involving a handcart?

You'll also hear people say the exact same thing about rock music too, of course. As Pete Townshend said, 'Rock is dead, they say; long live rock.'

However, in a simple twist of fate, moaning about what is wrong with football and rock 'n' roll is one of the most popular things about football and rock 'n' roll.

So what are my qualifications for undertaking this marathon task of delving under the bedclothes of football? Well, for ten years I've been writing about the game for the sprawling, off-beat, influential and hugely popular website Football365.com.

My column has a by-line, 'A Very Northern Mind'. This isn't because I write about northern football, but because it was thought I brought a northern sensibility or, perhaps more accurately, insanity to proceedings.

I was born in Hull, grew up on Teesside, went to college in Newcastle and now live in Edinburgh, apparently getting further north as I progress through life. I have been a Middlesbrough fan since 1970. I am happy to be a northerner. I love the north: the timbre of its vowels, the feel of its weather, its epic how-do-you-like-me-now nature; its gritty industrial grandeur and its wild Viking and Celtic heart with an admirable dedication to intoxication. I feel it in my bones, in my water.

I had to leave Teesside to fully appreciate it and my love affair with the place has always been conducted from a distance. When I was growing up there, it was impossible to get a perspective on the region. These days it seems a lot clearer.

Stand on a cold February afternoon on South Gare, a spit of land that juts out into the Tees, guarding the entrance to the river with the multi-coloured lights of Teesside's fading steel works and chemical industries twinkling like fireworks in the distance, as dark rain clouds gather in a cold sky like billows of ink in clear water. It is a unique, potent mixture of raw industry and raw nature; brilliantly contrived and brilliantly natural all at once; innate and man-made power side by side.

That is my Teesside: mythic, epic, rough-hewn, challenging and frankly, a bit pissed, and you will come across all sorts of references to people and places in the north east of England in this excursion into the belly of British football because it's what I feel and know best. It's also where I ventured out into the world with an armful of albums and an armoury of cheap guitars.

I've always seen a connection between football and rock music; they plug into the same socket in my psyche. Both are at their best when uninhibited, wild and intense. The best gigs and football matches are not far apart as an experience. From my first concerts in the mid-1970s at places such as Middlesbrough Town Hall and Newcastle City Hall, seeing the likes of Alex Harvey, Uriah Heep, Hawkwind and Bad Company, the whole experience and culture got right into my DNA.

My parents had brought home Beatles, Searchers, Gerry and the Pacemakers and Dusty Springfield records when I was small and putting eight singles at a time on our Dansette record player had always been an important part of growing up.

The first record I bought with my own money was The Kinks' 'Supersonic Rocketship', which was luckily quite a cool choice. At the time I had no idea how significant a decision that was to be in later life, when buying a good first record showed you were cool from an early age. I mean, you couldn't respect someone whose first record was something such as 'Granddad' by Clive Dunn now, could you?

I followed it up with 'Run Run Run' by Jo Jo Gunne, a fantastic record by Jay Ferguson's now long-forgotten band. I played those two singles and their respective B-sides over and over along with my parents' early Beatles records, which they'd bought and loved 'before they went all weird'.

Albums, on the other hand, were expensive for us nippers so we only got them for Christmas or if we'd had a serious disease and had only just avoided an early death. My first Christmas album was *The Best of Status Quo*, an early compilation on Pye of their 1970–72 period before they became the massive denim-and-hair band of the mid-1970s.

I loved the riffs on that. I followed it up the birthday after with Wings' *Band on the Run*, which I considered a record of much sophistication and it's one which has certainly stood the test of time. But it was the Christmas of 1973 which delivered a hugely important album into my juvenile synapses. *Meddle* by Pink Floyd. If you're familiar with the album, the first side is songs – and some crackers too – and the second side is 'Echoes', a twenty-minute sonic epic full of great riffs, enigmatic lyrics and all sorts of weird sections of noise.

It blew my mind.

That record altered me. I can remember how it felt. There was a pre-*Meddle* Johnny and a post-*Meddle* Johnny. It exponentially expanded everything I thought music could be. I would sit and listen to 'Echoes' in the dark wearing a massive pair of padded headphones – the kind which are ironically rather fashionable again – the volume up to distortion point. It took me away from Stockton-on-Tees, took me to another place in my mind, and I liked where that was. I also learned aged just twelve that it was a place you could go to in your head at any time in a state of meditation or contemplation.

Later, when I experimented heavily with psychotropic drugs, it was to this familiar place that they took me; my own corner of the universal mind, a place behind the sun, just a step beyond the rain. Which is just as well, really, as it rains an awful lot in the north east of England.

But it didn't stop there because in a perfect synergy, *Meddle* also connected to my football world. On the first side is a track called 'Fearless', which concludes with a recording of a football crowd, allegedly Liverpool's Kop, singing 'You'll Never Walk Alone'. This might not sound much today, but at the time, the blend of progressive rock and football was a thrilling juxtaposition and proved to me that the two things need not inhabit separate universes.

By the time I was sixteen, I had an album collection approaching 500; by the time I was twenty it was nearer 2,000. It's now over 8,000 in total across all formats. I ate up rock music in all its forms and deviations. Even at a young age – around thirteen or so – I was mad about jazz-rock. I'm not sure if Mam was putting drugs in my baked beans but the first album I bought with my own money was *The Inner Mounting Flame* by the Mahavishnu Orchestra.

I was just a kid but I found the music just breathtaking; high-speed, frenetic and overdriven guitar in a complex stew of rhythms, electronic keyboards and violin. I should have been listening to pop music but somehow jazz-rock had captured my pre-pubescent soul. However, as soon as puberty kicked in I embraced the heavy rock trinity of Zeppelin, Purple and Sabbath to better soothe my newly lustful psyche. Massive riffs and male puberty form a perfect match now as then, and it was inevitable that I'd end up as an axe victim.

My first example of what Ian Hunter called a six-string razor was made by a company called Satellite. This may have been because it was constructed out of space debris. It was sixty quid in the mid-1970s, which was a bloody fortune, and a bloody fortune for a piece of crap, as it turned out.

It wouldn't stay in tune, the action made your fingers bleed and the jack socket malfunctioned, making it cut in and out all the time. But it was a guitar and I learned G, C and D and thus could play the blues, albeit a mutant messy form of blues. A love affair was formed right away and I would never be without a guitar again: playing on my own, playing in bands or just recording stuff for my own pleasure, it's been a crucial part of life ever since and not a day goes by without my picking up my old Fender Squire and cranking out a riff or lick or two. As I write it sits six feet from me, plugged into a Marshall and waiting for me to finger it lovingly once more. It remains an irresistible mistress.

As a kid I was completely, totally, utterly obsessed with rock music. It occupied every waking hour that wasn't committed to school. I crammed up on it, reading the *NME Book of Rock* cover to cover and back again, memorising the discography of bands I loved and others I had never heard yet but liked the sound of, such as Irish proggers Fruupp or blues-rock innovators The Electric Flag. I knew the evolution of line-ups of bands, where they were from, what were their best-regarded albums, what label they were on and the year of their release.

In exactly the same way, I was utterly obsessed with football and would read the *Rothmans Football Annual* from cover to cover, learning all the clubs' colours, grounds, along with players, FA Cup winners and any other fact I could cram into my brain. It all seemed to go in and stick. I was the only kid in my class who knew that Exeter City played at St James Park or that Workington Town's best league finish was fifth in the Third Division in the 1965–66 season or that Barnsley won the FA Cup in 1912.

I had no reason to know these facts, I just enjoyed knowing them in the same way I enjoyed knowing that Jimmy Page did session work on Tom Jones records and that David Coverdale came from Saltburn.

I watched all the football I could on TV, which wasn't much. I devoured all football and rock literature I could, be it comics or books or magazines. I went to see Middlesbrough play from 1972 onwards, addicted to the match-day experience.

I wasn't to know it at the time but all of us born in the 1950s/early 1960s are lucky people. We saw England win the World Cup, and we witnessed the golden days of working-class football in the 1960s and 1970s, an era of outrageous skill and outrageous aggression, when players were still part of the community, not separated from us by the tinted windows of wealth.

We grew up when football was more tribal, more about your local culture and your local club. It wasn't an arm of the entertainment industry and we were not customers making a 'leisure activity' purchase. It was our art, our culture, our civic pride. This lasted till the mid-1980s in the top division and indeed still pervades the lower echelons. However, the increase of hideous violence inside and around the game, the playing out of one tragedy after another, and the steady but relentless commercialisation of the game changed things. We set off down the road to where we are today: a world of millionaire players and billionaire owners.

Unlike many of my generation, I don't wring my hands too much about this. Change is inevitable. We have all changed in the last forty years, we live differently now and want different things out of life, so it's no surprise that football should also have changed. Its flexibility and adaptability to society's needs is the reason it remains on top of the sporting tree. It is a social and emotional landscape as much if not more than a purely sporting one.

It's also undoubtedly the case that the footballers of today live like the rock stars of the 1970s. Only without the badly conditioned hair, high-end narcotics and twelve-hour bus rides across the Midwest to play Peoria, Illinois. But they have the groupies, the outrageous wealth, the adulation and the unpleasant diseases from the girl in the Marriott hotel.

In many ways we have the best of all worlds today. We have the Premier League with its comedy cavalcade of money, mercenaries and the marvellously talented. It bears little relation to the game I grew up with, but as long as you accept it for what it is, it can be tremendous entertainment. The old school game that we grew up with still exists in the lower leagues and in the Conference, where it is still an unpretentious local game, played for local people, often by local people.

Issues about the distribution of money from top to bottom still need addressing and wages remain seriously out of whack with income, but football persists, it is resilient and as the figures prove, still massively popular.

Personally, I've given up worrying about the effect the Premier League has on the game as a whole, preferring to see it as an amusing soap opera to be enjoyed rather than bemoaning the latest billionaire takeover or 30 million quid transfer. It will probably implode at some point but it won't kill football because the people love football too much and will always want to watch and play it. Even if clubs go bust, they will be resurrected, start again and work from the bottom up. It's inevitable. Football is a Terminator that you cannot defeat.

It's the same with rock 'n' roll. We sixties kids grew up with rock music as it grew up itself. In perhaps ten short years from 1965 to 1975 the vast majority of the best rock 'n' roll was recorded. It was a thick seam of gold that was mined in such a short space of time. We took it for granted, thinking that this was always how it would be. But we were wrong. They were halcyon days of utter originality.

Periodically someone comes along and thinks they'll sweep away the old guard, make the past redundant. But rock, just like football, is a resilient beast and refuses to leave the stage just because some people think it's briefly no longer fashionable.

We rock 'n' roll acolytes are in it for the long haul. We don't care if you think the bands we like are now uncool, cool, fashionable or cringe-worthy. We really don't. It's our art and it will prevail.

Oddly for a football obsessive, I'm not really very competitive and I simply don't care what other supporters think of my club. People occasionally think they can write in to Football365 and insult the Boro, calling them rubbish or boring or whatever, but it's water off a duck's back to me – I keep a duck handy for just such occasions. I've never understood why people care so much what other anonymous people think or say about their team but, as you'll learn, I'm not a normal football obsessive.

It was the same over music at school when punk arrived. Kids newly adorned in punk clothing – often little more than a pair of black drain-pipe jeans and an old T-shirt with a safety pin – would deride us long-haired, cheesecloth-and-denim hordes, as though their disapproval would change how we felt.

Well, I suppose for some it did, but for me, I just thought, in my non-competitive way, just because you now hate Steely Dan, it doesn't alter the fact I think they are musical and lyrical geniuses – why would it? I'm not you. It also seemed to me that kids would like a band for a few months then go off them and take up with a new obsession. I wasn't like that. I've never stopped liking a band once I get into it. I don't love *Meddle* any less now than I did at Christmas 1973. Maybe that's really conservative, narrow or just consistent, I don't know. But it makes total sense to me.

In the twenty-first century football is a less visceral but safer place. We have lost the intense atmosphere that games could have in the 1970s, trading it in favour of not getting our head kicked in. Well so be it. I have no hatred for other clubs or countries and their fans – so much so that someone once said I was a football hippy – and along the way in this book, I hope to illustrate why this is. I've certainly watched a lot of football while stoned and occasionally while wearing tie-dyed T-shirts, not to mention purple loon pants. No one should mention purple loon pants, except in a blackmail letter.

Football acts as a pressure valve for society, allowing people to release tension and transfer negativity from their everyday lives on to footballers, managers and just about anything else inside a football ground. It's a place to feel part of something and a place to get away from everything. Football facilitates all manner of emotional responses and needs, which is another reason why it's so hugely popular. It's a big-tent philosophy. It fills up our lives and, some would say, keeps us down; it's an opiate for the masses. There's no time for revolution when you're worried about relegation and your striker has ruptured something.

Like the fickle music fans who flit from band to band, for some football is a passing interest that they pay attention to only when the big games roll around; to others it is a fundamentalist religion to observe which they worship several times a day via a series of rituals, incantations and superstitious practices.

There are newspapers and Teletext, a service which seems to exist only for footballers and their managers, the rest of us having got on board with computers fifteen years ago. There are websites to be read each day for news about your club. There are fellow travellers on the football road to commune with, preferably over some alcohol, and there are memories to wallow in and future glories to hope for. Then there's the mocking of other teams, players and fans and the humiliation of defeat to be assuaged and all of this in just one waking day. It's a wonder any work gets done at all when there's so much football to fret over.

Football is a universal language. It's oddly easy to communicate with anyone no matter what language they speak when there's some football to watch. You can get into a fight or make a friend within a few minutes of watching football, be it on the terraces or on a TV in a bar anywhere in the world. More usually it is a unifying thing, bringing people from vastly different cultures together in their love of football, be it at a game or in a bar.

It's the same with rock 'n' roll too. I once walked into a diner on California's Pacific Coast Highway, ordered coffee and eggs and sat back to look out across the infinite blue Pacific Ocean. Mist swirled in and out and around this little wooden shack near Big Sur and it felt like I was somewhere just west of heaven when this guy walked in. He's a hundred foot tall and wide and covered in hair and tattoos. This was before tattoos were fashionable and they were sported only by sailors and Hell's Angels and the mentally insane. This guy looked like he was all three.

He sat down opposite me. The chair creaked under his vast bulk. He looked like a bear that had recently stolen a Hells Angel's clothes. He grunted. It *was* a bear, I thought, maybe it's Big Foot! He grunted again and then pointed at me. I looked down. I had on a Jimi Hendrix T-shirt. The bear slowly appeared to smile from behind a beard.

'Cool. Very cool,' he said in a rich voice. If a redwood could talk, it would have talked like this guy.

So we got talking about Hendrix and other great guitarists. He'd seen Jimi in 1969 and was a big fan of British musicians such as Peter Green, Clapton and Jeff Beck. We didn't talk about anything else. Just rock music. Then we shook hands and went our separate ways, never to meet again. Without that connection, that would never have happened.

Later that month, I was in a bar drinking – a bit of a theme throughout this book – this time somewhere in Ventura, California. The 1994 World Cup was just starting and even in the football-averse USA, tribes from all the participating countries, and a lot of English too, all gathered to watch games in bars. It was fantastic. All united in their love of football. I made friends that day who remain friends today. That's what football can do.

Other sports are just not loved on this humongous scale. No other sport attracts the kind of crowds that football does every day of the week year in, year out. Even clubs that are unsuccessful, have never won anything and have a ground located on a windswept moor so cold that your extremities go an unpleasant icy blue colour will routinely pull in two or three thousand hardy souls. People will say, 'Oh, we don't get much of a crowd' if only 1,500 people turn up, but most other entertainment venues in your town would be delighted with 'only' 1,500.

Even when football is low-skill, poor-quality and boring; even when it is physically uncomfortable to watch and you may end up being punched by a mad man; even when all of these elements are in play, a football match can still attract a crowd bigger than you can reasonably expect to attract at a provincial theatre on any given night. And they have warm, plush seats.

What used to be largely a game played on Saturdays and Wednesdays is now played seven days a week, even on Thursdays, which to those of us of a certain age fools as unnatural and creepy as buying underwear for your mother or listening to Gary Glitter records.

And still we can't get enough of football's sweet, sweet lovin'. It is astonishing that 75,000 people will pack into Old Trafford to watch Manchester United without any guarantee of it being a good game, good value or of even being very comfortable. It's not like going to see

Springsteen, where you know they'll play to a certain standard. Any football game can be so boring as to make you want to claw out your eyes. There is no guarantee of quality even with the best clubs and yet still they come, paying upwards of £50 per head twice or more a month.

Football has the capacity to inspire, to thrill, to make you howl with laughter and weep bitter tears. It brings joy and misery. It brings glory and heartache. It is all human life, rolled up into ninety minutes and played out across the world to millions and millions of people, eager to feast on the experience.

I don't believe it's just me upon whom it has exerted a life-changing influence. I'm sure it has done this to millions of people worldwide, perhaps without them even knowing it.

Football is Britain's big sporting love and has been since the inception of the game in the 1860s. We have hungrily devoured all things football from Victorian newspaper reports to hideous polyester duvet covers from the club megastore plastered with a tasteless picture of the latest greasy, amoral, poorly educated millionaire.

We have gone to matches in shockingly large numbers for over 140 years; we have made up obscene chants, abused thousands of referees and linesmen, eaten indefinable protein wrapped in pastry and drunk hot brown liquid of dubious origins. All because of Association Football.

So now you know about me, where I'm coming from and where we're going to, get yourself a big drink, put your feet up, put on a good album, feel free to don a football shirt and a scarf, or if you're more continental-minded, let off a few distress flares and discharge a firearm at a fleeing referee. We're about to take a journey into the culture of the beautiful game.

For those who are about to rock, I salute you.

Johnny
May 2010
Edinburgh

1
Shirt

O N the face of it, a shirt of man-made fibres, plastered in logos and advertisements for companies you couldn't care less about and had probably never even heard of previously, is an unlikely object of worship. Add a big number on the back, a seemingly limitless amount of odd gussets, vents and seams, top it off with a stranger's name and it's easy to see why the non-football follower considers supporters' passion for wearing their shirts to be an act of lunacy of the highest order.

And while I bow to no man in my obsession with football, I must admit to having some sympathy with this notion. However, I am in a minority in the football community of, well, about one, I think.

I don't own any football shirt, let alone one of my club's. I never have. In fact the whole collective culture of football shirt wearing has never appealed to me at all. I totally understand why most people do it. But I'm different. It's OK, you don't have to back away from me like that.

To understand why the football shirt has become one of the great loves and great binding forces in football, we need to have a look at what's going on in most of our heads. It's OK, I won't tell anyone about that fantasy you have about the otter and the black lace panties.

A football shirt is a kind of uniform and a lot of people love uniforms, and I don't just mean getting the wife to dress up as a nurse on a Saturday night. Uniforms give people a sense of purpose, unity and respectability. They confer status and let the world know you are part of something; you are useful to a group in some way.

Would the police have the same kind of authority if they were dressed in Arran sweaters and chinos? No. Authorities need a tailored uniform to give them some sort of seriousness. It shows you mean business. Everyone from the army, to nurses and traffic wardens, has an official one for that reason. You can't invade a country while dressed in a range of garish leisurewear. The Nazis didn't wear soft V-neck sweaters and Farah slacks in their attempt at world domination, now did they?

No one would fear the Gurkhas if they came at you wearing a silk smoking jacket and slippers – though perhaps this could be a new military strategy: lure the enemy into a false sense of security by advancing in a silk kimono, only to whip out your weapon at the last minute and shoot them.

Even the security guards in those depressing emporiums catering for low life, £1 stores, are issued with those indestructible brown polyester shirts and trousers in the belief that this gives them more authority when stopping heroin addicts stealing razor blades, or at least provides them with the opportunity to administer a severe static electricity shock by rubbing their thighs together very, very quickly.

'Drop that after-shave, son, or I'll shock you with my trousers.'

But it's not just official uniforms that bind groups of people together. City workers in their dark suits, white shirts and ties are all wearing a uniform of sorts. No one turns up for work at the Bank of England in a pair of Lycra shorts and a Metallica T-shirt. It's probably a sacking offence, even though it couldn't look any worse than the ill-fitting, shiny-arsed, style-free suit so beloved of the British male.

But would it make you worse at your job? Well, given that the collapse of the whole financial system was brought about by people wearing shiny-arsed suits, you probably couldn't do a worse job if you were dressed in a pink taffeta ball-gown and diving boots. Indeed, it is my firm opinion that all bankers should be made to wear pink taffeta ball-gowns and diving boots as part of their punishment for making such an almighty bollocks of things.

Uniforms, be they official, or cultural, are an important indication of being in a team and, as every middle-management executive called Justin will tell you, there's no 'I' in 'team' – not unless you're illiterate or speaking Croatian, *ekipa* being the Croat word for 'team'.

The only concession to individuality in a uniformed environment is perhaps one of those 'wacky' Daffy Duck ties, or a pair of hilariously mismatched red and green socks. In a strict, conformist environment, this marks the wearer out as 'a real character', and the rest of the time as 'a bit of a wanker'.

So many groups of people have a cultural uniform; the black T-shirt and mid-length black shorts of the thrash metal community or the hideously conformist three-quarter-length cargo pants of the British tourist.

There are the landowners in tweed checks and jumbo corduroys, often in startling pinky red or yellow hues. Or how about the middle-class student girls in their Ugg boots (worn down on one side of the heel is the look *de jour*), carefully messed-up hair, skinny jeans and extra-long T-shirts. It makes them virtually indistinguishable from each other, which must surely be the point. It's all, at core, a uniform to help people recognise one of their own.

Now, I have never had a job. I've always worked for myself. I've never owned a suit and never had any intention of doing so. I've never worn any kind of uniform and actively sought a lifestyle that would mean I'd never have to. Having to wear clothing to impress your boss, or to conform to some corporate branding decision, was always total anathema to me. I am an awkward bastard though. Most people would just accept such a thing as part of life, but not me. I took it as a personal insult, as an infringement on my civil liberties and anyway, I looked rubbish in a suit. I'm the sort of man that could make a £5,000 suit look like it was from Primark.

So I set about avoiding having to make this choice by first being a student for as long as possible, then deliberately going on the dole at a time of mass unemployment, better to learn all the stuff they forgot to teach me at school, which was just about everything. That took a few years. But when I'd had enough rest and recuperation from the process of growing up, I started working for myself, reasoning that no one was good enough to be my boss.

These days, working just involves sitting in front of a computer in my flat in Edinburgh. One of the great advantages of working from home is that you can dress like a derelict, a Regency dandy or a tramp, and no one ever knows. We self-employed home-workers rather pride ourselves on this fact and, as a consequence, are some of life's more reluctant joiners-in, fearing it might dilute our individuality, especially if it might involve wearing bloody Ugg boots.

This attitude of going my own way and not being prepared to confirm to some group identity has its roots in how I felt as a kid towards owning and wearing a football shirt. I deliberately avoided owning one, even though it proved awkward.

However, there are many times in life when it's advantageous for your football allegiances to remain undeclared.

This was made clear to me for the first time in 1970, shortly before the FA Cup Final between Leeds and Chelsea. On my way home from junior school, two of the local evil hard lads stopped me and wanted to know who I was supporting in the game. I didn't have anything on that could be construed as a football colour, so they couldn't tell. What was my best chance to avoid the kicking they wanted to find an excuse to give me?

I weighed up my response; it was fairly obvious from their respective scarves that one supported Leeds and the other Chelsea. This was a clever ploy because one of them could – indeed, would be obliged – to beat you up no matter what you said. If you claimed not to like football, that constituted reason enough for both of them to break you into tiny pieces.

Neither boy was a fan of either club but they had struck upon this ruse as a way to better exercise their innate violence upon nice little boys like me. Ah the good old days before Broken Britain.

They were skinny, nasty, aggressive kids from the Hardwick Estate who took pleasure in their young reputation as psychotics. I was a nine-year-old nascent hippy with an early love of The Beatles and Pink Floyd. I wasn't the fighting type but I decided to go down with all guns blazing. There was no winning this one.

'Fuck off, they're from down south, I'm a Boro fan!' I bellowed proudly, even then feeling that 'The South' was a place to define yourself against. As I did so, I took off at high pace in the full knowledge that, if they caught me, my reply had given both of them reason to kick me unconscious.

Fortunately, I out-ran them easily, being a nippy little kid and also because my violent pursuers were already both smokers and lacked the lung capacity to keep up with me. There's a lesson for any would-be juvenile thugs: lay off the fags or all the non-smoking kids you want to violently assault will be able to run away from you and thus make you look like a bit of a dick.

Had I been wearing any football colours, I wouldn't even have had the chance to get away. I would have been jumped and rendered senseless without discussion. It was a lesson learned early and so I set about appearing neutral in public. No football shirt, no scarf, no bobble hat. As this was before the mass commercialisation of sportswear this wasn't quite as freaky as it would be today.

For games lessons at school I deliberately sported a cheese-grater-rough, plain mustard-yellow nylon shirt, worn with black shorts and mustard-yellow socks, because it didn't look like any team's strip except perhaps a mutant version of Hull City's and not even the mad kids wanted to beat you up for having a vaguely Hull City-looking shirt on, largely because they wouldn't even know what colours Hull played in. So I was the Switzerland of the sports fields and parks, blissfully neutral.

After a while, the evil mustard crimplene creation had exfoliated my tender young skin so thoroughly that I had to opt for a soft 100 per cent cotton option, but what colour to choose for maximum non-commitment and thus preservation of my immature undescended testicles?

Back in the mid-1970s, giant nylon nirvanas such as Allsports and JJB Sports, JD Sports, Jim Beam Sports or KC and the Sunshine Sports didn't exist. Instead, we had small, independent sports shops that sold everything from boots to tennis rackets, table-football accessories, shuttlecocks and jock straps. Most towns of any size had at least one that was run by a local ex-player; in Stockton it was the Boro legend and much-missed Willie Maddren, a magnificent centre-half whose career was ended in his mid-twenties by a knee injury. These were the only places to buy sports goods, including football shirts, apart from the market stalls.

The lack of merchandise wasn't much of an issue, really, for us as kids; after all, you can't miss what you've never had nor ever seen.

There was no heinous concept of 'official' merchandise, which meant there was no valid or invalid product to wear or buy. It was all down to your intention. If you bought a red football shirt and said it was Liverpool then that's what it was. If you bought a white shirt and said it was Leeds, no one could say it wasn't. This was a much healthier state of affairs, to my mind. It was impossible to be bullied at school for having last season's shirt on because there was no such thing. That whole feeling of inadequacy that I sense some kids have today if they don't have the newest version of shirt, trainer, boot or whatever, didn't exist so intensely for us. We just got bullied for other more traditional reasons: being ginger, having big teeth or just being alive.

So if you wanted a scarf or bobble hat in your club's colours, there was no club megastore at which to buy one; instead you got your mam or gran to knit you one. To subsequent generations, I'm sure this seems very quaint, something that belongs to the Victorian era, almost. But knitting was, for many households, an omnipresent thing. The click of the needles was the soundtrack of life at home.

Both my gran and mam knitted all the time, not to an especially high standard, but well enough to clothe us in outsized, ill-fitting jumpers and strange socks that were too wide and too long and which when worn looked like a kind of woollen Wellington boot.

As I didn't want to show my club colours, I deliberately requested jumpers, scarves and hats that were not in Boro's red and white but rather in obscure shades of brown or purple. One time I had a jumper that was knitted in space-dyed wool. This wasn't wool dyed in space; rather, it was wool with lots of different colours dyed into it in sections so, when knitted, it came up in random bands and blotches of different shades. It was yellow, brown, black and orange. I looked like a psychedelic fucking wasp when wearing it, but at least it wasn't in a football club's colours.

I may have had odd-looking jumpers and scarves in purple and white, but I once again felt clever that I had avoided an obvious reason for someone to give me a pounding. The veracity of this notion was proved to me one evening at the Boro in a mid-1970s game against Manchester City.

It was late winter, not too cold, as we set off. However, after ninety minutes of goalless boredom, an icy roake had blown in off the North Sea up the Tees and right into Ayresome Park. It was freezing, so I took out my home-made woolly hat and pulled it over my frost-bitten head as we made our way out of the ground on to the streets.

We hadn't gone far before someone ran up behind me, and kung-fued me hard in the back so that I fell to the ground. (Kung fu was very popular at the time with many a skinny kid worshipping Bruce Lee and buying Carl Douglas's number one 'Kung Fu Fighting'. I liked Hong Kong Phooey myself. A crime-fighting martial arts dog is my kinda animal.) Anyway, to whoops of delight, he grabbed the hat off my head, threw it over a wall and ran off at speed.

As I looked up to see the hat disappearing, to my horror I realised that it was a light blue and white affair, Man. City's colours. I'd had a brain fart and not even thought that wearing it would make me appear to be a Man. City fan. It only confirmed the danger of such clothing decisions.

The next game I made sure I reverted to my plain brown hat and as a result I went unmolested.

And of course, this was before the idea of official merchandise. It just didn't exist. But we were no less satisfied with life because of this. A stall on Stockton market sold long-sleeved T-shirts that looked like a traditional crew-neck football shirt, with a contrasting coloured rib. Ideal.

But red with a white trim was too obviously Manchester United or Liverpool. Royal blue was Chelsea. White was Leeds. Oddly enough, no one had thought of making a Middlesbrough shirt red with a white central band after 1974 but you could buy a plain red shirt and many lads had that as their Boro shirt. I had a strong notion that I had to avoid this at all costs.

Then I saw what I wanted: a coloured shirt I could wear in games lessons or in Ropner Park in the summer without any obvious allegiance. For 50p I took home an orange shirt with a white collar and cuffs. Yes, I could have been a Blackpool fan – they played in tangerine – but no one was going to hit me in the face behind the gym for being an alleged Blackpool fan, at least not in the north east of England.

I felt clever, believing, controversially, that avoiding getting your head kicked in is actually quite a smart idea and not having severely bruised bollocks would pay off in later years while entertaining ladies. Later, a Californian Buddhist monk told me that orange is the most positive colour, and that it emboldens and cheers the spirit. He may have been smoking too much carpet or maybe he's right, who knows. But I loved that shirt and wore it until it was threadbare.

From an early age, I realised that playing football was a gateway into being more popular. Kids on the school football team tended to attract more admiration from girls and – just as important – from other boys. It was a pity then that I was never good enough to get picked for the school. I was once a substitute but only because flu had decimated the regulars. I never got on the pitch so my career as a top-flight footballer was stalled early on.

I always wanted to be a tricky right winger and I had the pace to beat most other kids but, sadly, not the ball control to go with it. I was a prototype Theo Walcott: blistering pace but not much else. I could never quite work out how to cross a ball while running at top speed. It seemed impossible to do and sometimes as I tried I would either do an air shot or simply fall over my own feet.

On one occasion, in trying to deliver the ball with my right foot, I somehow contrived to bruise a low-slung testicle. I still can't work out how I did this but I managed to crush it against my standing leg. The pain was so bad that I had to go off injured! The humiliation has never left me.

I had to content myself with playing on the wing for the rugby team, which I was much better at because all you had to do was catch the ball and run like stink, which I was one of the best around at doing, but such is the way of these things, it gave me much less pleasure, not least because rugby is a cruel game which hurts a lot and requires a degree of physical intimacy with men that I never felt comfortable with.

After two years as a rugby first-team regular, when I moved up to the sixth form, the first training session was a real eye-opener. Playing against kids as old as eighteen who had grown into absolute beasts was all too much for me. The opposing winger essentially just ran over me. He was fast and built like a rhino. I came off the pitch hurting and thought 'Sod this, I'm off to the pub', thus abandoning my rugby career right there and then.

We were not really trained as kids at school in the art of football. There was no attempt to make us more skilful or fit. Most games lessons were just a kick-about with the games teachers notoriously more interested in chatting up the fifth-form girls. Our man, who we called The Pink Panther because he wore pink-tinted glasses which gave him a vaguely sixties psychedelic appearance was what we used to call 'a fanny rat'. He was especially fond of the more grown-up girls in the fourth and fifth year and, indeed, even dated an especially delicious one if I remember rightly. Wouldn't that be illegal these days?

But throughout my school football years, anyone who knew me knew I supported the Boro, but unlike most of my contemporaries, I never felt the need to broadcast it via my clothing. I was a pragmatist, even at an early age, and reasoned that all of these battles were, at heart, pointless and best avoided for a peaceful life.

It seemed to me that anyone who wanted to hurt you because you supported one club or another was, in essence, a daft bastard, possibly evil and, certainly, a twat. Even at an early age, fighting just seemed a monumentally stupid thing to do and fighting about football doubly so. Even as a boy I knew it was supposed to confer a special kind of masculinity on to you; it was a badge of manly honour. But to me, no amount of bruises and painful groin swellings was worth it just to be thought of as hard by kids who were often a bit thick.

And it was two such hard, thick kids who one day after games lesson confronted me as I was about to go home.

'Why don't you support the Boro?' one asked with the kind of tone that suggested whatever I said would not be a good enough answer.

'I do support the Boro,' I said indignantly, I knew they didn't go as regularly as me. But this wasn't about that. It was just a reason to be cruel.

'Fuck off! No you don't! Where's your Boro shirt then?'

'I don't have one,' I said, knowing logic was not going to be a defence here.

'Why not, like?' said the other lad, as though it was a personal insult to him. Wanker.

'Lads, I'm only allowed one shirt and my mam and dad bought me this orange one.' I was always good at making up a story to excuse my eccentric behaviour and shrugged as though to say, parents huh?! What can you do?

'Fuck off, Nicholson, you cunt. Get a Boro shirt by next games lesson or we'll kick your fucking head in! Right?'

It was the sort of pathetic aggressive confrontation I hated so much and which used to worry and weigh me down at school. I didn't want a kicking but, then again, I really bloody objected to being coerced into doing what they wanted. It was pointless to fight them. I'd already worked out that to get the better of such kids you needed to be clever and make important allies to help you out. I built capital with important allies throughout the year for occasions such as these.

One such ally was my pal Paul. Paul was a great lad. His nickname was Knocker. I always assumed this was because he was a 'hard knock' but it may have been because he knocked on doors and ran away for all I know. Somehow he'd acquired a reputation as a tough kid but I never saw him have a fight at school so this must have been achieved out of school or through his innate menace. He was also one of those lads who at fifteen looks twenty-five and has a decent beard growth despite terrible acne. He went on to do hairdressing. Clearly there was something of the artistic, sensitive soul in Knocker and he liked me, so that was in his favour as well.

I knew which estate these kids were from so I went to Knocker, who lived nearby, and told him what had happened. Like a kindly older brother he told me not to worry about it. Next week after games, performed as usual in my tangerine dream shirt, I saw the two kids at a distance. My stomach knotted and I got ready to run. They saw me but walked right past and did nothing. Though he hadn't said anything to me which was very much his style, he had clearly had a word with them and this had been sufficient to stop their evil intent being exercised on me.

Good old Knocker. Later, I'd occasionally go drinking with him and was amazed that he knew and was apparently friendly with every hard bastard on Teesside. All the blokes I'd run a mile from when out boozing, he'd shake their hands and exchange pleasantries. His presence made them friendly to me as well, which was very weird. 'All right Nic, out for a few pints are you?' they'd say like we were regular mates and they didn't spend the daytime punching boys like me behind the gym.

Through him I acquired immunity from aggro without having to become a hard kid myself, for which I was always grateful.

There were relatively few rewards for being a hard kid. The chance to put your hands down the rough-estate squeeze Dawn Minton's knickers perhaps, which had an exotic and mouth-drying temptation about it because she had the look of a girl who knew her way around both her and my erogenous zones, but it still wasn't worth a Doc Marten to the head to achieve, in my humble opinion.

Nor was it worth having to appear to be more stupid than you really were in order to fit in with the hard kids. It was important not to appear too clever in such company because being clever was frowned upon as weak, possibly homosexual and certainly an indication that you could be beaten to a pulp with little effort. So it was never going to be my thing because I was an irrepressible smart arse and liable to shoot my mouth off to impress someone.

By the time I was fifteen I was already devouring modern poetry and trying to decipher Jim Morrison lyrics; I quite fancied being a lizard king. But all this had to be kept under wraps if you were to get through a day without some form of humiliation or violence.

The fact was, to join the hard kids you had to properly commit to it. It was a full-time job being an evil twat. You couldn't just go in for an occasional bit of GBH on sickly boys; it was all or nothing.

If you took on one of the tough kids and beat them up, this would not give you entry to the hard kids' club, which I always thought was a tad unfair. To the victor the spoils, right? No, in this case, to the victor, the broken spine, legs and bollocks because beating up a hard kid inevitably meant that the hard kid's bigger brothers and his mates would wait for you after school and put you in hospital.

It was a kind of instant karma for knocking the snot out of their kid, which was exactly what happened to a mate of mine, Colin. He took on the hardest kid in school, a skinny, wiry streak of piss called Mickey, and over-powered him. Colin was a big rugby-type dude with hands like a bunch of bananas and thighs like those of a beast of burden and he utterly kicked the crap out of Mickey, creamed him and left him grovelling, weeping, covered in his own blood. A day later six older kids jumped Colin, broke his legs and other vital bits. He was in North Tees General Hospital for months.

This sort of thing was normal life. We had to deal with it even though it was, frankly, shit and damaged me psychologically for ever.

Ironically, I was perfectly able to 'look after' myself if so inclined, at least on a part-time basis when up against the second-division psychos. I'd had an impressive growth spurt up to five foot ten by age fourteen and was taller than most kids my age until I was about sixteen. No one could out-run me. That speed I'd had as a ten-year-old that had allowed me to escape a pre-Cup Final beating had developed into an ability to sprint 100 metres in around eleven seconds. This had continued to prove useful in evading beatings all across Teesside and would continue to do so in post-pub escapes from pissed punters looking for trouble. A bit of pace is the best defence you can have. Of course, you will be called a coward for turning and legging it by those who can't keep up with you, but better that than lose something important in the fleshy, blood-engorged organ department, even if it did mean being denied access to the council estate bike's lacy black knickers. Ahem.

So, had I wanted to have a teenage career as a high-paced thug, I could have given it a go, but it was just never in me so to do. As a sixteen-year-old, when the testosterone was flowing in rivers around my nervous system I was playing on the wing for the rugby team, and in the course of tackling someone accidentally delivered an upper cut that Alan Minter would have been proud of. His face exploded in bloody tissue and bone. The guilt and sorrow at what I had done still haunts me. But of course, I was lauded for this apparent random act of macho violence by my team-mates. It seemed wrong at the time but I kept quiet and briefly wallowed in my status as a pugilist.

So my attitude to football shirts had been formed early in life and I've stuck with it ever since. I love football and I am forever bonded to Middlesbrough FC, but wear a shirt? Nah, not for me pal; haven't you noticed, everyone else has got one on? Seriously, that was always a problem for me. That and the nipple rash.

The politics of the herd mentality aside, I still totally understood the new fashion for wearing club shirts and I loved the way some of them looked. Obviously, not everyone who wears a football shirt is some sort of lunatic, would-be fascist or psychotic and most get a tremendous sense of pride and identity from their shirts. Fair enough. My issues are my own.

The strange thing is I've never felt shy of declaring my allegiances over rock bands. I grew up feeling that was an entirely cool, sexy thing. So much so that for nearly ten years I've owned and run DJTees, a company dedicated to designing and selling T-shirts of bands and musicians.

While in the 1970s there was little or nothing in the way of rock merchandise available, I took much pleasure and identity in turning up for school clutching an album under my arm, preferably with a gatefold sleeve.

I even had a Wishbone Ash T-shirt in the mid-1970s, which my parents had got me for my birthday. I'm not sure where they picked it up from, probably the same market stall that did the football-style shirts. It didn't fit me, it was too small. My parents were seemingly unaware of my size despite the fact that I was in front of them all the time. But it didn't stop me wearing it until it was as threadbare as my orange football shirt.

To be out in public declaring my Wishbone Ash love was a noble, wonderful thing to me. In my mind, it set me apart from the mainstream kids who liked Abba or chart music, even though at the time Wishbone Ash were a top-twenty album band and hardly obscure. Liking a rock band was still an act of rebellion in itself and decidedly not a mainstream thing to do in the way it is today.

But being set apart from things is probably as important an emotion as belonging to something when you're in your teens. From an early age I knew which side of the fence I was on. I was a rocker. How this would later manifest itself I had no idea, but as a young teenager I had already figured out that not conforming to the path laid down for you by the rest of society was greatly to be desired.

Not unless that path involved playing very loud guitar and listening to Mahavishnu Orchestra albums anyway, and even as a kid, I knew that was unlikely.

As puberty took hold of me, it also seemed undoubtedly true that rock 'n' roll was infinitely cooler than football. Holding a guitar was infinitely more preferable and to my nascent male self, infinitely sexier. Even at an innocent fourteen I'd figured out it was a phallic symbol and was much better than your average phallic symbol or indeed your actual phallus because it made a very loud noise.

Girls loved rockers but they could take or leave most footballers apart from George Best. This wasn't surprising as most 1970s footballers looked like a brick wall or a wild animal, or both. Then again, so did the blokes in bands unless they were in prog rock bands, in which case they looked more like librarians.

So by osmosis I hoped to acquire rock sexiness by appearing in public in the Wishbone Ash T-shirt and holding a copy of *Back to the Future* by Man or *Pawn Hearts* by Van Der Graaf Generator. Obviously, this only made me seem weird and less desirable to almost every female of the species. But hey, what did I know?

But the totemic power of a uniform of any kind should not be underestimated. It can bind people together in a common cause and it allows you to spot potential friends and potential foes at a distance, which is very useful, especially if you're in Glasgow on a Saturday afternoon and walk into the wrong pub.

'No pal, I'm not looking at you; now, can I have my kidneys back please?'

Britons had been obsessed with football for around a hundred years before they started buying football shirts in large quantities, but the wide availability of merchandise allowed fans to publicly declare their allegiances, gave them an easy-to-wear item of clothing within which to cram their ever-expanding bellies and which stopped them having to think for too long about what to wear on weekends. For people who didn't mind nailing their colours to the mast, this was ideal.

During football's formative years in the 1860s, players sported jaunty-coloured caps to distinguish themselves, which sounds jolly polite and gentlemanly, if fraught with difficulties when playing on a windy day in Grimsby.

It was in the 1870s that clubs worked out that actually being able to spot a team-mate across a foggy Victorian field was quite a good idea if you wanted to pass the ball to him, and a team all dressed the same would aid this basic ambition.

But what colours to choose? As clubs were often founded by men who had all attended the same public school, many used their old school colours as an inspiration. Reading sported a lovely salmon-pink and pale blue outfit; Wanderers wore eye-watering pink, black and cerise. Oooh, suits you sir.

This wasn't as outlandishly silly as it might appear. As crowds were often stood around the pitch, a plain shirt wouldn't necessarily stand out against the massed ranks of fans. You could be quite certain, however, that none of them would be wearing cerise or pink, because it was illegal for the working class to wear pink.

OK, it wasn't actually illegal, but it might as well have been. If your average mill worker was seen sporting a lovely salmon-pink and blue shirt they would be hounded out of town by a howling mob with burning torches, fearful of the homosexual interloper in their midst, worried that their children would stop wearing brown clothes, start wearing cravats and calling themselves Cynthia.

This attitude was still present in the north of England in the 1970s. My dad's boss once asked him whether I was 'a pansy' (it's hard in the twenty-first century not to love the word 'pansy' – it seems such a gentle insult though at the time it was anything but) because at fourteen I sported bright orange loon pants and had long hair. In the old buffer's mind this was clearly the early showings of transvestism. Dad explained that it was a fashion even though he wouldn't have been able to spot a homosexual if one had put his hands down his trousers and called him darling. It's always seemed odd to me that colour is caught up with sexual orientation in our culture. How is blue a boys' colour, exactly? Does it have a penis? Me, I always liked a bit of pink.

This fear must have been behind Newport County's players refusing to wear their new strip of fluorescent orange shirts and orange-and-black striped shorts in 1972. Apparently, in the first two games this kit attracted wolf whistles and general mockery from the crowd who were probably already getting the burning torches ready to drive out this latest gay incursion into their macho lives. Feeling suitably humiliated by appearing in public in striped shorts, the players refused to wear them and pulled on plain black shorts instead. Orange on shirts was seemingly fine for South Wales's macho men to wear, but not on shorts with black as a stripe! There's not lovely, boyo.

The male of the species' sensitivity to insults to their innate masculinity has always amazed me. OK, so you're in orange-and-black striped shorts; do you really think this is evidence that you're keen for some cock-on-cock action? No. But male pride is a weird thing. It is ruled by fear. Not fear of what women might think but of what other men might think about you. Once you stop worrying about that, most of these problems go away – this much I've learned. I speak as man who was prone to wearing mascara and very tight pants in the late 1980s and rather enjoyed it.

Anyway, after a few years, clubs realised that the psychedelic miasma of colours on the pitch, while making it easy to tell the difference between the front row of the fans and your left winger, actually made it hard for players, fans and officials to distinguish one side from another in the foggy grey sleet of a late Victorian January afternoon. It all looked far too complicated and confusing, so the kaleidoscope of colours was dispensed with, at least for a hundred years or more, and shirts became plainer, simpler and of contrasting primary colours. The fancy-coloured shirts were left to the rugby types, who still sport them to this day.

So by the turn of the century the fanciest shirts were just hooped or striped, most strips looked pretty much as we came to know them in the following hundred years and all the macho folk were very pleased about that, and folded their arms, nodded sagely and put away their flaming torches, safe in the knowledge that shirt-lifting was not being encouraged by the wanton display of pink clothing in their fine town.

This also had the much-needed economic effect of making the

shirts cheaper. Players had to buy their own shirts, which was fine for the public-school, upper-middle-class football pioneers who had spare cash for such fripperies, but as football became a working-class sport, initially in Scotland and by the 1880s in England, the players didn't have much money to spend on kit and they certainly didn't want a colour combination inspired by a public school located somewhere they'd never heard of and could never hope to even visit, much less attend to study Latin, Art History and how to discipline a poor boy with the aid of a large stick and the house lynx.

Players wore knickerbockers instead of shorts; a pair of pants that buckled at the knee in the old New York Dutch style. After winning the league in 1889 several Preston North End players celebrated by filling their pants with ice cream, jelly, fruit and cream, thus accidentally inventing the Knickerbocker Glory. I'm not making this up. OK, I am.

Players were not allowed to expose their knees to daylight or non-consenting adults until the turn of the twentieth century. The sight of knees was considered a very dangerous thing that might destroy society in an orgy of lust and immorality, as opposed to the consumption of delicious, still legal, opium, which was ideal for numbing the pain inflicted by a brutal centre-half in an away game at Roker Park and a treat to be enjoyed on pre-season tours of the Far East.

But in 1901, with the end of the Victorian era, caution was thrown to the wind and the knickerbockers were hoisted further up by daring libertines, eventually becoming admittedly still very, very long shorts. These were always white, black or navy. Socks were always in dark colours. It was the 1950s before anyone was secure enough in their manhood to wear pale sock colours. Well you've got to have standards, haven't you?

'I am not a girl, sir; as you can see, I have dark-coloured socks on. That is the only proof you need. Now kiss me, you big brute.'

Until the 1930s shirts were a collar-less granddad style with laces up the front, then replaced with a rugby shirt-style collar with a button, first worn at Arsenal. Their boss, a revolutionary Yorkshire chap called Herbert Chapman, also shocked the football world by introducing the contrast body/sleeves shirt. It was as modern as Picasso. People scratched their Brylcreemed heads and said 'Bloody 'ell, our 'Erbert's gone daft' in a broad Yorkshire voice, despite coming from north London.

Despite these changes, there was still no organised retailing of replica shirts and it has only been in the past twenty-five to thirty years that the mass wearing of football shirts as leisurewear has really taken off. It prompts the question, why did it take so long?

It's certainly true that football clubs for decades were run exactly as that: a club, not as a business. The idea that fans could or should be exploited for profit struck many a patrician chairman as simply wrong. And anyway, when football was a resolutely working-class game, there wasn't an abundance of disposable income to be spent on football shirts. In the 1970s, around 25 per cent of the typical household income went on food. It's under half that now, according to something I read in *The Guardian*, which surely couldn't be wrong.

It wasn't until business attitudes began to change in the 1970s and clubs started to look for additional income at the same time as the rise in popularity of sports-casual clothing so popular with footballers themselves – think Emlyn Hughes on *A Question of Sport* – that it became a cultural possibility for people to wear a football shirt down the pub or while shopping for a packet of Penguins and a Vesta chow mein in Presto supermarket.

Our fathers and their fathers before them wore a shirt and tie most of the time, often with a waistcoat and jacket. My dad's idea of being casual was to wear an open-necked shirt – still with a vest underneath, even in the hot summer of 1976. There was no way in a million years that he would have gone out of the house in any kind of sporting shirt. He wouldn't even have worn a polo shirt, much less a football shirt with the logo of a brewer on the front, and even if he'd wanted to, my mother wouldn't have let him leave the house dressed like that. It was common and scruffy, both things that aspirant working-class social climbers were keen to avoid because they represented their past.

It wasn't until the sixties generation grew up with their own fashions and a more relaxed attitude to dress codes that the football shirt industry could really take off. And as soon as it did, it became a default dress code for millions and shirts themselves evolved into iconic symbols.

Those worn by superstars of the past attract the kind of prices reserved for quality works of art. Someone paid over £157,000 for Pele's 1970 World Cup shirt, while a George Best Manchester United shirt came in at a handy £28,000. It's just a shirt, an assembly of cotton fibres, but it touched the body of a genius while he performed his art and so becomes a kind of religious artefact for worshippers.

In these agnostic times, people no longer try to pass off some dried-up crust as Jesus's foreskin, but when it comes to football shirts, there is no shortage of worshippers prepared to buy up these nouveau holy relics, though I would imagine there'd be a few takers for Pele's foreskin were it to come on to the market.

'It's yours for £10,000 in ten easy payments, sir; a gift for the wife, is it?'

However, as iconic as football shirts were, we never expected that they'd soon become advertising hoardings. Even more surprising to me was that nobody seemed to care. This development only hardened my attitude to not buying or owning one.

The next step was for clubs to invite sponsors to have their company name plastered across the front of the shirts. It was resisted for a while. Kettering were the first to rent out their shirts to the global conglomerate and international high rollers of, er, Kettering Tyres, but the FA got uppity about that and stopped them.

However, in 1977 Hibernian took Bukta's money (Bukta had been an early sportswear company dating back to the late 1870s) and then Derby did a deal in 1978 with Abba-loving wonky-shaped car people Saab, but wore them only in the club photo. Maybe they were too ashamed to play in them. Who wanted to drive a Saab, anyway?

Well, probably more than wanted to drive a Datsun, who were my club's first sponsor; Datsun Cleveland to be more specific. I couldn't drive and I didn't want to learn either, so this was wasted on me, not for the last time. They were replaced in 1982 by McLean homes, and I didn't want to live in one of those either. In fact, I'd have rather lived in a Datsun.

If only they had been sponsored by Yamaha guitars, which I was very partial to at the time, I might have felt more sympathetic. I played a Carlos Santana-style solid body Yamaha SG in the late 1970s and early 1980s. Its weight prevented you doing anything too gymnastic with it, unfortunately, as I was prone to a bit of guitar histrionics, and its price prevented you from smashing it up in an orgy of auto-destructive rock 'n' roll hedonism. It was also too heavy to lift over your head. But the sustain just, well, sustained. You could hold a note and go away for a three-course meal, get married, stand for Parliament, be appointed Minister of Sport, organise a coup in the Philippines, marry Bianca Jagger, divorce her, bake a potato and climb the Matterhorn and it would still be sustaining when you went back to it.

But no, there was no chance of Yamaha (or Yammer Hammer as my deputy headmaster used to call it out of wit or ignorance, I never worked out which) sponsoring the Boro because there's an unwritten rule in football that everything advertised on football shirts, unless it's booze, is almost always shit that no one wants and which everyone can certainly do without.

Liverpool was the first top-flight club to actually play in a sponsored shirt in 1979 after doing a deal with Crown Paints. It began a rush by all professional clubs into the eager, sweaty grasp of dozens of companies large and small, keen to exploit football's popularity and use shirts as moveable billboards. In a highly metaphysical move, boot manufacturer Gola sponsored comic-only club Melchester Rovers.

In the early 1980s, BBC and ITV wouldn't show games when clubs had the sponsor logos on their shirts, so briefly everyone had to have a 'for TV only' strip without a logo or cover up the offending words with gaffer tape, seemingly unaware that most people watching the likes of *Match of the Day* were slumped half comatose from alcohol or distracted by a stint of sweet weekend lovin' on the settee with the current lady of choice, and couldn't make out what it said on the shirts.

I should know because I was once manually brought to climax by a lovely Teesside wench while we lay on the floor of my mam and dad's front room, in front of *MotD,* and in doing so, soiled Jimmy

Hill's beard with the consequent expulsion of bodily fluids. If you've ever tried wiping sperm off an old-school cathode ray tube TV screen you'll know it's more difficult than some might think, especially if the screen is dusty and charged with more static electricity than a security guard's trousers. Flat screens are much easier so they tell me, like. Anyway, during the whole episode I was completely unaware of any advertising logos and even if a shirt had been sponsored by the Holy Ghost I wouldn't have noticed.

The old farts at the BBC and ITV had to give way in 1983 but insisted the logo should be no more than sixteen inches square. Whether they turned up on match day with a ruler to make sure this was enforced isn't clear, but these were the last dying cries of the old attitudes because a year later they gave up this plainly mad idea and the sponsorship genie was well and truly out of the bottle.

I genuinely thought that advertising would put people off buying the new plethora of replica shirts. Apart from my general aversion to declaring my allegiance by wearing a shirt, the last thing I wanted to do was compound that by endorsing a car, house builder or, in the late 1980s, Heritage Hampers. Yes, really.

I will say that again, Heritage Hampers sponsored Middlesbrough for two seasons. I mean, hampers, man! Who the hell buys a hamper? Why don't you just buy a basket and fill it yourself with stuff from the supermarket? Is it too much trouble to buy your own tins of chopped ham and Branston pickle? Perhaps they're aimed at the same people who buy ready-grated carrot or cheese; people for whom grating anything is just too much work that consumes too many precious seconds of existence.

In the early 1980s, I was living in Newcastle, and at the time Newcastle United had their club shop in the Green Market, a covered market area-cum-shopping centre, alongside cobblers, wool shops and people selling cheap watches and sewing machines. It was very small and more like an indoor market stall than anything. I picked up the current shirt for sale and showed it to my mate. 'Who wants all that on the front?' I said, referring to the advertiser currently despoiling the black and white.

The bloke behind the counter snatched it out of my hands and for reasons I have never been able to fathom, shouted, 'Well get back to your free shops then!' I stood, puzzled. OK, by now I was a long-haired rock 'n' roll grebo and I didn't like the shirt, but how this related to a some notional charge-free retail environment, I had no idea, so being a quizzical sort of chap I queried this outburst, 'Free shops, mate? What free shops are those, like?'

His reply was cryptic and very Geordie. 'You knaw,' he said, nodding with certainty. 'Aye, you knaw, alreet.' Perhaps he had been eating boot polish.

So you can see my anti-football shirt advertising stance has a long tradition of controversy. But I was very wrong. It made no difference. People bought replica shirts anyway, regardless of how uncool, silly, ludicrous or downright embarrassing the sponsor.

Meanwhile, the kit itself was evolving away from heavy-duty cotton and into the infamous shell suit hell. Shell suits, for those too young to remember, washed on to these shores in the mid-1980s like a polyester tidal wave breaking across the council estates of Britain.

They came in many colours, all of them garish and unpleasant. The fabric had a crumpled rough texture. People seemed to become deluded into thinking that wearing this notionally sporty clothing would make them appear athletic and lithe. However, it quickly became the clothing of choice for under-nourished, spotty, gaunt-faced chavs, sweaty chip shop princesses and twenty-stone middle-aged men from Dewsbury to wear while shopping in Kwik Save and thus immediately became devalued, both as sportswear and fashion. More typically it was identified with people who lived on the dole, sniffed glue, reproduced the species a lot and lived off deep-fried food covered in breadcrumbs.

It got worse as people started to wear shell suits with their normal leather shoes and bobbly old grey socks, having apparently totally given up on themselves and life in general.

I couldn't get with this fashion at all. I was a rocker, after all. This meant whatever you wore had to be blood-restrictingly tight. While any garment with an elasticated waist has an attraction to the man with a thickening girth, you knew with certainty that to pull on the shell suit was the final proof that all hope was lost and your dignity, along with your social skills, was being abandoned in favour of drinking cheap white cider out of three-litre bottles, eating chips and watching ITV.

Tight jeans, I was familiar with, ball-crushingly tight, worn with very pointy boots. It was a great look for us kings of the eighties riff. Even spandex had a wilfully tacky charm when worn by heavy metal men – think Biff Byford, singer with Saxon – and a girl in spandex was a camel-toe heaven.

You had to have balls to wear spandex; if you hadn't, everyone could have easily told, because even casual onlookers could see if you were Jewish or excited. Shell suits required no such chutzpah.

Sadly, rock 'n' roll had a brief flirtation with shell suiting as singers, keen to be distinctive, would don the multi-coloured jogging pants the better to entertain their public. I seem to recall seeing Fish performing in some headache-inducing pants and Yes's mystic-in-residence Jon Anderson could be seen sporting a white shell suit-type creation, which made him look like a man who ran a discount tanning salon in Accrington. Rock and shell suits were an awful, unnatural combination.

Before they finally disappeared, even old-age pensioners had taken to donning them, not out of a sense of sporty athleticism but because they were loose-fitting and now very cheap. Shell suits were, in short, an abomination. They seemed to take an age to go out of fashion and leave the market stalls of Britain in peace to sell leggings to fat lasses and stolen Calvin Klein underwear to mid-life crisis men.

The last time I spotted an original shell suit was in rural Lincolnshire in 1998 during a year living in the fine town of Boston, whose main feature is a church called The Stump. In the shadow of The Stump there was a market held on Saturdays where a chap was selling a particularly eye-watering turquoise, white and lemon affair for an unbeatable £5. There were no takers. But it will doubtless live on, at least in a landfill, where it will take a few thousand years to decompose or turn up via a charity clothing drop in a sub-Saharan village, being worn by a tribal shaman in a documentary while intrepid jungle explorer Bruce Parry vomits copiously.

However, the boil-in-a-bag shell-suit-style nylon fabric had one major advantage: it could be printed via sublimation. This opened up the possibility of shirts that were not just plain but positively hallucinatory just at the time in the late 1980s when everyone was rediscovering psychedelic drugs and staring at their hands for six hours while listening to the Stone Roses.

So everything went loved up. Goalkeepers wore garish shirts that made them look like a moving kaleidoscope; it was as though they were wearing a barf of many and varied hues. Some were so dense and detailed you could become convinced that, if you squinted hard enough for long enough, some image would magically reveal itself: a portrait of Chairman Mao, a plaster cast of Jimi Hendrix's penis or the X-ray of Bert Trautmann's broken neck. Someone missed a trick by not creating magic-eye goalie shirts.

But it didn't stop with goalkeepers' jerseys; strips began to change radically as well in the early 1990s. Norwich's shirt was an intense, radioactive green-and-yellow bird-poo splatter. For the 1992–93 season, Birmingham City had a blue strip covered with daubs of colour apparently in tribute to the school of pointillist painters.

Strips were exercises in hellish graphic design for the colour blind. Arsenal's 1991–93 cubist hallucination away strip could induce epilepsy on a sunny day and wipe your synapses clean of any memory whatsoever. This may go some way to explaining the state of Paul Merson and why Tony Adams talks so slowly.

My lasting recollection of that especially awful shirt dates to one April afternoon in 1993 near to Middlesbrough Railway Station. We had just beaten Arsenal 1-0 with a goal from the fleshy Scot John Hendrie and I was on my way to catch a train home when I saw ahead of me a small group of Arsenal fans all wearing the nauseating away strip of the time.

You could tell they were looking for trouble because they were making odd gestures with their heads and necks: a sort of forward spasm of the head accompanied, as tradition demands, with a flexing of the arms forward too. Think Tommy Cooper head butting someone and you get the idea. I don't know if this is something handed down through generations of Londoners as a street code but it looked hilarious. They strutted along like a gaggle of yellow roosters, twitching and shouting abuse at strangers. Now, this isn't a good idea in Middlesbrough because however hard you think you are, believe me, people in Middlesbrough are harder. If you come from London and think you're working-class, wait till you get to Middlesbrough; you'll realise you're middle-class. Experience told me it was only a matter of time before these lads would be dealt with.

As they were occupying the route to the station I thought it might be a bit dangerous to have to walk past them – my nine-year-old experience with the Chelsea and Leeds fan had stayed with me. I wasn't wearing a Boro shirt or scarf but my accent is a dead giveaway and I can't do an Arsenal accent, whatever that would sound like. So I did what any good northerner would do in such circumstances: I went in the nearest pub for a couple of pints of bitter and waited for them to leave. This took about twenty minutes.

I emerged to an empty street . . . apart from an Arsenal fan tied tightly to a lamppost with an Arsenal away shirt which was surely his as he was half-naked. He couldn't bloody move and was pink with fury and embarrassment, which clashed terribly with the yellow shirt. Where the rest of them had gone and what had happened was a mystery. Presumably, a group of local creative hard men had taken it upon themselves to disperse the baying north London massive, leaving behind this sole representative, securely anchored to a steel lamppost as a warning to other southern interlopers.

'That's fantastic, I'm all for street art happenings,' I said, smiling, as I passed him. In return he instructed me to go fuck myself, as though to do so would have been worse than being tied to a lamppost. As I got to the station and looked back, he was being released by a fellow Arsenal fan. I've often wondered if this was the only instance of fan-on-fan shirt-based bondage.

It was a remarkable period. Increasingly, going to the football was like taking mescaline and staring at the sun. Hull City's shirts even had tiger stripes printed on in orange and black. It had the cheap look of a social club stripper's underwear. This is a bad thing.

Every club developed a home, an away and a nakedly-for-the-money-only 'third' shirt for occasions undefined. Strips changed most years, making kids who sported the old strip look instantly dated and old-fashioned, thus causing a lot of tears before bedtime in households all over the country. Football clubs' lust for sponsorship money and shirt sales was making small children cry and fat men sweat like a pig in a leotard. But still, they sold in record amounts, especially on Tyneside, which holds some kind of record of shirts per household – all of them stained with bitter tears, no doubt.

Newcastle United brought out an away shirt that was denim-coloured to officially 'go well' with jeans. It also had the major advantage that blood could be easily washed out after a Saturday night pounding on the Bigg Market cobbles. It was, needless to say, a big seller.

Twenty-first-century technology has brought us the cool, wicking shirt which draws sweat, beer and blood away from the skin, and there's no doubt that most shirts are nicer to wear than at any time since natural fibres were abandoned. Some clubs have even got in touch with their feminine side and produced shirts in women's sizes. Everton produced a special pink shirt as part of a breast cancer awareness campaign to try and tap into shirt power.

Retro strips have become a large industry, if not as big an industry as the 'bootleg' shirts, which you can buy from a man called Mo on any market, anywhere in Britain on any weekday for a tenner, which are probably made in the same factory in the Far East, by the same people, as the 'official' shirts and come with the exact same 'unforgeable' holographic tags.

Umbro paid the FA a reported £180 million for the exclusive rights to produce the England shirts, which are the best-selling shirts of all time, anywhere in the world. Given that the large majority are almost certainly purchased by people from England, it goes a long way to illustrating how mad we are for football shirts as a nation. England's current shirt is little more than a polo shirt, so complete has the transformation of the humble football shirt into smart-casual leisurewear become.

AIG's £14.1 million deal with Man. United showed what a big business sponsorship had become. But who wanted a shirt with a company as nerdy as a 'leading provider of flexible investment solutions' on their chest? OK, Gavin in accounts does, but I mean anyone who isn't a virgin and who doesn't still live with their parents.

And since AIG was at the centre of the financial and banking disasters of 2008, almost bringing down the whole of the world's financial structure, and clearly couldn't run a piss-up in a brewery, it hardly cast a good vibe on the club and has now been dumped. It's hard not to see AIG's sponsorship deal as just another stinking, awful financial decision in their massive portfolio of stinking, awful financial decisions, born out of epic ego, hubris and greed. Where are those taffeta ball-gowns and diving boots when you need them?

Middlesbrough's sponsor is Garmin. The irony of losing your way in the league and getting relegated while sponsored by a satellite navigation company was all too delicious. It shows you that a sponsor can be little more than an embarrassment for the club, but people just seem to accept it without thought these days.

Is it worth the money the companies pay? Does it increase their profits? It seems very unlikely. Some people wouldn't even buy a Sharp TV when they sponsored Man. United, and how many Spurs fans had JVC equipment when they sponsored Arsenal? I'm sure no one gave AIG a call because they were plastered over Paul Scholes's chest.

Not everyone wants to be a billboard for the various shysters, environmental rapists, mentalist food purveyors and capitalist attack dogs that often sponsor our clubs. This is why the retro strips have become so popular. The retro shirts are free from advertising and are ideal for the fan who finds the idea of wandering around the streets advertising the likes of Perspex, Mita Copiers or Chupa Chups or whatever, just too low rent and humiliating.

There are plenty of people who are prepared to say, 'I don't care if this is this season's official strip, it's forty quid, it's bloody horrible and it's very uncool.' I'm extremely sympathetic. That being said, in a further twist of nostalgia, some see the early sponsored strips as iconic of a bygone era and they have retained an element of notoriety. There are even Boro fans that look back fondly on the Heritage Hampers days, though this may be more down to severe and persistent intoxication than anything else.

For most, a match day isn't complete without donning some sort of club shirt past or present. When a fan sings 'you're not fit to wear the shirt', it is still the biggest insult you can throw at any player, suggesting, as it does, a failure to match the status of the club's most powerful emblem. Shirts are an important part of football life. They are totems of allegiance. They are not merely a brand identifier, as the modern marketing men see them. They are part of a collective social, civic and cultural identity, despite all that nipple trouble and the fact that they may cause you to get tied to a lamppost in Middlesbrough.

For many, their football shirt is, in a very real sense, their club. The shirt is what you actually support. The club can change grounds, rename its stadium after an airline, change its players, managers, grass or toilet seats, but only the shirt is a constant. It might change colour or style but it remains the emblem you endorse with your cash or TV subscription. Not me of course, but hey, someone has to be awkward.

As comedy God Jerry Seinfeld, a man I turn to for much cogent analysis of life, once said, 'Ultimately, we're just cheering laundry.'

2

Drink

IT was the winter of 1976, I was just fifteen and a half and was about to enter my first pub, prior to going to Middlesbrough FC's Ayresome Park for an afternoon's football-based brutality. I could not have imagined that this would become a ritual for the rest of my life nor did I imagine just what a widespread phenomenon I was about to take part in.

To prepare for this occasion, I had made my first attempt to grow some Gary Neville-style facial hair in order to look older, ridiculously unaware that such paltry growth was a dead giveaway that I was actually only fifteen and a half.

Needless to say, it was unsuccessful in the extreme, looking more like a thin growth of mycelium on my top lip than anything resembling a real man's 'tache. I still looked about thirteen, so just about old enough to get served in a pub in Stockton-on-Tees, then.

Football and drink have long had an arm-in-arm, you're-my-bestest-mate-you-are relationship, which isn't surprising considering the UK's fondness for a tipple across all classes and age groups. In fact, if you look at it, football and drinking are Britain's most popular leisure activities; a marriage made in heaven, each of them enhancing the other and each helping to make the other more popular.

Many of the game's best players have had drink problems, George Best most obviously. One of Newcastle's finest strikers, Hughie Gallagher, was once accused of being drunk while playing. His impressive excuse was to blame his whisky and water mouth-wash. You'd think he could have come up with something more plausible than that. Poor Hughie later threw himself under the York to Edinburgh express and was decapitated; ironic really as he'd been an excellent header of the ball.

The original incarnation of West Ham, the Thames Ironworks, was created by Arnold Hills, a teetotaller who insisted the players followed his example. This didn't last long, as such a restriction meant that no one wanted to play for them. See, the British love to drink and will actively reject anyone who tries to stop them.

That cold afternoon in 1976 was the start of my journey into the football-related intoxication that has served me well in adulthood, and continues to serve millions of others too. The culture of football and boozing is one of our finest traditions.

There was an unofficial list of pubs in Stockton where the under-age drinker could get served: just about all of them. At the time, no one was bothered about kids drinking. All most landlords asked was that you didn't make a row or argue with the regulars. Just sit quietly in a corner, sup your ale and you were fine. It was all very reasonable, really. Despite looking like a young boy, the only time I didn't get served at a bar in my thirty-month under-age drinking career was at the bar in Newcastle City Hall at a Uriah Heep gig. Having to see Heep sober was a bitter blow.

I didn't really know what to expect. I had, until then, only been into what we used to call a beer-off, a counter to one side of a bar that dispensed beer to the public. These were the original off-licences, serving booze to be consumed off the licensed premises.

As a kid buying crisps or pop, you got a whiff of the stale beer and fag smoke. You could hear the hum of beered-up conversation and you knew this was the proper adult world. A place that didn't admit kids was always mysterious, scary almost, but also fascinating. What was the great evil we were being protected from?

My mam and dad didn't go to pubs. They almost never left the house on an evening. They were not social or gregarious in any way whatsoever. For them it was tea and toast and bed by ten. So having arranged to meet my older-looking mate, Bob, in the American Tavern that lunchtime, I really had no idea what I was going to experience. I had correctly guessed, however, that it would not, in any way whatsoever, have anything American about it at all.

The pub was set in a wasteland of gravel at the back of Stockton High Street. It stood alone, as though it was the sole survivor of a bombing raid by the Luftwaffe. The Camerons brewery red lion on a yellow background hung on a sign out front; I pushed the battered wooden swing doors open and went in.

In hindsight, it was nothing more than a typically basic, northern pub, untouched by modernity and full of regular old-school working-class people. What you've got to remember is that for places like Stockton-on-Tees, the 1960s, let alone the 1970s, had never really happened yet; indeed most over the age of thirty still thought the 1950s were a bit modern and risqué. Men with long hair, though common for six or seven years, were still considered by the over-thirties as likely to be cross-dressers and almost certainly homosexual, at least until they had beaten someone up with a crow bar in the car park outside after twelve pints of bitter.

Men drank beer, not lager. Spirits were for chasers, alkies and New Year. No one drank wine. Today's football managers are more progressive and freely admit to drinking wine, Mourinho famously buying Ferguson an expensive vintage after a game at Old Trafford. Ferguson himself is a big collector of the vino, which is about as far from the culture of Govan as you can get. Working-class people drinking wine in the 1970s would have been considered by their contemporaries as pretentious and, as one old lad in the Tav once put it, 'Why drink wine? You don't get as much in a glass as you do with beer.'

It would also have been considered exceptionally unmanly. This notion is still in the air even these days. In the alpha male world of football management, drinking white wine still has a vaguely effeminate quality to it. You'll never hear anyone say 'He'll enjoy his glass of Gewürztraminer tonight,' now, do you? No, it's always 'He'll enjoy his glass of red tonight.' In football it's still white wine for the lady.

Back in the 1970s, along with drinking bitter, a proper working-class bloke did manual work, considered the kitchen an alien land, embraced misogyny and would never be seen in public displaying any emotion. Emotion was for the weak, for women, or for southerners. It was into this northern, adult world that I walked that afternoon.

The American Tavern was a lino-floored, brightly lit public bar on one side, red Dralon seats and brass in the lounge. The windows were frosted glass as if to protect the drinkers from the non-drinking public's critical gaze. Convention for the under-age drinker was to go in the lounge. Urban myth was that it was easier to get served in the lounge than in the bar, which had to be untrue because it was the same bloke behind the bar wherever you went.

I walked through to the lounge. Bob wasn't there. My heart sank, I'd have to buy my own drink. I flexed my early facial growth and went up and asked the fat old bloke, who was actually the landlord, for a pint of lager and lime.

Lager and lime was a natural cross-over drink from pop to beer and thus proved your juvenile status too, of course. The tension knotted in my gut loosened as he pulled the pints, put in a splash of fluorescent lime-green cordial and pushed it over the bar at me in return for twenty-eight whole pennies. He didn't even look twice at me or my sparse facial hair. He couldn't have cared less if I was fifteen or fifty; my money was still worth the same.

As I walked from the bar, the thrill of my achievement spread all over me. This was living, getting served in pubs like a proper grown-up.

I sat down in the corner, behind a small wooden table, and surveyed my new home; and I say home deliberately. It instantly felt more like home than home did. It was cheerful, warm, well lit and people were talking. It lacked the joyless, grim, silent tension that was all too typical of our house. Over the following couple of years 'The Tav', along with a few other pubs, filled the role of home in my life very well. Rather than leading me astray, I actually think it made me more stable. Once I had the pub and I had drink, I was a happier kid, more outgoing and at ease. As I would leave the house to go out for a drink, the weight that was always on my shoulders at home, lifted immediately. If you're brought up in an unhappy house, it is brilliant to find somewhere else to go to where you can relax and find cheerful people.

Even now I can recall a young couple sitting opposite me that first lunchtime. He drank Camerons Strongarm, a ruby-coloured bitter, and she had a half of Harp lager which, contrary to the adverts, did not 'stay sharp to the bottom of the glass' but did make you belch a lot. As I say, at the time lager was not a man's drink. It was for women and 'trendies'. Indeed, drinking lager was, by some old-timers, seen as a betrayal of your working-class heritage and a sign of a Tory voter in their midst or, worse still, a fucking Liberal.

This couple both smoked Benson & Hedges in the distinctive gold packet. He had shoulder-length hair, parted in the centre, and sported a greasy thin moustache. She looked how Lynsey de Paul would have looked had she grown up on a council estate in Teesside: skinny with thick eye-liner, big lashes and yellow fag fingers. They were probably only twenty but they looked really old and grown-up to me. To my juvenile eyes, they seemed classy and sophisticated.

At the bar sat an old man on a stool. He was just staring into the middle distance, and occasionally sipping at a pint as though he was still waiting for the war to be over, time apparently standing still for him.

Two old women sat alongside each other and gossiped over two halves of stout. Old working-class women always drank stout back then. I've no idea why. Perhaps Ena Sharples drank stout in *Coronation Street* and they took her as a role model.

Bob soon arrived and got himself a pint of bitter, like a proper grown-up man. He actually knew a few of the blokes in there – well I say blokes, but they were probably just seventeen or eighteen. He nodded and said his hellos. I looked on in admiration at this social ease in the adult world. Bob was shorter than me but already had a beard and looked five years older, easily.

'What do you reckon to this place then, Nic?' he said, taking an impressively big gulp of the pint.

'It's fucking great,' I exclaimed too excitedly. It was, after all, a regulation, bog-standard pub. Bob laughed as I finished off a pint of lager and lime.

'So do you reckon you're going to be a fucking boozer then?' he said. It already sounded like as good an ambition as any to me.

'Fucking hell, yes,' I replied. Back then we swore in almost every sentence. I'm not sure why really. We were both grammar-school kids for a year before it went comprehensive and far from being the roughest of kids. The fact is we were foul-mouthed kids. When I hear parents criticise modern kids for their bad language I think they must have forgotten what life was like for us. Fuck, cunt, shit, bastard, piss, piss-flaps, arseholes, twats and tits were some of our most commonly used words. The only one of George Carlin's seven dirty words we didn't routinely use was motherfucker. But only because we'd never heard of it.

So we had two pints and then got the bus to Middlesbrough for the game. I was light-headed. The drink had changed everything. Normally, this was a ride devoid of excitement or much entertainment, but now it had become a colourful adventure. The ramshackle, broken and semi-derelict buildings on wind-blown industrial estates now had poetry to them.

Once we got inside the ground the pre-match atmosphere of Ayresome Park seemed noisier and the anticipation of the game even better than normal. The game itself was brilliant and the Boro won. I was happy. At the Boro! My mood was normally one of bitter resignation and a gnawing sense that I really should be doing something more constructive with my time than watching some hairy men kicking each other. I had been indoctrinated into football's drink culture aged fifteen years and six months. Life would not be the same again.

After the game Bob had to go home and get ready for his part-time job. I just wanted to go back to the Tav and have more lager and lime. So I did. I sat on my own for the rest of Saturday night. People came in and out and some of them had been to the game. They swapped opinions over a few pints and a packet of fags. I sat and had two more pints of lager and lime and soaked it all in. This might sound odd now, but at the time I thought it perfectly reasonable. This was better than being at home, so why not spend the whole evening there?

By the end I was thoroughly drunk. I don't even recall how I got home but I probably walked because like most kids, I walked everywhere, whatever the distance. Seven, eight, ten miles was not uncommon. From the Tav to our house was less than three miles, which was a short stroll to me. I'd be a feature in a documentary about drunken teens on BBC3 today, but back then it just seemed part of growing up.

Indeed, going to the pub, initially as part of pre-match ritual, was to become a crucial part of growing up for me. It helped me deal with the vortex of hormones and emotions that your teenage years bring in spades. It helped a lot. Booze was very useful for that. It was an entirely positive experience without which I would have been much less happy. You'll never hear such a comment today. In the black-and-white world of dominant tabloid culture, only the negative aspects of teenage drinking are raised. But I bet there are plenty of kids who like a few drinks and a chat in the pub and never get into trouble. We're encouraged to see the worst behaviour as the norm and many people buy into that view, if only to make themselves feel morally superior.

Pubs are places to meet and to socialise with strangers. Or they were in the north east back then, at least. You could talk to the old fellas who propped up the bar, or to the barmaid, or someone watching the TV in the corner. For me, having led a pretty sheltered life, it was where I learned about the world. I sat and observed. Other kids' parents wouldn't let them go out boozing and would have been horrified if they'd come home stinking of drink, but mine didn't care. If my life was a car, they had taken their hands off the wheel. They never said a word against it. Even if they had, I wouldn't have stopped. From day one I knew it was right for me.

But because most kids of my age couldn't go out drinking and because Bob had a series of jobs that kept him busy on evenings, I spent a lot of my early drinking years going out on my own, sitting in lounge bars and on bar stools, sometimes reading a book, sometimes writing ideas down, or just watching.

There was a whole new culture to absorb. In the days before the insane notion that pubs should be 'family-friendly' and before anyone had come up with the idea for those hideous 'fun' pubs with a grubby inflated bouncy castle outside, a pub was usually two rooms, just as it was in the Tav. One with carpet – the lounge, one with lino – the public bar. No self-respecting working-class football fan would go in the lounge before a game. The lounge was used only when out with the wife, for a wedding, or on Sunday lunchtimes if you were trying to impress your future father-in-law. It was rarefied, posh even. There were the Dralon seats, horse brasses on the walls and a photo of the pub taken in 1891. All superfluous adornments for the football fan with his mind on an important cup tie against York City to worry about, so naturally the football fan went in the public bar. If you wanted food to sustain you through the afternoon or to line your stomach before imbibing a gallon of beer there were a few timeless choices. First, crisps. You might take them for granted, but crisps are one of the UK's big snack success stories.

They're now an everyday part of life with twenty-five foot aisles in supermarkets dedicated to them, but in the 1950s and 1960s, they were far less common and were just ready salted, and came in tins because bagging crisps was technologically beyond us at the time. Luckily for football's authorities, by the early 1960s, Smiths and Golden Wonder started using bags, thus preventing hooligans filling the tin with a bodily fluid and throwing it at opposition fans.

It was Golden Wonder who shook up the world when it brought out cheese-and-onion flavoured crisps, just in time for the explosion of 1960s drug culture. Where would stoners have been without crunchy, salty snacks exploding on to their tastebuds like space dust while they listened to The Grateful Dead?

The crisps you bought at a football match would likely have been Smiths or Golden Wonder or, at Middlesbrough FC, Maxi crisps, which I never saw anywhere else. Every area also had its local manufacturers too. In the north east this was Tudor. Based in Sunderland, they could be bought only in the north east and though they were bought out by Smiths in the early 1960s, the brand remained. Growing up breathing the yellow air of Teesside gave you an innate taste for chemicals, so the nasal passage-clearing salt and vinegar flavour was always popular, along with other finger-staining artificial constructs such as prawn cocktail, tomato sauce, gammon (which had a weird pink hue) and smokey bacon, which would make your throat sore.

Tudor also sold a crisp they called 'beef-e' flavour. It was so powerful that the smell of it stayed on your fingers for days even if you put your hand in bleach for an hour. Dogs would follow you in the street admiringly, thinking you had meat about your person to dispense to a good-looking dog who paid you the right kind of flattering attention. No amount of talking to these flirtatious canines could persuade them you were actually meat-free. Many a teenager growing up on a north-east council estate in the mid-1970s was the leader of a pack of feral dogs solely due to their over-consumption of beef-e crisps.

Ready salted Smiths crisps came with a legendary twist of salt in a bit of blue wax paper. Somehow, this twist of salt has become emblematic for the older generation of a simpler time when you could salt your own crisps and didn't have to suffer the oppression of having pre-salted crisps forced down your throat by the Brave New World snack industry.

Ah yes, a self-seasoning society is a happier society, which is why they brought the concept back in recent years, though somehow, it seems less glamorous now that we have X-Boxes, cable television and the internet to distract us from the simple pleasures of salting a sliver of fried potato.

Recently I met a bloke who claimed to be a snack food executive, which isn't something I'd go around bragging about, but he seemed happy to do so and he told me proudly that Britain eats more crisps than any country in Europe. This was a huge success to his way of thinking; proof of his snack food executive qualities. He seemed less pleased when I exclaimed, with typical insensitivity, 'That must be why kids are so fat!'

He bragged that Britain gets through 10,000,000,000 packets a year – yes, ten billion. Over seven kilos of crisps a year each, which is more than half the total eaten in all the EU countries combined. It's a wonder the nation has time to do anything else. I almost never eat them myself. Seems like you get a lot of calories but not much food with crisps. So who the hell is getting my seven kilos?

If your pre-match rituals were conducted in a pub or social club, from the early 1960s onwards, and you didn't want to go down the exotic crisps road, there was always a card hanging up behind the bar, usually depicting a woman in a tight vest and knickers for no apparent reason, with minute packets of salted peanuts crammed into it. So that was at least first-class protein, albeit in a small amount and wedged under a woman's left breast. For me, any time you find peanuts under a woman's breast is a happy day, though less so if you find them in the downstairs department. That's just bad hygiene, though may offer a snack to sustain you through vigorous love-making.

Remember when dry-roast peanuts arrived on these shores around 1977? No, of course you don't. You've got a complete and wholesome life and the introduction of snack food is a commonplace event today, but let me tell you, it was a day of great taste sensation for the jaded boiled beef and carrots palate of 1970s Britain.

Planters dry-roast nuts were an orgasmic hit of MSG-based flavour. No night of drinking in the Stockton Arms was complete for me without at least one bag of them. No one seemed to have a nut allergy back then; if you saw someone who was a funny colour with a swollen head you'd just assume he'd had some sort of terrible accident involving industrial chemicals at ICI Wilton.

If you wanted something more challenging than crisps or nuts, why not go for a bag of pork scratchings? Whatever you do, don't eat them though. That would probably kill you or at least loosen your teeth. No, hang on to the bag because it may be useful if you're jumped by a gang of away fans. The contents of a bag of pork scratchings is so hard, sharp and angular that it can make an excellent knuckle duster in a fight.

When I started going drinking, many pubs had a large jar of pickled eggs on the bar. The eggs may have been in the malt vinegar for weeks and often looked more like the preserved specimens of some hideous tumour extracted by a Victorian body snatcher. The barman would fish the eggs out of the brown acetic acid with his bare, unwashed hands, grappling at the slippery vinegar-stained ovoid with big, pink, meaty fingers, before dumping it on the bar in front of you. Surprisingly, we parted with money in return for these sinister objects, the taste of which was not dissimilar to sucking a tramp's foot and which, once consumed, gave you evil flatulence, flatulence so sulphurous it burned your nostrils. Many believed the yellow fog of pollution that clouded the skies over Teesside was little more than one giant amalgam of pickled egg farts.

The largest jar of pickled eggs I ever saw was in a pub in Durham marketplace. It was so big, you could have got your whole head inside of it, lit a cigar and still had room to eat a stottie. It contained apparently limitless quantities of eggs, none of which was ever eaten, it seemed.

I even once witnessed a pickled egg being used as an offensive weapon by a football hooligan. This happened at Billingham Sinfonia, a great old club that plies its trade in the shadow of Teesside's chemical industries. A few of us turned up for this Northern League game, a few drinks worse for wear. One of our number had purloined three pickled eggs from the jar in the pub we'd done our pre-match drinking in. It was a boring game. Nil-nil with eighty minutes gone. Everyone was yawning and wondering where our lives went wrong and looking for extra-curricular entertainment.

'I bet I can hit the lino with this egg,' said Terry, one of the more drunk of our number.

'Bollocks man, you've no chance,' I said, reasoning that he'd had five pints of beer and couldn't even walk straight, much less throw straight. It was easily thirty feet to the admittedly violently bald head of the linesman.

'How much says I can?' he said.

'Three pints in the Tav says you can't,' I said, emboldened by intoxication.

'Right, you're on.'

He took a firm stance, waited until the lino was standing still on the halfway line when there was a halt in play, squinted heavily, took aim and chucked the egg.

It hit its target with unerring accuracy, splitting into a hundred pieces as it slapped into the back of the bald official's head.

We all cheered.

'Fucking run,' shouted Terry, and we took off at high pace out of the ground to evade any post-egg-assault consequences. There's nothing quite so satisfying in life as seeing pickled produce bounce off a head.

Anyway, for the egg-averse pub-goer in need of nourishment, help was on hand in the super space-age 1970s. There emerged a new and fantastic option to provide nutrition to hungry football fans and any other pleasure-seeker for that matter. It was modern, exotic and exciting and was served to you in a brittle brown polythene-style bag. It was the toastie.

For a while toasties were considered a very fancy, exotic foodstuff. Hot food in a pub! Amazing! You'll be telling me the barmaid has shaved her beard off next.

Ah yes, lovely molten hot food with the power to administer severe blistering to the lips and mouth if consumed without due care and attention.

In the 1970s men would look on admiringly as other men ordered a toastie, full of envy at the courage and cosmopolitan nature of this progressive fellow. So modern and upmarket, my god, he'd be eating caviar and voting Tory next.

Quite what the crinkly toasting bag had to do with the toastifying process wasn't clear, but we thought it must be something that the space programme had developed. Anything we didn't understand or seemed hi-tech was always assumed to be a development from NASA experiments while orbiting the moon. Teflon, TV dinners and Jimmy Hill's ties were all products of the space race.

The odd thing about the glamour of the toastie was – when all said and done – it was just a hot sarnie. We all ate cheese on toast and we all ate sarnies so it was hardly a massive culinary step to combine these into a new hybrid, but we had lower expectations in those days. So in such a culture, a hot toastie full of ham or cheese or, wonder of wonders, both, was a revolution of sorts and just the ticket to keep the gnawing cold at bay before an away game at Oldham Athletic. Though today it would be seen as a light snack, back then a toastie was a full meal. Genuinely.

A few of you would nip into a pub before an away game and the cry would go up, quiet at first, like a scarcely believed rumour, followed by a joyous yelp of, 'They do toasties!!' A cheer would rattle the rafters and, briefly, all was right with the world, at least until you had to start fighting the locals with only the aid of a bag of pork scratchings

Your other in-pub eating experience was possibly the most hazardous of all as it raised the possibility of proper life-threatening food poisoning. The sort of poisoning where your whole body goes into spasm and every orifice pours with unholy fluids as it tries to expel the evil invading bacteria. I'm talking about Roy Keane's favourite, shellfish.

This wasn't the prawn sandwich or anything quite so civilised. No, this was far more medieval. For many years, especially in towns that were near to fishing ports, a man would come round the pub carrying a big wicker basket full of bags of prawns, whelks and winkles, which you would eat with a wooden toothpick-style thing. He was a popular chap in the pubs of Newcastle.

A delicious salty taste of the sea, and excellent with pints of ale. However, this was before the age of refrigeration was common or mandatory, and after a few hours of being punted around hot, sweaty, hairy pubs, they would start festering.

If consumed before a game, by half time the only concern you had in life was not to pass the entire contents of your bowels on to the terrace. Grim-faced, sweating and with buttocks nipped together like the rollers of a steel mill, you'd have to waddle off to use the insanitary malfunctioning toilet facilities and thus miss the whole of the second half, which could be something of a blessing and perhaps even preferable to being present.

So for that winter of 1976, like thousands of others we'd always go to the Tav for a pint or two before every home game. Later on, we ventured into pubs in Middlesbrough too. Even now the first taste of beer in my mouth evokes those days, waiting for the game to start, the warm tingle of alcohol in the bloodstream keeping the bitter cold at bay. So it was obvious from an early age that this love of pre-match and post match drinking was all part of the match day experience. I doubt I'd have experienced it so early and so frequently if it wasn't for football. It created a context to do something that was basically illegal. Football gave me an excuse to get out the house, to get out and about and to experience the world.

But while Saturday lunchtimes were never less than great fun, the Wednesday-night game was really, really special. Football played under floodlights is just a better experience and when you add in a cold north-easterly and a skinful of local brew, you are talking living high on the 1970s hog. Even as the winter bit deep, it didn't dissuade me from getting two buses from my house to Middlesbrough, having three pre-match pints in the Corporation pub, walking to the ground, more often than not on my own, and enjoying Middlesbrough's brand of football.

I almost always went to evening games on my own. This was partly because few of my school friends liked football much and those who did were not allowed out on a weekday night on their own, and especially not to travel to the back streets of Middlesbrough to see the Boro kick lumps out of Stoke City or whoever in the company of that Nicholson boy who liked to go in pubs. Although I didn't know it at the time, I think some parents thought I was a bad influence.

But I didn't mind. In fact, I rather liked it on my own. As I got more confident of getting served, I wouldn't bother with the Tav and I would try out boozers in Middlesbrough on Albert Road. I avoided any pub that was thought to be or looked 'trendy'. This largely meant staying out of the Berni Inn or anywhere which had a new space-age-type theme. These places were dangerous. They attracted the nutter kids from the mentalist estates whose idea of a good night was to kick some poor sod into a bloody heap. They never went in 'old man' pubs, quite probably because they were the pubs their parents drank in and that would cramp their psycho style.

If a group of kids my age came into the pub, the old fellas would grumble and moan about 'bloody kids' and they'd shout at the landlord: 'Don't serve them, George.' The kids would be chucked out or told to sit quiet and not anger up the locals. But when you went in on your own, it was odd how much respect you'd get from the regulars.

I firmly believe that people in the north east are the most open and friendly you'll find in Britain; not everyone, clearly, but enough to make it a truism, at least back then. I'd get chatting to other solo drinkers at the bar of whatever pub I was in pre-match.

'Now then son, going to match are you?' some old lad would say in between draws on his fag. 'They'd be buggered without Hickton. I saw Wilf Mannion play y'know. Wilfy with 'is wings flappin'. Aye. What a player he was.'

I saw all of this as great experience. I didn't care that they were from a different generation; I just saw it all as experience to be absorbed: part of the folk culture of football. If I was short of money and couldn't afford another drink, a regular would put his hand in his pocket for me. I know today this kind of behaviour would be thought of as a bit dodgy – adults buying a kid booze; you can see the tabloid headlines – but nothing bad ever happened to me except it made me grow up quicker, which was something I was rather pleased about.

It made me feel different, or perhaps confirmed my difference to the kids who were sitting at home watching *Mind Your Language* or *The Rockford Files* and doing their homework. Stalking the dark streets of Teesside on winter nights with the drink in my bloodstream as a warming friend was a thrilling experience for me. I realised early on that booze was a friend, a sign, many have since told me, of an addictive personality and of an alcoholic in the making. I'm not so sure, but then I'm probably in denial, though if I was, would I say I was? Surely that means I'm not. Oh bollocks. Psychology is all bullshit. Let's have a drink and forget about it.

Later in life I met many other people who had undergone similar experiences through going to football matches because football brings all generations together, forcing them to mix socially in a way they never would otherwise in pre- and post-match drinking sessions. It could only happen in pubs. Drinking was central.

Oddly enough though, my football life was entirely separate and different from my emerging rock life. Having started going to gigs aged fifteen, the first being Ace at Middlesbrough Town Hall, I didn't go to gigs on my own, always with a gang. The Talbot, the great rock cellar bar at the top of Stockton High Street, was a place I rarely if ever sat and drank alone in. It was place to party, to turn up in a crowd, put Frigid Pink on the jukebox, get drunk and smoke dope in the bogs.

We'd get coaches to Newcastle City Hall to see the big bands. These were run by a small company called Beggs Travel. You booked a seat on the coach and got a ticket for the gig as well. They'd take us up there and take us back home; a coach full of hairy, heavy rockers going up the A19 to see the likes of Alex Harvey, Uriah Heep and Bad Company.

On one of these trips I had my first experience of being properly drunk. It was on a trip to see Wishbone Ash in 1977. They were touring their *New England* album, a damn fine record that is too. I was with Jimmy, Russell and Cav; someone had brought a bottle of Southern Comfort. We drank the whole bottle in the hour it took us to get to Newcastle. This was somewhat destabilising. The rest of the events of the night are somewhat hazy. I was the least worst, due to my drink tolerance being marginally higher than theirs. I recall there was vomiting inside the City Hall by some but, being made of sterner stuff, I held on to my stomach contents until the return journey. I tended to get travel sick anyway but with a third of a bottle of Southern Comfort swilling around in me, there was always only going to be one outcome.

When the nausea got irresistibly strong, I bent over in my seat and retched. To my drunken surprise, what came out of my mouth wasn't the expected stream of diced carrots and mush but instead, what appeared to be a whole fried egg, perfect in every way; a circle of white with a centre of yellow yolk. It flopped out of my mouth on to the blue vinyl floor of the coach. I'd had egg and chips for my tea so it seemed that the constituent parts of the eggs had regrouped in my gut and re-formed their post-cooked shape. I stared in disbelief, thinking this must be some sort of drink-addled delusion. I poked it with my desert boot and it slid under the seat in front on a trail of stomach bile. To my drunken mind, this seemed all the more shameful. To be sick was embarrassing enough, but to throw up identifiable dishes seemed plain weird. What next, a bowl of corn flakes and a bacon sandwich?

In all my subsequent years of debauchery, I never once threw up anything as distinctive as a fried egg again. Peas, carrots, oh yes; I have exhaled Bailey's through my nose, and on one memorable occasion in a motel outside of Santa Barbara, projectile vomited beetroot, but a whole fried egg? No, and I assume I'm the only man on earth ever to have done so.

I haven't drunk Southern Comfort since and I swear the smell of it brings that night back vividly. It taught me that getting totally shit-faced was no fun at all. Not that it stopped me repeating the experience time and again for the next twenty years. I seem to have learned my limits now and haven't lost a few days to the drink for ten years or so. So eventually, I learned the lesson.

So it was with the twin pillars of rock 'n' roll and football culture that I grew up, both supported and enhanced by drinking, and I am not unique at all in that.

The British really don't need any excuse whatsoever to start a drinking session, and if one presents itself we'll be quick to take it and exploit it to the maximum, be it a wedding, a bank holiday or a sunny afternoon.

We live in a society dominated by a boozing culture, from the cheap three-litre bottles of white cider consumed on the bereft housing estates by people in loose-fitting sportswear, to the G&T golf club brigade who put the world to rights from behind half a bottle of the hard stuff, to the lads and lasses down the town on a Friday night drinking for oblivion, drinking to free themselves of the torment of normalness.

Drink is what defines us in the same way that food defines American culture. This is well illustrated by a wine tour a friend and I once went on in Monterey, California. Naturally, we thought it was a chance to have a bit of a piss-up. We were driven around several vineyards on a trolley bus – why a trolley bus I have no idea, but a trolley bus it was – driven by a guy who looked like he'd been the guitarist in Blue Cheer in 1968: lots of grey-blonde hair and eyes that had been to the other side.

So there were maybe thirty Americans there and us two English. The first concern for the Americans is when lunch would happen but for us, eating was a strictly peripheral activity to drinking. So we went about necking several fine vintages and some of the best Pinot Noir that has ever ticked my tonsils (if I had tonsils) from the Bernardus winery.

A few hours later we roll up to the trolley bus, not exactly caned but we could certainly see caned from where we were. The rest of the Americans are eating sandwiches and waiting for us. We have bought more wine than all of them put together. The first thing I see is a moon-faced mound of blubber with mayo on her face, pushing the last morsel of a massive sandwich into her meat-hole. Technically this had once been a woman but was now a largely inanimate blob of fat who had replaced all human joy with the consumption of food.

'You guys sure like drinking dontcha?' she said sneeringly as though this was the moral equivalent of horsewhipping small children. It was all the more galling to hear this from a giant sack of cholesterol wrapped in little more than a tarpaulin. Had this been Britain, rolling up somewhat unsteadily with an armful of drink would just be normal. Indeed, we might well have received a small cheer as a reward for our consumption of lovely, lovely booze.

You can always spot a Brit who is in America for the first time because he walks into a bar and, rather than sit down and wait for someone to bring him a drink, even when it's obviously table service, he will march purposefully to the bar. We like to be in control of our drink. We want it when we want it, not when someone else wants to bring it to us. That being said, there are fewer finer things in life than being served drink by an attentive waitress.

Last summer, a group of us were in Bill's Gamblin' Hall in Las Vegas, trying to lose money slowly on the poker machines. A pretty Filipino waitress kept bringing us free gin and tonics, maybe one every ten or fifteen minutes. Getting the guests pissed will earn you a bigger tip and the casino more money as your customers fritter away cash in a drunken stupor. After a couple of hours, she came back with the latest round and said, 'Wow, you guys can really drink', which we took as a compliment, as any Brit abroad would.

There is much phoney outrage about binge drinking today, as though this is a new thing. If it is new, it is only new to the middle class, to the nice kids. I was drinking three or four pints of Heineken most nights when I was sixteen, and I was not alone. The cavernous clubs and pubs of the north east were packed with people drinking heroically. Let's not pretend it's ever been different. The gin laws were brought in nearly 300 years ago to try to combat the same habits that we condemn in our so-called broken society today. We just detail, document and hand-wring about it more than ever now. Just because it's new on your TV doesn't mean it's a new thing in itself.

For most of the Industrial Revolution it was normal to see pubs near factories have the bar counter completely loaded with pulled pints of beer just before knocking-off time to slake the thirst of hundreds of men as they left work. Men who had spent all day shovelling coal or pouring molten iron didn't go home and eat a nice alfalfa sprout salad and read Proust; hell no, they piled into the nearest boozer and got leathered on pint after pint of foaming ale; usually ale that was brewed locally.

I recall seeing this on Teesside in pubs near Head Wrightsons works in Thornby as late as 1979. A major local employer, it was a massive ironwork factory that made all sorts of heavy industrial stuff. Hot, hard work.

It was quite a sight to witness hundreds of men streaming into a pub and draining glass after glass of bitter ale. Because there was less hysterical media coverage and fewer hysterical people around at the time, no one called it binge drinking at the time it was just a working man slaking his thirst after a hard day's graft. And who can complain about that?

That all being said, we don't consume nearly as much booze as the Germans and others in Europe. France has as many if not more alkies apparently. But it is the central place that drink occupies in our culture that makes it such a dominant force in British society. The idea of doing anything on a day off while not sinking some alcohol fills the majority of us with horror.

Some are snooty and conclude that we might *need* to drink to have a good time, but I beg to differ. We don't need it but it's just that it makes every day brighter, more colourful. Perhaps it's our weather. The dark skies of a rainy summer, the short dark cold days of endless winter lead us naturally to the fireside at home or in a boozer to oink a pint, a dram or a glass of the grape.

We celebrate with drink, we commiserate with drink. So it is no surprise that drink is crucial in the majority of our football lives. So when sponsors such as Carling and Worthington started to put money into football, it was a natural home for them.

There are moves to ban alcohol advertising in sport, but does the fact that Carling sponsor the League Cup make us drink more?

Certainly not more Carling, which is an insipid lager that is neither strong nor cheap enough to compensate for its taste.

The pre-match drink-up doesn't seem to have changed at all since the mid-1970s. It was always popular and it still is. What has changed markedly is the culture of drinking at home in front of the telly. That simply never happened until Sky bought football and put it on live on our screens. Even when I started my boozing career, drinking at home was regarded as something only alcoholics and stressed-out mothers did. There was something almost seedy about the idea unless it was Christmas or New Year or a party.

Hard to imagine now, but coming home with a couple of mates and a bag of a dozen cans was the stuff of special celebrations only. You didn't do it just because Blackburn were playing Bolton on the telly. Obviously, there was little live football on, so the pre- and post-match drink in your local was the only place drink and football could interface.

It was also where a match was reviewed, dissected and players assessed. This might seem to be stating the obvious, but these days there are so many other options via electronic communication. You can email your mate on the beach in San Diego and tell him how rubbish the goalie was. You can go on message boards' phone-ins and send emails to websites. You can read a thousand different views of the game you've just seen. All we had in the 1970s and 1980s was the pub, a table and a pint. Ironically, the conversation is just the same, vulgar, largely biased, irrational and over-focused on the short-term!

When Sky bought the rights to live football, they quickly understood that football is a communal game, best enjoyed with your mates, so they set about selling their service into pubs up and down the land. Soon signs stating 'Sky TV Here' had sprung up everywhere and sucked in football fans for a game, all keen to drink and watch football.

Initially, the cost of subscription inhibited sales, so the pub became a surrogate terrace for games and it's been like that ever since. The big-screen game is commonplace and this year the first 3D broadcasts were done in pubs. Drinking and football have become best buddies and nowhere do we see that more than in the way pub culture has adapted to absorb the wish to see live football.

The drinking culture that had always existed before and after a game from the mid-1990s was transposed into the boozer and to the front room as people stocked up with drink for a big game on their TV. This is now a way of life and unexceptional, yet when it first started it was neither. A Sky pub was a very desirable destination for a night out and having Sky became a highly prized asset for pubs because it guaranteed a full boozer when there was a big game on.

On such occasions pubs have become surrogate terraces, packed to the rafters with fans chanting and singing just as they would if they were at the game. No TV news report of a big game is complete without footage of people going bananas in a pub.

As it became a seven-days-a-week sport, football excused and facilitated seven-days-a-week drinking. Hurrah! Get in!

If you're under the age of thirty you won't remember a time when the football-in-a-pub phenomenon didn't exist, but it's been a huge cultural shift.

For most of my early drinking years, the idea of any TV being on in a pub was frowned upon because it was a conversation stopper. In fact the few televisions that were on in drinking establishments were usually in the Social Club.

I vividly remember watching Bob Wilson on *Football Focus* in the late 1970s in a club in Sunderland. For some reason I'd gone to Roker Park to watch the Mackems play Luton. It was 2-2 and bloody freezing, Roker Park being set by the North Sea, seemingly as a test of your northern masculinity.

The old wood-encased black-and-white TV was propped up on a shelf and was turned up to Hendrix-style distortion levels. Standing at the bar drinking Federation Ale as Bob talked to Asa Hartford was a rare and exotic experience and stands out in the memory as such, which just shows how unusual football on a telly in a bar or club was.

But today you can go to almost any pub and watch the latest game on screens small, medium and humongous. Indeed, with the price of tickets for some grounds being so high, this is the nearest a new generation of fans gets to the community aspect of the live football experience. And it's all to be welcomed really; drinking while watching football is enormously pleasurable.

However, oddly enough, we are not allowed by law to drink booze in a football ground while in sight of the pitch. This is illegal, presumably because the law-makers consider the sheer raw excitement of seeing a footballer kicking a ball, combined with sweet, sweet booze, will cause a riot. But if you consume the drink while watching it on an in-ground TV you won't tear the place down. No of course it doesn't make any sense. In fact it is total bollocks. And it's total bollocks because the Tory government of the 1980s drew up the legislation in a panic in the wake of Heysel and thoughtlessly rushed it through to look like they were doing something.

Apparently on European nights no booze is allowed to be sold in the stadiums at all. There's even a Facebook page set up to complain about that, so you know it must be a serious concern. And you've not been able to buy drink in a Scottish ground since the Scottish Cup Final 1980 when some drunken Celtic and Rangers fans indulged in an orgy of violence so heinous that the government, in another 'something must be done' spasm, banned the sale of it, conveniently forgetting that most fans were hammered before arriving. A Scotsman needs several hours to get properly drunk; he can't do it in an hour and a half inside a football ground. Do they know nothing?

But the relationship the authorities have had with football and alcohol has always been an uneasy one, which culminated in the mid-1980s with drink being banned from sale in grounds. But this deprived clubs of much-needed income, so eventually the ridiculous compromise we have today was introduced.

You might be interested to read the relevant bit of the Sporting Events (Control of Alcohol etc.) Act 1985. It's

> an offence of trying to enter a ground when drunk or in possession of alcohol; of possessing or consuming alcohol within view of the pitch during the period of the match; or being drunk during the period of the match.

This is the bit that means that even if you're in an expensive executive box you're breaking the law if you watch the game with a glass of Chardonnay in your hand. Mad isn't it? And frankly, I've been to many games while drunk and stoned and no one tried to stop me. Of course not. Unless you're being an arsehole and causing trouble, what's the problem with being drunk? Most people when drunk are fine; some are admittedly nutters but frankly, they're usually also nutters when sober.

Christ knows, being pissed was the only way to get through several seasons of watching the Boro. Talking of which, one poor sod was kicked out of the Riverside for falling asleep during the game after a skinful. He even had his season ticket revoked. After a public outrage which understood that being asleep and intoxicated was an entirely reasonable response to watching Middlesbrough play, he was forgiven and allowed to torture himself once again and pay for the privilege so to do.

Some of the more readily outraged members of British society are snooty about drinking and football, seeing the worst aspects of some fans' behaviour as the direct consequence of their consumption of lager. But this is largely an urban myth. Social scientists who have studied the relationship between drinking and violence at football have found little commonality between drunken fans and violence. The Italian Ultras are rarely heavy drinkers but are some of the most violent fans, yet the Danish *Roligans* like a big booze-up but rarely cause trouble. The Scots, once the most feared of drunken hooligans, capable of dismantling your entire stadium and taking it home in a million different pieces, still drink heavily before games but the Tartan Army rarely gets into any bother these days. They moderated their behaviour. The Irish can drink your whole country dry and ask for more and will still almost never cause any trouble.

So despite the tabloid culture that grips this country insisting that boozing causes trouble at football, the reality is that people who like to fight and break up a cafe in a quiet Belgian market town or overturn a burger fan in Barnsley also like to drink. The drink doesn't make them do it; they're prone to do it already. Many are in fact sober when doing it. However, why anyone wants to behave like that in the first place is a deeper cultural issue.

The truth is, all parts of British society drink and get rowdy. Have you ever been to the Henley Regatta? It's a nightmare. Middle-aged women off their face on gin, ruddy-faced Home Counties colonels flushed with burgundy, hooray Henriettas and their vile male counterparts barking out their Pimms-enhanced vowels. It's worse than anything you'll see outside a pub in Middlesbrough on a Friday night.

The nice middle-class rugger buggers quaff yards of ale and then light their own farts. What fun. If that was done by the working class it would be viewed as one of the signs of the on-rushing apocalypse. Wimbledon is the home of those frumpy, dumpy potato-looking women of the Home Counties getting over-excited after too much rosé, emitting high-pitched squeals as Andy Murray hits a ball over a net. It's not hooliganism but it's pissed-up public behaviour nonetheless.

Glyndebourne's champagne tent does brisk trade, as it would at any of those 'light opera in the park' events. In fact one of the most pissed-up events I went to recently was a food fair in Edinburgh's Inverleith Park. It was one of those weekend affairs where lots of posh nosh producers turn up and sell their wares. You can sample everything and there are bars and such everywhere. It was attended largely by wealthy middle-class Edinburgh society, by the end of the Saturday night there were gangs of respectable women cackling and whooping while their belly-heavy husbands staggered home with bags full of pricey wine.

OK there were no fights, pissing in people's gardens or songs sung about anally violating a footballer's wife, though there was a nasty argument over the last truckle of a fine Orkney cheddar, but it was as rowdy as any pub when there's a big game on.

The difference is, when the middle classes get drunk, they are not judged harshly by the working class, who understand that getting drunk is an important and necessary part of life. But the more judgemental among the middle class see the working-class drunk as morally reprehensible scum and can't see how similar their own behaviour sometimes is.

All these occasions have one thing in common: communal drinking.

There is something life-affirming about collective intoxication among people who enjoy the same sort of things in life.

This was brought home to me in 1979 when I went to see Led Zeppelin at Knebworth. It was a one-day festival in a massive field filled with upwards of 150,000 people. I had never been in a crowd bigger than the 20,000 the Boro would get occasionally.

This was almost beyond comprehension.

I'd gone with my brother and his girlfriend. We'd travelled down overnight and arrived early in the morning in time to get a position around 200 yards from the stage, so quite near the front really. As the day went on, the crowd stretched out behind us into the distance. It took thirty minutes to walk out to the giant trenches of turds that professed to be toilets.

By the time Zeppelin took the stage at sundown, the crowd was collectively hammered. A biker chick stripped off near to us, revealing a pair of breasts so huge they could have assuaged the hunger of a small Third World nation's children.

After a day boozing in the sun, the crowd was in high spirits and it was very much like being at a big game. The only difference was that everyone supported the same team and there was no enemy or opposition in site, though DJ Nicky Horne did get some abuse and Chas 'n' Dave, weirdly booked as the opening act of the day, were largely ignored. There is a powerful bond between a large crowd all in support of the same thing. After the encore, the band stood on the stage and took their bow. The noise that greeted them was profound. It vibrated through you like a nuclear explosion; so much love and excitement and passion in one direction. It was another twenty-seven years before I experienced a similar out-pouring of joy.

When Middlesbrough went on an epic UEFA Cup run in 2006, twice they came from behind to win 4-3 on aggregate. Against Steaua Bucharest, after twenty minutes they were 2-0 down on aggregate, had to score four times to go through to the final and had their captain injured. Middlesbrough had never played in Europe before. It was an amazing time for all of us. As Maccarone rose to head the winner with minutes to go, the Riverside, not normally a noisy ground, erupted into a visceral explosion of sound. It was very moving and very life-affirming. Very like witnessing Zeppelin's epic Knebworth concert in fact: that same bond and unity of the collective celebrating the same thing simultaneously and also, mostly, to some degree, drunk.

Nearly thirty-five years on since that first pre-match drink in the Tav, it's remarkable how, as a ritual, it has changed very little. I still wouldn't go to a game without a drink in me if at all possible, though these days it would be a decent wine rather than a few pints. While so much else about football has changed, this element remains true and constant up and down the land. Proof if it were needed that the British are still a right old bunch of drunks and, what's more, we always have been.

Football and booze still form the perfect marriage, together for ever and ever, amen.

3

Anger

IF you write for a very popular website such as Football365 and gets over 1.4 million unique visitors every month, a lot of people will read what you have to say. Naturally, football being a divisive sport, you will often encounter those who agree with your point of view and many who disagree. Some will love your work and others loathe it. It's the way it's always been, but in days gone by, if you wrote for a newspaper, you'd rarely hear from the public. The occasional letter to the editor was about as interactive as the process got.

Even when I first started writing for F365 in 2000 there was simply a readers' letters page. But it has all changed in the last couple of years. Now, we have, along with most publications, a blog under each piece which allows registered users to post their comments. These comments are moderated. In other words, someone in the office looks at them and deletes anything libellous or racist. But outside of the main taboos, all comments make it on to the site on the principle that even if it's a witless, stupid remark, it will be critiqued as such by the posters' contemporaries.

In these circumstances, as a writer you need to have both balls of steel and a very thick skin. It's not always dominated by critics and there are a lot of positive comments, but the criticism, when it comes, is often vitriolic and insulting and often utterly misinformed. The most annoying thing is when people assert that you've said or assumed something that you blatantly haven't. It's amazing how many times people just don't read what you have actually written and instead respond to what they think you have written. Others seem less interested in any point you are making and more in trying to find some perceived hypocrisy or contradiction. Weirdly, I occasionally get accused of self-indulgence, as though being a writer is anything other than self-indulgent.

I suspect those who say that do so when I write about football with reference to something in my life or an incident in the past. But the idea is to create something personal and unique, not trot out a load of facts and figures; that's for journalists to do and I'm not one of those. If it doesn't interest you then fair enough but why have a pop at me for not being what you want in a football writer? This doesn't just happen to me, it happens to everyone who writes online.

Imagine if in your job you routinely got called 'moron', 'tool', 'dickhead', 'wanker', 'nasty', 'bastard', 'cunt' or 'total fuckwit', 'terrible writer' or regularly attracted comments like 'absolute shite', 'I hate this', 'waste of my time' and 'utter drivel', how would it make you feel? There are not many jobs where this happens routinely. Equally there are few jobs where strangers praise you for your work.

I often write a piece purely to see how a specific idea plays and the kind of responses it gets, regardless of my own opinion or view of it. Sometimes it's like lobbing a grenade on to the site and seeing what the explosion provokes. I don't buy the idea that as a writer I have to hold a consistent position or be even-handed. My job is to entertain and stimulate. That's how I see it, anyway. Each column isn't supposed to be part of one big John Nicholson manifesto.

Many criticise me and others too for not being fair and balanced, thinking that a journalist should be both those things. I'm not sure where they got this idea from. For a start, as I say, I'm not a journalist, because that would involve more rigour and adherence to the facts than I could handle.

Second, F365 and most other football writers' work are clearly opinion-driven. It's an individual's perception at that time, not intended to be some even-handed assessment of events. Indeed, if it was, the pieces would be very boring. So such criticism is based on a prospectus that was never on offer.

There are a few fans of clubs – by definition the least impartial people – who write and accuse me and the rest of the team of bias against their club, as though their view is the most objective available. It's something that is regularly mocked and rightly so.

It's also curious how these critics define bias. To most it would seem that being biased against, say, Arsenal, is proved by your writing a critical piece about Arsenal. The more rational members of the world can see that these two things are entirely different. But in some fans' minds if you're not 100 per cent on board, you're 100 per cent against. They will accuse you of not being similarly critical of other sides, as though in order to critique one club you must also do the same for each of the other nineteen to keep things balanced.

The truth is I don't hate any team and am not in any way biased against any. Maybe I should be. Most football people have a blind dislike of at least one club. But I never have had and I don't see the point of trying to pretend otherwise, even though I know this is relatively unusual. I've tried it on but it's a coat that doesn't seem to fit me well.

As kids growing up we were encouraged to dislike all London sides. London was always to be despised. However, I found this hard because I liked the early-1970s flash Chelsea side. I liked Bobby Moore at West Ham, Charlie George at Arsenal and Jimmy Greaves at Spurs. I do admit to having a soft spot for some sides. QPR is one. Their 1974–75 side was one of the best to watch ever and for some reason I've looked out for them since. Similarly I liked Liverpool for its history and for Shanks. I always was in awe of Old Trafford and Man. Utd; it was like going to see the biggest band in the world play to go there, like seeing Led Zeppelin, maybe. Across at Maine Road, City were full of mercurial talent like Summerbee, Marsh and Lee, who were a pleasure to watch.

So even now, I really don't have any irrational hatred against any club. Not even Hartlepool. It'd not be fair to hate Hartlepool; it'd be like hating a three-legged dog.

But even stating this won't stop people making up shit in their head and telling me it's the truth.

When this fashion for blogged responses first began three or four years ago it was easy to get caught up in the anger directed at you, often very personally. People will lay into the most innocuous remarks in an article as though you have expressed a fondness for torturing kittens. People don't just disagree with what after all is just a point of view; they take it as a personal insult to them. Oddly, others patronise writers with comments such as 'not your best work', 'fail', or 'must try harder' or some such withering – so they think – criticism.

I recall one poster who said he only decided to read the piece based on the responses to it! Another claimed, after being criticised by other bloggers for slagging off an article, that his motive was to make the writers better at their job. Only someone choking on their own hubris would entertain for a moment that any writer worth their salt would take guidance from some bloke idly posting on the internet. That is to seriously overrate yourself, son.

At first I found this anger disturbingly over-sensitive and out of all proportion to the importance of the subject matter. But I soon realised that this was all part of one of football's most important cultural roles in society; it's a place to release all your negative emotions and frustrations. Websites, blogs and message boards are just a new version of the terraces. That's why they've grown so huge and so many people use them. They facilitate the whining, moaning and bitching which is the birthright of every football fan.

Football has long been a pressure valve for society, allowing thousands of people to vent emotions that would otherwise be stewing inside of us. We scream blue murder at opposition players or players on our own sides who we think are not pulling their weight. It matters not whether the subject of our wrath deserves the ire being poured on to him – he probably doesn't – but he's there, you've had a hard week and so you give it to him with both barrels. That's how it works, now more than ever. So it is with message boards and blogs. Your life is rubbish and here's a bloke saying something mildly disparaging about a footballer you like. Right, let's get the twat . . . and out it all comes.

For years I've assigned the characters of people I dislike in life to footballers I don't even know. I had an unwarranted dislike of Billy Bromnor for years merely because he, like a boy who bullied me at school, was small and ginger. By shouting abuse at Billy I was, in some way, getting revenge on the bully. It certainly let out the hurt and emotional trauma. I was never happier than when Mick Mills was getting a kicking because he looked like an especially vicious teacher I had. To see someone ploughing into him was almost as good as doing it yourself.

I knew a bloke who would shout insults at Peter Osgood every season on the basis that Osgood bore a resemblance to his boss. Even now I find myself disliking someone such as David Bentley not because I have any idea what he's like as a man, but because he seems emblematic of the bling and bollocks celebrity culture that so many people seem obsessed with and which I loathe. It's unfair really; should I expect him to read Kurt Vonnegut and collect Italian Poor Art? No. He's just a regular, if uneducated lad and is behaving like many would in the same circumstances. So it goes. It's not him, it's me.

For me, as someone who is loath to get properly angry, I've always found watching aggressive football releases what aggression I do have. In fact, non-aggressive football really bloody annoys me. In the 1970s and 1980s when hooliganism was rife, there were people who said that the physical nature of the game was making people angry and violent. This was a right load of old bollocks.

There was little trouble at rugby games and that's a much more violent sport So the correlation between on-pitch violence and crowd violence was always spurious, being born out of wider social issues and problems. Personally, growing up seeing Graeme Souness plough through some poor sod, kicking him to the ground like a Kung Fu master, released any pent-up violent tendencies I had. It didn't make me want to go out and emulate it; quite the opposite, in fact.

No, from an early age I saw the on-pitch aggression in football as the perfect release for any violent tendencies I had. When you've been brought up watching Souey stamping on players, you walk away from the game a spent force, all too painfully aware of man's inhumanity to man. OK, maybe that was just me.

Aggression between sets of supporters is now more usually fought out on the message boards than on the back streets of Britain, which is progress of sorts, I suppose. But occasionally you do see vestiges of the seventies state of mind.

I was at Hibernian to see Middlesbrough play a pre-season friendly and there was a small section of the Hibs fans that were almost insane with desire to wind up the few Boro fans that were present, gesturing at them to come have a go if they thought they were hard enough. It wasn't witty banter; it was just pointless, raw, naked aggression. Naturally, Boro's fans were indifferent to this abuse, being largely a few drinks in and a bit sleepy in the late-July sun and anyway, who wants to have a running battle with a few Irn Bru- and vodka-fuelled Scotsmen in Leith?

My football education, indeed my early life as a whole, in common with all my contemporaries, was played out against a backdrop of simmering aggression and violence. I thought it was normal because, for years, it just was. You learned to get a sixth sense, an antennae that twitched if something was about to kick off. You could almost see it before it happened. While I took it for granted as a way of life, it always seemed wrong. Wrong at school, wrong on Stockton High Street on a Friday night and wrong at football. Others were more ambivalent, thinking it was all part of life, all part of growing up and of being a man. But I was certain, being violent didn't make you strong, it made you weak. But I couldn't say that to anyone. In fact, I'm not sure I could have cogently expressed such a notion. I just felt it. I may also have been a soft git too, of course.

By the time I was a teenager this anti-violence state of mind was entrenched. It's easy to forget so many years later, but violence and aggression were almost demanded of you at a state school. Mine wasn't the worst school in the region but nonetheless every day was an assault course to be carefully negotiated. I had a permanent siege mentality, always aware that someone would be looking to pick on me for some reason.

Nowhere was safe. Even when eating school dinners someone could and would put a fork to your throat and demand your sausages with menaces. For a couple of years there was a group of hard lasses from the appropriately named Hardwick Estate who, en masse, would take your food under threat of violence. They'd also eat cast away food from the slop trays. I presume they were either very hungry or had terrible tapeworms. These girls were, if anything, worse than their male counterparts because they could humiliate you sexually as well as bully you for food or money. We called them the Slag Bags.

One time I was sitting there eating the weird gloop that was defined as cheese pie and two Slag Bags came up to me.

'Stop looking at my tits,' one said. I looked up and glanced at her chest. It was impressive for her age but I hadn't been looking at it prior to this prompt.

'He's doing it again! You dirty little cunt. Do you want to have a wank?' the other said, charmingly.

This is guaranteed to make any fourteen-year-old boy go puce with embarrassment. I mean, what can you say? I chose to shake my head, hoping this would make the humiliation stop.

'You don't want to have a wank? What's wrong with you? Don't you like girls, you fucking poof?' she responded, so quickly and with such good timing that it suggested this was a well-rehearsed strategy, oft repeated.

'Give us your pie or I'll tell Smez that you're a poof.'

Naturally I handed over the pie. Smez was the king of the school bullies and not to be messed with. His name struck fear into the hearts of pretty much all boys.

Nasty, aggressive little incidents like this were commonplace at school. It was brutal really and it all helped me to form this kind of hippy-ish, anti-war, anti-violence mentality, and this was further entrenched when I was fourteen when my dad, for the first and only time, told me about his experience in the war. The fact that thirty-five years later this is still imprinted on my consciousness, tells me how deep it went and how much it affected how I thought about life subsequently.

My dad was a Desert Rat and fought Rommel in the North African desert, aged just eighteen; a skinny, scared kid from the sleep-five-to-a-bed back-to-back terraces of Hull, who had never been out of Yorkshire, let alone out of the country. He was a gunner. It was his job to aim the guns on the enemy, to sight them accurately. He won medals for it. Which, it later occurred to me, meant he was responsible for killing a lot of Germans. At the end of the war, he threw all his medals away. Binned them. I knew this only because my mother had told me. He wouldn't talk much about it. Then in the third year at school, I had to do a project about the battle of El

Alamein, a battle that, as a gunner, my dad had taken an important part in. So I asked him about it. He was a Yorkshireman and, as such, intrinsically emotionally repressed from birth, but he briefly opened up what must surely have been a whole vault of experience and emotion. He didn't say much but I wrote it down and used it in my project.

'We captured a load of them. They came through our camp in a long line. They were kids, just like me. Scared out of their minds, a long way from home and petrified they'd get killed. They had a different uniform on to us but they were just the same as us. Young lads, conscripted, doing what they'd been told was right. They weren't like the Nazis in the war films. Some of them had shit themselves in fear of us. We looked at them, they looked back at us. We knew we'd killed their mates, they knew they'd killed ours. No one said anything. We didn't try and lord it over them because we'd captured them. We were all in the same boat really. I remember thinking, "How has it come to this, us lot blowing the shit out of each other in the desert?" But no one was allowed to question anything. It was traitor talk. We all shut up and did what we were told. But I know, from what people told me after the war, that probably most men there felt the same.

'It was hard after that, knowing that you were fighting people who were, really, just like yourself. The next time I was told to sight a gun, I felt sick. But I did it anyway – I didn't want to but what choice did I have? I hope you never find yourself, in your life, in that position. I wish I had never had to.'

That was literally all I ever got out of him about over five years of service in the army. You don't have to be Carl Jung to do the psychology. It really upset me at the time to think he was only eighteen and blowing the crap out of people and I think this all added to the idea in my teenage mind that there was little glamour in fighting.

While I enjoy a muscular game as much as if not more than most, and the odd on pitch fight is always a joy, by and large violence has never had an attraction for me the way it does for some blokes. I even find watching boxing a bit disturbing. I can't watch those programmes on TV which feature CCTV footage of violence in city centres; the sort of programmes that purport to be addressing a serious issue but are really just fight-porn. I think it brings the worst out in humans so I purposely turn away from it.

I think the culture of fans has changed from the one I grew up with as a kid in the 1970s. We always sang vulgar songs – a surreal one about Alan Gowling fucking Alsatians sticks in the mind, why Alsatians I have no idea – and we always booed the opposition. We would jeer at players like Chopper Harris for removing the legs of one of our players with a scything tackle, but it was never really personal and we knew it wasn't. It all happened within the context of the ground and the game. We didn't know anything much about the players as men. We didn't take their actions to heart as somehow emblematic of a greater malaise or condition. It was just football. We were glad to have the emotional release of shouting for an hour and a half but that's where it ended.

Today, with the growth of the interactive culture which has encouraged everyone to believe that they have a right to be heard, alongside the growth in what we have to, through gritted teeth, call celebrity culture, things have started to take a weird turn.

For me this started when fans began reporting players to the police for 'incitement to riot' when a player made a gesture at the crowd. This would never have happened until recently and I see it as part of this culture of 'me me me'.

There are people who feel they have paid their money so they've a 'right' to abuse a player, but if he so much as gives a hand gesture back, they are outraged and demand the player is hauled up for incitement to riot, as though spectators have no control or personal responsibility for their own actions.

Just because Gary Neville is thrusting his groin at you, as he did once famously in front of Liverpool fans, there is no need, nor any reason, to feel the urge to become riotous let alone report Mr Neville to the police. His groin is no threat to you.

There are too many who have become emotionally incontinent, raging at perceived injustices when no such injustice exists. And yet at the football it is allowed and this continues to be a strong attraction of the game. Where else can you vent virtually any emotion or publicly insult people who cannot answer back or do you any harm. It's an opportunity you don't get in any other walk of life. Indeed, in most other walks of life you are required to repress these emotions.

However, I draw a distinction between frustration or moaning and actual anger. Anger is a much more powerful emotion, a bigger measurement on the emotional ruler. Call me old-fashioned but I reckon if you're getting really angry a lot, especially at football, then you've either got too much sugar and caffeine in your diet or you're a whack job.

If frustration or indignation at something a player does gets ratcheted up into outright anger, then surely it's gone too far. I feel sorry for players who become hate figures. We've seen this for England players such as Downing, Lampard, Bentley and Ashley Cole, all of whom have been booed and abused at one time or another. Personally, I'd never boo one of my own players. But football is there for everyone and if you want to do it you can.

I was brought up in an environment where showing emotion, especially as a male of the species, was regarded as weak. Be it happiness or anger, it showed too much about you. Stoicism was the philosophy of choice and frankly, since I was a kid who felt things quite deeply, being encouraged not to break down in floods of tears of rage and hurt was not always a bad thing.

I've noticed that there is a lot of crying at football these days; it is a very modern affectation. I just saw Leeds get promoted recently and there were Yorkshire folk in the crowd weeping with the joy of finishing second in the third tier!

This would never have happened in the past and especially not in Yorkshire. Crying was reserved for a death in the family and pretty much nothing else and, even then, it was only for women.

Geordie fans have become famous for their incontinent tears of loss but this phenomenon is not confined to St James' Park. You'll see any amount of sobbing fans of relegated teams at the end of a season, picked out by the TV cameras. However, take a look at the 1966 Wembley crowd and you'll see no tears of joy like we saw at Leeds. Bobby Charlton shed more himself than the 100,000 assembled fans. The idea you would cry in public was bad enough but that you should do it over a game of football would have been seen not just as weak, or over-sensitive, but as a sign of some kind of mental breakdown. Children cry, adults don't. Not at a football game. That was the mantra and even as a tearful kid you'd be told not to be so silly and grow up. We now live in a world where some adults behave like kids, it seems.

In hindsight, though I fought against it as a teenager, I rather liked Britain when it was uptight and emotionally repressed; when we swallowed our anger and hatred down into a small ball of iridescent bile in the pit of our stomach and let it fester there until one day you find yourself on the roof of the town hall with a high-powered rifle creating the kind of news report that always ends with the words, 'before turning the gun on himself'.

Yes, at its extremes we were way too emotionally repressed – my family was full of repressed people who avoided talking about anything personal – but again in hindsight, there was much to be said for not getting yourself into a lather about stuff you can't control or that isn't really important.

I think this upbringing at the Boro gave me a perspective on life. Just because a bloke has scored against my club, even if he used to play for us and he celebrates a goal in front of me, I am just not going to lunge forward and try to choke the air out of his throat, reasoning that what a footballer does is never important enough to justify making any physical effort to hurt him or to get into a fury over. He's just a footballer, not a vicious dictator. This isn't because I'm some sort of saint; it's just a matter of perspective, though some have said it means I'm not a true fan. They would say a true fan *does* go ballistic and is manically defensive about his club. I'm just not wired that way.

When I was a kid going to watch the Boro, if anyone had gone into a rage, contorting their face in twisted hatred at a player or screaming abuse because a player had made a gesture to them, they would more than likely have been laughed at.

'What's wrong with 'im? Bloody big girl's blouse,' the old-timers would have said, having seen such levels of emotion only from their wives or mothers. After all, it had taken Hitler to incite these old lads into action, so a player making a wanking sign at the crowd was hardly likely to stir their ire. They'd more likely just laugh.

Sadly it doesn't stop there. Whether consciously or subconsciously, some fans have started to make public their moral judgements on footballers and managers, presumably feeling that they have a right to do so, based on tabloid news reports. I find this appalling. Ashley Cole was booed by some England fans because they didn't like him, his various affairs being in the papers at the time. Similarly, after John Terry had been in the news for his supposed infidelities there was a banner held up at Wembley at the next England game which declared 'John Terry: We Forgive You', as though the fans were some kind of priest or vicar. I take this as the same kind of self-reverence that leads people to believe that their criticism of writers will make the latter better at their jobs; they are the same people who claim they are being incited to riot. It's all part of the one mind-set.

It's quite something when a crowd of people act as moral arbiters. It suggests that they have something of a personal relationship with footballers. As though they are people they really know, so they're able and entitled to judge their behaviour accordingly. This is the monster that the up-close and personal saturation of modern media has created.

We don't behave like this in other walks of life, do we? We tend not to think, 'Well, I've paid to see this guitarist but he's taken cocaine and has syphilis so I shall boo him to express my displeasure at his lifestyle.' We go to see people whose art or talent we enjoy but who we might or might not like to have as a friend. That would certainly be the grown-up attitude.

Because of my upbringing at football and in life generally, I could never take it on myself to judge someone like that in public. We all have our thoughts and make our own judgements in private, but to publicly put up a banner proclaiming you've forgiven someone is a big step too far for me. I'm not that morally assured – or deluded. My first thought is always, hang on, who the fuck are you to appoint yourself as judge and jury? Maybe these people have been encouraged to think that their view matters, when frankly, I suspect it doesn't matter at all.

Growing up in an environment where being phlegmatic and stoic was the norm seems to have stood me in good stead for these more hysterical, hyperbolic times that, symbolically at least, seemed to start with the death of Diana, a time when wallowing in grief seemed for some to constitute proof of their own worth, of their own good morality even. It made some adults become childlike in their emotional overload.

Blogs on popular websites are there for one main reason: to boost page impressions and thus advertising fees. People love to see their own posting up there, will return to see if it's been published and then again to see if there are any responses, thus taking the traffic numbers skywards.

If the bloggers knew the degree to which some of them are mocked, disregarded and laughed at by the people who publish their entries, I wonder if they'd continue to write in. Probably. It's become an important release mechanism. Why not insult someone you don't know and will never meet as a way to relieve your own lack of self-worth and fury at life? It makes sense. There was a running joke on F365 for a while back when we just had the letters page. People would write in to complain about something and end by saying they'd never read the page again. To which editorial often added '(except to see if this letter has been published)'.

That being said, I should also say that there are some excellent, insightful and witty comments posted on F365 too, and that they make it all worthwhile. Indeed, thanks to an early policy not to go down the 'You're shit', 'No, you're shit', 'No, it's you who is shit', 'I think you'll find it's you who is shit' route by not publishing those pointless abuse-fests, a high quality of debate has been encouraged on some occasions and that is genuinely enjoyable and enlightening. The interactive culture is a very mixed blessing providing, great highs and deep lows.

Talking of lows: hand in hand with this more emotionally over-wrought behaviour of some sections of the football public has been an increase in genuinely hateful chanting directed at individual players.

Crowd chants are one of football's more notorious phenomena; sometimes quirky and witty, sometimes vicious and nasty. There were always the generally intimidating chants that you'd hear at all football grounds in the 1960s and 1970s such as 'You're going home in a fucking ambulance' and 'You're gonna get your fucking heads kicked in'.

But these had no melody as such. The best chants must be based around a familiar melody often lifted from a current pop song. A few songs have been regularly adapted by football fans and updated generation after generation. These are, for no special reason it would seem, other than their catchy tunes, 'When the Saints Go Marching In', 'Guantanamera', 'Go West' and 'Lord of the Dance'. I suppose it would have been hard to fit a chant around Genesis's 'Selling England by the Pound' or Black Sabbath's 'Fairies Wear Boots', though I for one would like to try. Recently, White Stripes' excellent 'Seven Nation Army' riff has been adopted by some fans. I first heard it sang by Italy fans in the 2006 World Cup.

Collective chanting is clearly one of those communal activities which thousands have always loved about football. I loved it from an early age. Standing on the terrace, arms aloft singing together, it binds you with strangers in a common cause, and the sheer physicality of singing is an uplifting experience per se even if, like me, you have a voice akin to that of a wounded animal.

Quite where the songs spring from and who orchestrates them is never really clear; they just seem to emerge organically. The crowd noise can also intimidate the opposition. Anyone who went to Liverpool in the 1970s on European nights could attest to that. The Kop could almost literally suck the ball into the net as they en masse sang the old Rodgers and Hammerstein song 'You'll Never Walk Alone'. It was spine-tingling and inspirational even to me as an outsider as I stood there feeling this blast of noise. It was the same sensation as being at a gig when the first power chord is struck. It physically alters you.

This is football chanting at its best, almost spiritual and certainly uplifting.

However, there has always been a darker side to the football chant and it's one that I sense has only got darker in recent years as contempt for players has risen to new heights through that over-exposure in the media.

Take this one, directed at Sol Campbell by some Spurs fans when he played for Portsmouth (to the tune of 'Lord of the Dance'):

Sol, Sol, wherever you may be,
You're on the verge of lunacy,
And we don't give a fuck when you're hanging from a tree,
Judas cunt with HIV.

Such vile, charmless chants offend against the best traditions of the game and against any sane sense of decency. All the more ironic that some Spurs fans should engage in them when they are subjected to chants such as this:

Gas a Jew Jew Jew
Stick him in the oven, gas mark 2
In his head, in his eye, jump up and down on him, make him cry.

Awful, isn't it? Then there's the hissing noises made to simulate the gas chambers. Whose idea of a bit of fun is that?

There are those who argue that this is all part of football's banter. That the chants, however nasty, are merely designed to put an opposition player off his game and don't represent much beyond that. Now God knows, I'm no politically correct, wilting flower and, as you know, I favour industrial language, but I just can't agree that we should expect to hear let alone take part in such vitriol.

This is what I think; if you let that kind of evil into your soul, it doesn't leave and it will infect you in the rest of your life: with negative consequences. You don't get to summon up that kind of nastiness without it having repercussions. Taking the piss is one thing, just being outright vile is quite another. If you put out that kind of bad vibe, it doesn't just dissolve after the final whistle; what you've summoned up will live on with all those who heard it and most strongly in you.

Letting off steam and venting frustration is part of the reason football exists. It's great for that. But these chants seem to represent a deeper, nastier, sicker worldview created in those people's minds in their everyday lives. In their life chants like this must be acceptable:

Adebayor
Adebayor

His dad washes elephants
His mum's a black whore.

There is nothing witty or clever about this. It's not even crude or vulgar, just hateful.

I wonder if, as violence on the terraces and in the surrounding streets has decreased, the chanting has got worse? Has violent language replaced actual violence? It seems so to me. Chants were always insulting, aggressive even, right from my earliest days of going to games, but rarely outright personally vitriolic.

There is no excuse for it but I do think it's connected to or fired by the greater alienation fans feel from players. Now footballers are paid so much, some fans feel anything is justified, as though the players are no longer humans simply because they're rich.

It's not that I think we should be quiet – quite the reverse – I just want some wit and humour in the songs.

Football has never been a polite place, that's for sure, and I'm not too precious or sensitive about it, but you have to draw the line somewhere. You have to have standards and I would consider singing this to have gone beyond them:

Ryan Giggs is illegitimate
He ain't got no birth certificate
He's got AIDS and can't get rid of it
He's a Munich bastard.

Contrast this with a chant in the 1970s when Tommy Docherty was managing Manchester United. He had an affair with the physio's wife, a woman called Mary Brown, whom he would later marry, and fans would sing:

Who's up Mary Brown?
Who's up Mary Brown?
Tommy Tommy Tommy Tommy Docherty,

to the tune of 'Knees Up, Mother Brown'. Now I think that's very funny in a way that enquiring as to whether Victoria Beckham takes it up the arse just isn't.

I also recall a George Best chant in the early 1970s, 'Georgie Best, Superstar, walks like a woman and he wears a bra', to the 'Jesus Christ Superstar' tune. Again, that's quite affectionate and funny.

Nathan Blake, a journeyman striker who was once prosecuted for stealing money from a fruit machine, would be subjected by his own Cardiff fans to 'He's black, he's mean, he'll rob your fruit machine', which always amused me, as did Spurs chanting 'You're just a fat Paris Hilton' at pony-tailed striker Andre Voronin.

Yes, they're mildly insulting but are done with some wit and no real nastiness or hatred. This one, to the tune of 'Yellow Submarine', was sung at Peter Reid:

In the land where I was born
Lives a man with a monkey's heed,
And he went to Sunderland,
And his name is Peter Reid.
Peter Reid's got a fuckin' monkey's heed,
A fuckin' monkey's heed,
A fuckin' monkey's heed.

I think most people, even Peter Reid, probably enjoyed this. At the time he was leading Sunderland to two remarkable top-seven finishes and it was an acknowledgement of his increased profile and success. They don't sing it now he's an assistant coach at Stoke. So in a way, it was a back-handed compliment.

Others are more concise and to the point, such as 'You're shit and you know you are, you're shit and you know you are', to the Village People's 'Go West'. This was once hilariously adapted by Manchester United fans to 'You're drunk and you know you are', aimed at a recently self-confessed alcoholic, Paul Merson. There's almost a sense of affection about that, too. I'm sure Merse would have seen the funny side.

The purveyors of the worst chants are a small if vocal minority. It's a culture that can be changed less by the authorities outlawing them – though that needs to happen too – but more permanently by fans self-policing.

This has already happened on racist chanting. Indeed, I was at Middlesbrough last year and when someone shouted, 'You black bastard!' when a black opposition player had clattered a Boro player, he was shouted down by everyone around him with comments such as 'Shut it!', 'Racist!' and perhaps more wittily, 'Who let the twat in?' He didn't make any more such remarks and it's rare to hear anything like that any more.

Crude racist chants were commonplace in the 1970s though they rarely featured the specific player's name. There were, shamefully, also a lot of monkey noises.

People tell me Boro fans used to sing 'Nigger on the Pitch' to the tune of 'Brown Girl in the Ring' whenever a black player arrived to play at Ayresome Park. I never heard that personally but do recall 'You black bastard, you black bastard' being chanted against West Ham's Clyde Best.

I never uttered any such words and I'm not saying that to try and look good. It was because I heard this sort of stuff at home. It had always seemed unjustified on any rational basis and because I heard it at home and was busy building a rebel stance against everything that home represented, there was no way I'd be co-opted into the same attitude.

When Rock Against Racism came along in 1977 or 1978 I wanted to be part of it because I hated the idea that anyone should be bullied or abused just for what they looked like. I hated that when it happened to me at school, so on the basis of 'treat others as you like to be treated yourself', it made total sense. I didn't need a diversity lecture or some sort of pc training to feel that. It's just basic human empathy. And anyway, I didn't have money to waste on throwing perfectly good bananas on to a football pitch.

I didn't know anyone who wasn't white or Asian until 1979, but even so, it was something both me and my mates all felt strongly about and, looking back, was the start of a wider change in attitudes throughout society.

Just how far we have come from the 1970s was shown clearly when

England players suffered racist abuse when playing in Eastern Europe. I think even those of us who had grown up with the monkey chants were shocked to hear them again, so long had it been since we'd heard them. I'm sure I was not alone in feeling defensive on behalf of 'our boys' when that happened. Insult one of us and you insult us all.

The fact that racist songs are not sung any more proves progress can be made. Notice the Sol Campbell abuse doesn't specifically mention his skin colour. It's interesting how even the fans who sing such horrible words still feel somehow bound by the non-racist behaviour code. They seem to be saying that hoping he is hanged or dies of AIDS is all fine, but hey, we've got standards, we don't hate him for being black.

Football is society in microcosm and it would be naïve to expect it to be otherwise. In fact, it's that close reflection of the everyday world that makes the game such a universally loved sport. We can't be too wet about it. There always will be vulgarity and swearing; I just wish it could stop at that.

If football allowed me to grow up as a less angry, more laid-back type of dude, thanks to the various on-pitch psychopaths dispensing justice with the aid of a strong thigh and a size twelve boot, rock 'n' roll also had a major role in soothing the angry teenage soul; indeed there is much in common between noisy rock music and football.

Without a constant diet of heavy rock while growing up I'm firmly convinced I would have fallen apart completely. While football gave the weeks a structure and a context, rock 'n' roll was lifeblood to me. It fed my creative soul and filled up my world like nothing else. Noisy guitar-based music syncs in with the teenage male psyche so well. The lyrics, the riffs, the music all expressed my state of mind. It was in tune with my heightened emotions and hormones.

Hearing Ian Gillan screaming on *Made in Japan* by Deep Purple, one of my favourite albums of the 1970s, was like hearing all your own frustrations and emotions bellowed out at 120 decibels. It was in a very real sense cathartic. Listen to the opening track on that album, 'Highway Star'. As the drums and bass provide the intro, Blackmore's razor-edged guitar slashes out the riff with an elemental power that still thrills; it's so raw and primal – just noise really, but glorious noise. It seemed to leech the more toxic elements of growing up out of me. It was also a place to retreat, a world within itself that would never let you down.

One girlfriend at this time memorably asked: if I had to choose between her and my fast-growing album collection, which would I pick? Being a guileless boy, I said it had to be the albums. When she asked why, I replied, 'Because rock 'n' roll will never let me down and it will always be there for me.'

Not unreasonably, she said she hadn't let me down and would always be there for me. We both suspected that wasn't going to prove to be true in the long run and when we broke up, I went back to the collection, pulled out UFO's *Strangers in the Night* and felt vindicated and soothed all at once.

Heavy rock and metal, along with association football, have always had the industrial areas of Britain such as Teesside, Tyneside, Glasgow and west Yorkshire, Lancashire and the Midlands as their heartlands. It's often said that the metallic pounding of the music mirrored the noise from the factories and engineering works and thus connected to the male industrial labouring classes' psyche.

This always seemed a bit patronising to me, suggesting, as it does, that if you spend all your days making pig iron then you will be desensitised to everything other than pounding heavy metal music. In fact, if you'd been in that kind of environment all day, there's a good argument to say that you'd want to listen to quieter music. As a theory it also ignores the fact that folk music has always had its place in the labouring classes' lives, both culturally and politically, and there's not much heavy riffage in the likes of Ewan MacColl's music; try shaking your head to Dick Gaughan.

The truth about heavy rock's popularity, whatever incarnation it has reinvented itself in over the last forty years is, as with football, down to its ability to release pent-up feelings and emotions while being exciting, dynamic and unpredictable. If you go to a folk gig or to a jazz show, it's all pretty much sit down, shut up and listen. But go to any decent rock 'n' roll gig and it's much more like life on the terraces, only with extra moshing and head-banging. The arms-aloft cheering and the collective singing all find parallels with the beautiful game.

Whether you're at the game or just shouting at the TV the result is pretty much the same. Football and rock 'n' roll are, among many other things, important anger management devices, giving us a sop to soak up negative emotions that would otherwise leak out into society and make a terrible mess.

Football facilitates many, varying attitudes and emotions. It is a place to be happy, joyful, ecstatic and also furious, frustrated and miserable. You can praise and abuse people in public. You can even express your moral disdain for a player if you so wish. This is all part of the relentless pulling power that football has. It is a stage for all human expression and emotion in a way that few public gatherings ever can be. With that in mind, it's no wonder millions turn out every week to watch it. And if you don't agree, I shall burst into tears.

4

Food

BEFORE I sat down to start this chapter I ate a light lunch of beetroot dressed in balsamic vinegar and a splash of walnut oil. I roasted Californian walnuts in a little butter with a few chilli flakes and salt. I sliced the beetroot and stacked it alternately with a slice of ripe, salty soft goat's cheese and the walnuts, making two stacks. I served it with a handful of watercress and a squeeze of lemon juice, all topped off with a few roasted sesame seeds. It was bloody magnificent if I do say so myself.

This is the sort of food I eat all the time. I don't claim it to be haute cuisine or some unique kind of gastro-science. However, it is a million miles away from the stodgy, bland food I was brought up on. It's also the sort of food you can purchase at a football ground's restaurant these days. I know this because I first had a similar dish at Norwich City.

How times have changed and, I would argue, much for the better. Indeed, I would argue that food has been an important component in the positive and enjoyable experience of watching football and in the twenty-first century has helped it maintain its primacy as the sport of choice for so many.

I am hugely in favour of the new in-stadium restaurant culture. The combination of decent dining and football is a winning one for me and I suspect many from my background, even if some clubs' dining facilities, especially at the lower levels, look little better than a carvery set in a 1980s DSS office.

Whereas many aspects of the culture of football and rock 'n' roll guided and inspired me as a kid, the influence of the football food culture did likewise, only in reverse. It made me realise that there had to be a better way than a life lived off chips, greasy pies, pickled eggs and fatty sausages bought from evil-looking men on the street. It set an example which spoke loudly to me, and it was shouting, 'This is absolute shite; never eat like this again.' The food in and around football grounds was, to my tastebuds, usually rancid garbage, food poisoning waiting to happen. But remember, I am a food ponce.

Today, if you were to look at my shopping basket, it is the very embodiment of aspirational, middle-class food, containing everything from fresh coriander, organic Swiss chard and okra to hand-pressed organic apple juice, almond butter and camomile tea.

I do like to eat well and I eat quite healthily, I suppose. I've got to balance out the destruction the drinking brings upon my body somehow.

I've made a long journey from the typical working-class fare of my childhood to what my parents would have considered incomprehensible top-class restaurant food. 'You've fried some walnuts in butter with chilli, our John. Why have you done that!?' is what they'd have said, with a sneer.

From my mid-teens I had started to learn how to cook the basics, and by the time I left home I was keen to expand my repertoire and set about doing so with a great book called Madhur Jaffrey's *Eastern Vegetarian Cooking*. Regardless of whether you eat meat or not, it's a fantastic source of inspiration for all dishes originating east of Turkey.

It opened my mind to a whole new world of ingredients and spices. I hadn't even heard of a chickpea before reading that book. You have to remember that Britain was in the culinary dark ages in the 1970s with much of the population thinking that garlic was fancy foreign muck, despite the fact that garlic is as English as roast beef.

I don't know where they got that idea from. My mother was especially disparaging of it, considering it little better than flavouring a meal with dog shit. I can't emphasise enough just how much garlic was reviled as a foreign invader.

The cultural schism that separated most Brits from a cosmopolitan palate was vast. So much so that I reached my twenties without ever tasting, not just chickpeas, but fresh ginger, broccoli (or calabrese), aubergine, avocado (a word only ever used to describe a bathroom suite), any sort of bean apart from butter or Heinz, peppers, any sort of cheese that wasn't Cheddar, Cheshire, Edam or Dairylea, any pasta other than spaghetti, sweet potato, courgettes, squash and artichokes of any variety, or any herb apart from parsley, mint or sage. Yoghurt, which came into our consciousness only in the mid-1970s, was also viewed with much suspicion.

'It's just milk that's gone off isn't it?' my grandma once said, confused as to why this would be edible. She thought it was a Swiss conspiracy. She seemed to think the Swiss were out to get us, what with the fashion for muesli and the Toblerone. 'I don't care if it is triangular, it doesn't even taste like proper chocolate.'

Such fruits as kiwi, lychees, melon, mango and pomegranate were literally unheard of let alone tasted. Fresh fruit juice pressed or from concentrate was simply never drunk and barely ever available. We had Tree Top orange squash, a fluorescent teeth-rotting concoction that kept many a seventies child hyperactive.

Salad never varied from lettuce, tomato, cucumber served with a stick of celery and a spring onion, usually on a Sunday. It was never ever anything else. The idea that you might grate a carrot and eat it raw was no more a viable option than slashing a sofa cushion and adding its stuffing to Sunday tea. You would even have been laughed at for putting fresh peas into a salad. 'Why have you put cold peas on my plate?' That would have been the response.

What I'm about to say will, if you've been brought up in the last twenty-five years, sound ludicrous. It will sound as though I'm fabricating it. But it is absolutely true.

Food which tasted strongly of anything was mistrusted by my parents, especially my mother. The milder, the blander everything was the more wholesome they seemed to think it was. This was a common view, certainly among the grim-faced Yorkshire folk who comprised my extended family. They associated strong-tasting food with foreigners and not in a good way. Even the Cheddar was always mild, never mature. I suspect they felt if it tasted strongly, they feared it had gone off.

The only exception they made to this menu of blandness was

pickled produce. Beetroot, onions and piccalilli were all eaten in large amounts to cut the grease of the cheap meat. The only spice used was white pepper, never black, and you could forget curry powder or any such exotic nonsense.

'You don't know what they put in it. They make it in the streets. It's full of dirt,' were just a few of the comments about spice and curry powder that my mother and her mother would offer as food knowledge.

My mother and her mother would routinely dismiss non-British food, or what they perceived as non-British food, as 'foreign muck'. They would even ascribe the behaviour of people they saw on the evening news to what they perceived their diet would be.

So the trouble in the Middle East was all down to garlic and chilli.

'That hot food makes them all mad. Just look at them,' Granny would say as some sort of Palestinian protest was featured. She'd say the same thing of any news from the Indian subcontinent. Amusingly, she didn't really know what the Chinese ate (though she'd heard they ate cats) so couldn't disparage Mao or whomever for their diet. She did offer the view that they were 'a cruel race' though, despite never having met anyone Chinese and knowing nothing at all about China.

The French were hated for the dreaded garlic and for eating horses; the Germans for eating sauerkraut, which was thought by my mother to be an expulsion of the devil. The Spanish and Italians were condemned for consuming olive oil. Olive oil! This was considered a heinous crime as olive oil was – and again, this is not a lie – available only from the chemist! It was for loosening ear wax and loosening bowels, not to be enjoyed drizzled on salad leaves. Not for the working class anyway. That was akin to being poisoned, surely.

Salad dressings were not something I knew about until I left home. There was salad cream and nothing else. Putting oil and lemon on salad would have seemed like a joke to my parents.

I ate roast beef which had been cooked until so dry that it crumbled apart. It was tasteless. I ate liver so hard and rubbery that it was like eating a tennis ball.

I'd have dry chicken breast every Sunday with vegetables that were boiled until they were a soggy, sulphurous mush. We had chips almost every day. The kitchen revolved around the chip pan. We filled up on carbs to a ludicrous extent.

This low-grade eating was partly down to lack of cooking skill by my mother and no skill at all by my dad, but it was just as much a reflection of the narrow culture they'd been brought up with. Even watching early TV cook Graham Kerr, the Galloping Gourmet, didn't make a difference. Neither did Fanny Cradock. I was frightened of Fanny, a weird old witch with eyebrows, for no good reason, painted on her forehead, giving her an expression which suggested she had just received a parsnip up the arse.

Even Delia had yet to permeate the nation's consciousness in quite the way she was later to do, though she was on TV throughout the 1970s. My mam and gran thought she was too young to know what she was doing. And she used garlic, so that demonised her from the get go. But they watched anyway, just so they could bitch about lovely Delia. They preferred *Farmhouse Kitchen,* which was on Yorkshire Television presented by some large-bosomed old woman in a flowery pinny who would bake pies and pasties without the aid of the filthy garlic and would take pride in gravy and custard. Like A Proper Woman.

By the time I was in my mid-teens I began to associate the food of my childhood with the conservative, narrow culture that it came from and that was just not cool. But there was little opportunity to expand your horizons.

I was never encouraged to cook as a kid at home or at school. If you're under thirty it might sound weird now to hear that boys were not allowed to do Home Economics. That was women's work which, if you indulged in it, would turn you into a raging homosexual. No one said that of course but that was the received opinion. However, I rather liked Graham Kerr and he was married with kids so it hadn't made him gay, I reasoned logically enough. Could just being in a kitchen make you fancy lads anyway? It didn't sound likely to me.

So by the time I was seventeen I'd turned my hand to frying steaks properly so they were not dry and tough, and making spaghetti bolognaise. Admittedly not Michelin-standard nosh as such, but I enjoyed it nonetheless, especially once I discovered it made me more attractive to girls.

This was a real surprise. My parents had gone to my grandma's one day so I'd invited a girl round and proceeded to cook my speciality steak. This seemed to go down very well and it wasn't long before we were dry humping on the living-room floor; dry humping being my generation's ultra-safe form of safe sex. No sperm could ever leak from the industrial-strength 1970s Y-fronts.

I had clearly impressed her by getting in touch with what was, rather ridiculously, seen as my feminine side. This was to be the case time and again when I went away to college. It was ludicrously easy to impress girls by making spaghetti bolognaise. In these days of Jamie Oliver et al. I expect women think it less amazing that a bloke can cook, but it was a tremendous social advantage in the late 1970s and I'd still highly recommend it; after all, it means you can look after yourself and not have to rely on pre-made crap or your mother.

I had my horizons expanded even further by dating a girl called Jane who was 100 per cent unadulterated middle-class. I was punching above my social weight in dating her.

Her parents lived in a big three-storey detached house, more like a mansion to me, off Oxbridge Lane in Stockton. They were proper middle-class people, at least to my eyes. Well educated, erudite, loved their kids, doted on them in fact – a pleasure to talk to and to be around.

I never told Jane how in awe of her, her parents and their lifestyle I was. I was trying to be cool, but it was way out of my experience to have such space to live in, such a full life and such social ease. It was almost uncomfortable to see her and her sister being so loving towards their parents. I just didn't live like that.

So I was seriously impressed even though my emerging would-be beat poet, free-thinking soul told me I shouldn't be so materialistic as to admire their wealth. They seemed to glide through life with what seemed like such ease and social grace, not crippled by the lack of self-worth that was handed down to us with mother's milk and by school. They knew how to behave and what to say in any social circumstance – or so it seemed to me, a gauche, eager-to-be loved boy.

Crucially, when I visited they'd have bottles of wine in the house. It doesn't sound much now but back then this appeared to me to be very sophisticated. I thought it was tremendous. When I talked to them, they were so much more open-minded. Not for them the suspicion of garlic as 'foreign muck'; they had holidays overseas and embraced other cultures and were not afraid of them. They had black pepper!

This was in 1979, just before I was due to leave Stockton and go to college in Newcastle. I was open to many and indeed any new ideas. Jane and her parents, though they had no idea about this, were hugely influential. I was emerging from the gloomy swamp of my upbringing and realising you could live a better life, or at least one which was more cultured and expansive.

Better still, they were not nasty or snobbish. They treated me as if I was worthy.

Such open hearts and minds still echo back down the vista of years. Jane gave me access, without knowing it, to a different kind of life at a time when I really needed it.

I broke up with her while at college. It was a long-distance, unsatisfactory break-up during which I was unintentionally a bit of a bastard, largely due to being socially inept. But I was a kid with few social or relationship skills from my upbringing. However, the girl I left Jane for was Dawn, who I'm sitting next to now as I write. So it didn't turn out all bad.

But that summer was a great time of awareness and awakening. I hadn't realised fully just how food was part of the class war in the UK until I left home and was cooking more spaghetti bolognaise in my halls of residence kitchen during the first week of college. A new lad arrived with his parents, a bluff Yorkshire couple from the snooty part of Doncaster – yes, there is a snooty part of Doncaster; OK it's not in Donny, it's a few miles outside: a place called Thorne.

The mother was one of those women who self-consciously affect a posher voice than their own. She spied me at work and asked what I was cooking. When I explained, she was most impressed. Pasta was still a new thing to the working class. I'd had it for the first time – apart from tinned spaghetti and hoops – only earlier that year in

1979. I could tell she thought I was well brought up because here I was cooking that there fancy pasta for dinner. She stood looking over my shoulder, asking for my recipe, almost flirting with me despite the fact she was god knows how old.

I now realise this was illustrative of the culture of food in the UK and how it is tied into a sense of class, representing not just who you are, but who you aspire to be. So it's inevitable that this plays out in football culture.

Remember Roy Keane's infamous outburst? 'Away from home our fans are fantastic, I'd call them the hardcore fans. But at home they have a few drinks and probably the prawn sandwiches, and they don't realise what's going on out on the pitch.'

When he made this comment after a Champions League game against Dynamo Kiev at Old Trafford in November 2000, all British football fans knew exactly what he meant. So deep did these two sentences bury themselves into the football psyche, that very soon we all referred to such people as 'the prawn sandwich brigade', as though they were an invading army.

It was shorthand for a new type of supporter and it is no coincidence that food lay at the heart of it. While football fans all over the world eat before, during and after football matches, only in Britain is it so closely tied into the politics of class and social identity. Understanding this is the key to understanding how and why food and football have gone hand in hand in British football culture, so let's take a trip to the supermarket. Bugger, we've got a wonky trolley.

So we arrive at the fresh fruit and vegetables. Now, such humble plants as watercress, rocket and chicory are middle-class salad items. If you are spotted buying or consuming them you may well attract the ire of some of the working class, who think it marks you as a ponce or a snob.

Other reactionaries will think you are some sort of weird vegan or anarchist, especially if you have dreadlocks, in which case, you probably are. However, to the educated middle class, eating such things is entirely normal and a regular part of life.

But to others still, such foodstuffs are part of an upmarket, cultured lifestyle that they aspire to and they may look on enviously as you purchase expensive salad items, assuming you must be successful, educated, sophisticated and interesting. You may even get off with a skinny woman called Emily who likes cats and reading imagist poetry, merely by presenting her with a nicely dressed green salad, so powerful is the aspirational food culture in this country. It's just a bit of greenery, but in Britain it implies so much.

On the other hand, potatoes, turnips and carrots are legs-apart, jaw out, solid and trustworthy and as such are acceptable for traditionalists and the working class, unless they're obscure heritage varieties or organically grown, which magically transforms them into middle-class food.

Meals such as burgers, chips and beans are looked down on by the middle class as culturally narrow and the foodstuffs of the stupid and the poor. However, if consciously eaten as a 'retro' meal or rebranded as 'rustic', then it becomes middle-class again.

It's amazing how the word 'rustic', a word to describe something basic and rough, has been acquired by middle class food culture along with artisanal. A rustic meal served with artisanal bread is not eaten by the working class in Britain, nor by the rustic artisans. Oh no. It's eaten by soft-handed middle classes who like the idea of eating in a basic way, connected to the labouring classes by this food and in no other way at all. It's an affectation based on a sense of class.

Confused?

No. You know exactly what I mean, unless you are from another country, in which case this will all seem like a form of insanity to you. That's because it *is*, but it's how we live in Britain and we must either rather like the class politics of food or need it for some deep seated psychological reason.

A couple of years ago I was buying a humble aubergine in a shop in a Northumberland village, Haydon Bridge. As the girl, who was maybe twenty years old, on the checkout picked it up and inspected it closely, I assumed she was assessing the quality of this fine, though admittedly phallic egg plant. But no. She didn't know what it was.

'What's this?' she said, thrusting the purple vegetable back at me aggressively, as though I had set out to humiliate her with an obscure exotic foodstuffs examination.

'It's an aubergine,' I said, not unreasonably, I thought, because that's what it was.

She picked up a price list and ran her finger down it, straight down to the O's. Naturally, it wasn't there.

'Are you sure?' she said, more confident now, assuming I was the produce fool.

'Yes. It's spelled with an A, though,' I said helpfully, trying to not sound patronising, but failing.

'Well, that's stupid,' she said grumpily, adding, 'Who wants to eat these things anyway?' as though to do so was the most pretentious, wilfully elitist act on the planet.

With such narrow attitudes to things as culturally innocuous as an aubergine still present in British society, it's no surprise that food plays its part in football's cultural and class politics.

Against this backdrop, Keane's prawn-based critique was the perfect summing-up of the new, modern fan who goes to football for almost every reason other than to watch football. It's significant that it was a prawn sandwich he referenced. It couldn't have been a cheese sandwich – that's too run-of-the-mill, too everyday – it had to be something just slightly upmarket. Lobster or monkfish would have been too distant and elite, roast pepper and haricot bean pâté too weird and vegetarian. Prawns worked because they are somehow an expression of the socially aspirant and smug; a bridge between basic working-class food and truly posh nosh.

Thus, by extension, merely eating a prawn sandwich at a football match is a betrayal of the history and culture of the game itself, proving the consumer has little or no interest in the very thing the rest of us feel so passionate about. In this worldview, it seems impossible for a member of the prawn sandwich brigade to actually know anything about football. Keane's comment precludes this as a possibility.

These people are out of touch, have no place at football, and are thus actively diluting our heritage. It's enough to make the veins on the neck of your average eighteen-stone West Ham fan bulge. Gertcha!

But regardless of the negative attitudes of players, managers and some fans to crustacean sandwiches, the growth of finer dining facilities at football grounds has been unstoppable in the twenty-first century, as people called Jeremy, with wives named Clarissa, try to give the appearance of being ever more interested in the game and demand a decent bottle of Chablis to go with their carpaccio of horse ears, and finely shaved beetroot served with a cappuccino foam of trouser milk . . . or something.

Chelsea Football Club opened a restaurant at Stamford Bridge run by celebrity chef (whatever that might actually mean) Marco Pierre White. When it opened in 2004, the menu included fish and chips, shepherd's pie and something called 'Eton mess and trifle', which sounds like some kind of masturbation contest held in the dorm of public schools that future Tory ministers indulge in while horse-whipping a scholarship boy from Wakefield.

Currently on offer are that chip shop fave, fish cakes, served with buttered spinach and a slice of Bakewell tart; two courses for a recession-busting £35, about equal to the cost of watching half of a game at Chelsea only without the outrageous diving or padded headgear.

But this isn't something confined to the rarefied atmosphere of monied west London clubs; you can find it from Norwich to Newcastle as clubs seek to garner income from as broad a social and income spectrum as possible by selling a quality dining experience. Indeed, at Carrow Road, Canaries director and the always delightful Delia Smith (still using the filthy garlic too, I've no doubt) has a restaurant and bar serving pre- and post-match meals, as well as a New York-style diner doing bar food and beer. This sounds excellent.

As I write, the restaurant is offering a three-course meal for £32. Dishes on offer include minestrone soup, asparagus, Thai beef salad, Thai curry, risotto and chocolate trifle, among many other tasty treats. That sounds tasty, not outlandishly expensive and despite it being Norwich, none of it is canary-yellow either, which is a bonus.

Having spent some time in Norwich, and buying one of my favourite Mahavishnu Orchestra albums there (*From Nothingness to Eternity* – which is what it often feels like driving around Norfolk), I must say this sounds like one of the best ways to spend your leisure time in the town.

This aspect of modern football is an easy target for the old-school hardcore fan. There is much sneering from the traditionalists towards the new executive box, posh nosh interlopers and their dietary habits. Some are jealous of their money, some feel their presence is diluting the old passions of the game; others just hate people called Jeremy and Clarissa on principle, and who can blame them for that?

The more rational fan finds it a bit odd that football has become an extension of the middle-class social whirl. Who wants to entertain influential people with vol-au-vents and bottles of New Zealand sauvignon blanc, or impress other couples called Jeremy and Clarissa, in an environment where thousands of people are chanting 'You're shit and you know you are', or are loudly enquiring if a specific player's wife likes to engage in rough anal sex, possibly with some sort of farmyard animal or a carrot?

Some have said it's class tourism or, perhaps most controversially of all, that some people today just like going to the football and want to watch it in comfortable surroundings while supping a nice glass of wine. What kind of crazy people are these?! Next they'll be asking not to be beaten up by the away fans afterwards. Is nothing sacred?!

Either way, it is a new development and one which some feel is embarrassing, especially at Wembley Stadium, when the most prominent, centrally located, executive boxes and 'Gold' seats remain glaringly empty after half time as their former occupants hoover up food and drink, blithely ignoring England's attempts to play football to an international standard. It's a hard choice to make: do you watch England's lion, John Terry, getting caught out of position again, throwing himself in front of a striker and losing the use of a major limb in the process, or do you go back to the seafood bar for one last feast of champagne and oysters?

These are the choices for a member of Club Wembley. It's a hard life. Had the FA – a body not known for its ability to walk and talk at the same time, let alone spend the vast fortunes available to it wisely – thought about both the practical and PR implications of their decision to offer the most prominent seats to the least committed or interested customers (and I do mean customer as opposed to fan), perhaps, just perhaps, it could have offered the visibly uninterested people seats that were not so visibly prominent.

Some see it as a very public betrayal of the game and even rather unpatriotic for fans to shun their national team so publicly. Others just wish they could afford to sit in the padded seats, get their hands on the smoked salmon and chat up those women you only see in the executive boxes at Wembley, who wear décolletage, revealing silk ball-gowns, as though dressed for a night at the opera.

'Hello darling, are you a fan of having a man in the hole, then? Ow! That hurt.'

But for most fans, this kind of fine dining, whether at club or international level, is an untried and unwanted luxury. For most, the food they eat before, during and after football hasn't changed much over the years. Indeed, the remarkable thing about the food sold at football grounds, outside of the luxury dining niche, is that it's almost identical no matter where you go, no matter what level of football you attend.

Go to Manchester United to see a game and you can buy the same crisps, pies and burgers as you can buy at Barnsley or Blyth Spartans. There are a few regional variations, it varies a bit in quality though many source the same stuff from the same supplier, but by and large, football food is surprisingly predictable and homogenous in its breadth and quality.

To many this is very reassuring and is part of the appeal of the game, another reason we fell in love with football in this country. The consistency and predictability make supporters feel part of the family, part of the tradition and culture. It pulls you in, issues you with a few broad rules and choices and will not change throughout your lifetime. All other things may be in flux. The economy might go down the toilet, the value of your house plummet along with the wife's underwear in a Holiday Inn for that bloke who works in the Fiat garage, but football food will be constant, a fixed point around which your life can rotate.

It's important to have things that are unchanging as we're tossed around by the stormy waters of life, and so much of football's culture is to do with giving you an anchor. It makes you feel more secure, comforted and at peace. Even when your life is falling apart, the whiff of Bovril is always there for you, if only to remind you there are worse things in life than whatever current tragedy has struck you, worse things such as Bovril.

So here we are in the twenty-first century; football is hugely popular as a live event and on TV and we clearly have a divide between the traditionalists and the modernists: pies vs Pinot Gris, posh vs proletarian, if you like.

To understand how we got to this state of affairs, there are a few, admittedly odd, basics to grasp.

First is the riddle that food tastes better to the British when it's eaten outdoors, despite the fact that in normal circumstances we feel uncomfortable eating outside.

Britain is a nation that has, until relatively recently, spent most of its life inside, often huddled by a fire, wearing a stout pair of trousers and possibly a brown hat of some sort, as skies darken and wind lashes rain into the windows. Our only tradition of eating outside was the consumption of potted meat sandwiches on days out at run-down, melancholic seaside towns such as Bridlington and Saltburn.

As a kid born and brought up in Hull, I knew this all too well. Our holidays in the 1960s meant going on a train to places such as Filey, or, if we were really lucky, Withernsea, for a day out. We'd catch the train from Paragon Station full of excitement for the adventure, as well as the vague dread that being in public with your parents always brought. Mother would, on some wind-blown cliff-top, produce a blue Tupperware box of potted meat sandwiches and, if times were good, a tomato, wrapped, for no obvious reason, in some tin foil, with a pinch of salt. This, let me tell younger readers, was totally, bloody marvellous. We felt like kings as we sat braving the onslaught of a stiff north-easterly, consuming what otherwise would have been distinctively average-tasting food. Add into the equation a tartan flask of tea, and you had yourself a sixties working-class feast.

The important fact to remember here is that my generation, like that before it, realised even crap food tasted 100 per cent better for being eaten outdoors, and when football grounds started selling food, we hadn't forgotten this important insight.

We didn't go to restaurants in my youth. This was probably

because we didn't have enough money but also because my parents felt uncomfortable in such surroundings. They were out of their social depth and didn't know which knife to use. Very occasionally, we went to a pub that 'did' food and ate steak and chips. I seem to recall thinking that if you went out to eat you always had to have steak.

So my first experience of eating out wasn't in restaurants, it was in pubs before and after football matches, and I'm sure this was entirely typical for working-class kids.

If you're fortunate enough to live in a climate that is warm and sunny most of the year, eating food outdoors is all perfectly normal. It's what you do. A bowl of chilled soup as the sun slides into the sparkling silver and blue crystal of the Pacific Ocean isn't that unusual if you live in California, but try doing it in Hartlepool on a blowy Thursday afternoon in November, and something will freeze and fall off you.

On top of that if you're eating such posh food as gazpacho in Hartlepool you will most likely be beaten up for being pretentious under the unspoken but nonetheless strict food culture rules of these lands. Roy Keane will probably hate you for it as well.

Football's food culture became established at a time when the industrial cities were choked with pollution from a million chimneys burning wood, coke and coal. While the working-class football fans couldn't sit in the park, eat salad and drink mineral water for climatic as well as cultural reasons, football matches offered an opportunity for al fresco dining that was irresistibly attractive even to the uptight, inhibited British.

It was unpretentious, unfussy and easy to understand. You could do it regardless of the weather, for a start. There was no complicated and unfamiliar cutlery involved, no pressure to behave well, no pressure not to swear, fart or burp; all usually somewhat worrying aspects to eating out for the uneducated working class. It was free from the burden of the pretence to enjoy yourself on a picnic, when you'd really rather be sitting in the pub, on the toilet, or scratching your back with a fork. You could just stand there and eat. And no one would think the worse of you. Ideal.

The quality of the food mattered little because you were eating outside, and so the over-priced greasy pie served to you at a football ground from behind a chipped melamine counter by an old woman with cat food under her nails on a blowy January afternoon in the third round of the FA Cup, remained vaguely thrilling and luscious, whereas when eaten indoors it would more than likely induce vomiting.

Post-war, as football became established as millions of people's favourite sport and clubs saw the potential for profits in providing some basic nourishment, the more progressive ones began selling enamel mugs of weak tea, and thin beef tea, and perhaps, if they were very adventurous, a small bar of chocolate. The idea that stadiums would house restaurants and become destinations for fine dining would have been looked upon as a kind of lunacy brought on by sniffing too much mustard gas in the war.

A cursory look at any ground of the time reveals a ramshackle collection of wooden and steel stands, brick huts for turnstiles and crumbling terraces. Many hadn't been changed for fifty years or more. They struggled to find a home for a tea counter, let alone instal a kitchen to cook couscous and a lamb tagine.

However, since those early days, one comestible has been elevated to mythic status in football food culture. It is worshipped by millions as perhaps the ultimate foodstuff. It is available at every football ground with paying customers and even in today's health-conscious world, millions are consumed. It is, of course (drum roll please, Maestro) . . . the meat pie!

Pies have become a legendary football ritual that many feel obliged, compelled or delighted to indulge in. Recently, it was claimed on the BBC news website that one in three people who went to watch Scottish football had a pie on match day. That'd be over 20,000 just at Celtic Park! A volume of pies so huge it would need to be transported in the sort of big trucks normally reserved for Emerson, Lake and Palmer in their seventies pomp.

The first pie I ever ate at Ayresome Park was memorable. It was a freezing cold afternoon in 1974 – it always seemed to be freezing at the Boro; I don't recall one warm day in the whole of the 1970s.

As I bit into it, a belch of hot air was released in a steamy cloud into the smog-filled grey afternoon. It smelled fantastically savoury and meaty but it tasted somewhat different. First, the filling was bouncy, as though partly comprised of rubber bands. This is because it was padded out with gristle: eyes, lungs and arseholes. The flavour was peculiarly tangy and unlike anything I had ever tasted previously. It was salty but oddly perfumed. Looking back, this was probably because it was past its sell-by date – not that such a thing as a sell-by date existed back then. But I was used to vaguely unpleasant food at home so I ate it all.

It left me with a sore throat! I'm no doctor but I'm sure a pie shouldn't make your throat sore. God knows what was in that thing but whatever it was it wasn't in me long as it had exited out of my arse at speed a couple of hours later.

So that wasn't a good start and it put me off the whole football pie experience for many years. Indeed, I'm fairly sure I've not actually eaten a pie inside a football ground since! But as usual I was very much in the minority in this regard. I did have an especially good curried pasty at Boston United once though and a vegetable samosa at Leicester City too. Both highly recommended.

Eating a pie full of thick, viscous gravy and a few pieces of undefined protein while standing on a terrace surrounded by thousands of people is actually a tricky business. The tendency is for pie innards to burst and pour down your arm, giving you third-degree burns in the process, rendering your lips numb and blistered, as though you had just witnessed a nuclear explosion at Bikini Atoll. Then the whole thing falls apart and you are compelled to cram the last half of the now fractured miasma into your mouth, all in one go, to prevent losing the whole lot on the ground.

These days a TV camera will inevitably be trained on you as you inhale the bloody thing and you will briefly be the laughing stock of the watching football nation

But this has not diminished pies' desirability – quite the opposite.

Go to any ground and you'll hear the chant 'Who ate all the pies?' directed by fans, ironically often on the chubby side themselves, towards a 'husky'-sized player. It is the only foodstuff to regularly feature in such mantras in any sporting venue, so deeply entrenched has the humble pie become.

While in days of yore, pies would have been made by a local bakery and taken to the ground at dinner time on big metal trays, in these more corporate days, football clubs award pie contracts to manufacturers who then have exclusive pie-rights for the season. This has evened out quality but also eliminated much variety.

Shire Foods, a pie manufacturer of note, proudly shout from their website that they supply more football clubs than any other firm and that their most popular creation is the chicken balti pie, a kind of curry-in-a-crust affair. This boast could be made only about football pies. No one gloats about supplying the most cucumbers to Lord's Cricket Ground, now do they? Nor will you find a company keen to tell the world that they are the biggest suppliers of butter to Wimbledon's sandwich makers. But football and pies are different.

Another legendary company, Pukka Pies, hold some sort of record for supplying the biggest volume of pies eaten in one afternoon at Rotherham's Millmoor ground. They managed to cram over 40 per cent more down their meat-holes than the average. All very impressive, but who is paying such close attention to pie consumption at football grounds that they even know what the average amount of pies typically consumed might be? An expert in the science of 'pieconomics', perhaps.

At Merseyside clubs you can enjoy the treat of a Scouse pie, which in its finest form is a kind of Irish stew in pastry. Some say it should have no lid, others have cruelly suggested that Scouse pie did have a lid but it has been nicked, as though it were a kind of pastry hub cap. I would never dream of even thinking such a thing, though.

Go north of the border to Scotland and you will find that the Scotch pie rules. It's made from grey, greasy mutton and is served in a sharp, hard, gum-bleeding-inducing pastry crust. So hard are the pies that they could quite easily be used by hooligans to assault opposition fans and, if you think that is unlikely, meat-based violence is not unheard of at football matches.

In 2008 someone threw a leg of lamb on to the pitch in a Ballymena United vs Distillery match. Catching a glancing blow from a speeding raw ovine limb can do a player a serious injury and render a fan comatose. The culprit was never identified, so be warned: if you're at a football match in Ireland and you end up next to a man who smells of raw meat and he has a leg-shaped bulge under his coat, it'll either be the phantom lamb flinger of Ballymena ready to strike again, or simply a pervert pleasuring himself in public.

The Scotch pie has an advantage though: its top is sunken and thus allows for a spoon of starchy fluorescent jade-green marrowfat peas and vinegar or brown sauce to be plonked on top, thus providing Scots with an edible vegetable, something they are normally averse to, fearing that consuming vegetables is a pretentious English plot to undermine their Braveheart culture, so-called because you need a brave, indeed very robust heart, to keep on beating after a few years of the indigenous Scottish Irn Bru and pie diet. In fact, I'd go so far as to say, if you are English and find yourself in Scotland, under no circumstances opt for the Scotch pie; you will not have sufficient anti-bodies in your system to repel the poison it will certainly contain. It takes years to build up that level of immunity.

If you're especially fortunate you may get served a pie that was, until very recently, frozen. Some of the smaller clubs seem to specialise in this radical food. The sensation of biting down on a roasting hot pie, only to find ice in the centre, is a culinary and physical experience not to be missed, even though you risk some of the worst forms of botulism by eating it. However, like bungee jumping or insulting the girlfriends of men with 'hate' and 'love' tattooed on their knuckles, it's dangerous but kind of thrilling. Will it make you incontinent? Will it make hair grow on your forehead? Will it actually taste sinfully good? Could you start a new business selling meat iced-lollies? All these are questions that pass through the mind of the semi-frozen pie eater. Yes, you could just cut out the middle man and throw the pies straight down the bog, but where's the fun in that? Actually, now you come to think of it . . .

Elsewhere in the world, food is also sold outside and inside football grounds, ranging from chicken porridge in Indonesia, sunflower seeds in Greece – can you imagine that in the UK: sunflower seeds? Save mine for the budgie's cage, pal – and sausage sandwiches in

Uruguay. While Germans enjoy various wursts, Turkey loves its meatballs and Russians may serve you fish, it would appear only the UK has put the pie together with association football to make one of the great sporting/food interfaces.

Indeed, even the land of never-ending food, America, has yet to link savoury crusty pies with sporting events. In fact, Americans, though mad for anything meat- or pastry-based, simply doesn't have a pie culture outside of fruit pies. The day someone starts selling meat pies at baseball games, they'll have a million dollars overnight.

So pies rule.

But as dominant as pies are, they are just the crusty pinnacle atop a pyramid of foodstuffs available. While eating a pie is fraught with potential difficulties and health issues, the consumption of Bovril or, in days gone by, beef tea – often no more than an Oxo cube dissolved in a lot of water – is more understandable and far less dangerous, even despite its traditional boiling-point serving temperature.

In the freezing cold winters between the wars when this whole beef tea thing got established, a steaming mug of savouriness was a much needed barrier against the biting cold. And for the poor it provided a kind of budget roast dinner in a cup with just enough nutrition to keep body and soul together for another twenty-four hours pouring pig iron or hacking coal out of a big hole with a small child.

None of which helps to explain the persistent presence and popularity of Bovril at all levels of football in the twenty-first century now that much nicer alternatives exist, such as drinking piss. The Govan Stand at Rangers' ground was even referred to as the Bovril Stand, not because it had a salty, meaty taste, though it may well have done, but because of a massive advertisement for the gloopy brown stuff on it

I first had Bovril at Middlesbrough's old ground, Ayresome Park, on a winter's day around 1972 or 1973. We were playing Hull City. It was a still, cold Saturday afternoon, and the air was filled with nostril-stinging smog. We were 1-0 up, as usual, a Hickton goal. Half time came and with it the savoury beefy odour of Bovril as people bought steaming cups of the stuff. It actually smelled lovely, I thought, and was despatched to purchase some by my dad. I returned clutching my prize, feeling somehow slightly more grown up now I had joined the Bovril ranks.

It took almost until the second half kicked off before it had cooled down enough to drink but, when I swallowed it, I was shocked. Despite its rich savoury odour, it tasted watery, bitter and intolerably salty. It somehow managed to taste of nothing and yet be thoroughly unpleasant. I handed it to my dad and asked him if it was off? He drank it all down and said, no, it was always like that. That was my Bovril career over with until the early 1980s when as a student I used the stuff to mask the taste of powerful magic mushroom infusions – a task which it is eminently suited to and one that should be adopted by all clubs as a way of making the football more interesting.

Bovril, liked by a few, is tolerated by some and loathed by millions but continues to be served at most grounds purely out of tradition and because the British masochistically consume things they really dislike rather than actually complain that they're horrible. We like to wear a hair shirt in Britain; not really enjoying ourselves makes us feel morally more pure. This must be the reason for Bovril's survival because it certainly can't be due to the flavour.

For many years the beef Bovril was actually vegetarian, being derided not from boiled cows' parts but from yeast extract. Presumably the vegetable Bovril is actually made from boiled underpants and wood and has never seen a vegetable.

Recently, in a startling fit of logic, they started making beef Bovril out of beef again. Phew. Not that anyone could tell. It's an aroma everyone who has spent any amount of their lives at football games can recognise instantly, anyone that is except members of the landed gentry, it would seem.

Because it was once my pleasure to attend a Hartlepool United game and as the distinctive scent of boiling Bovril wafted in on the stiff north-easterly, a chap in front of me, a strange interloper dressed in obligatory landowners' uniform of green tweedy coat shot through with an orange check, with matching cap, yellow jumbo corduroys and brown leather shoes, raised his chinless face up, sniffed the air and declared in one of those braying, unself-conscious voices that only the old money has, 'Is that miso I smell? Yes, I think it is. Miso! Hurrah. How frightfully progressive.'

He was lucky to get out alive. Mind, I'm partial to a spot of miso soup myself and would love to see it on the menu along with some sashimi. I am a food ponce though, remember.

For decades football grounds have been surrounded by vendors selling hot dogs or burgers from greasy-looking vans or those funny little mud- and vomit-splattered trolleys, which in the trade are known as 'static' and 'mobile kiosks' and in equally corporate language are now said to deliver 'innovative meal solutions'. And you thought your cooker was just a cooker, didn't you? Turns out it's a delivery mechanism for food solutions. Who knew?

Typical examples of these 'kiosks' could be found outside Newcastle United's ground when I used to go there in the late 1970s and early 1980s. Tattooed ex-cons used to sell Westlers hot dogs that certainly tasted like an over-heated canine. I'm sure they're a better product today – certainly Westlers current 'Premium Pouched Hot Dogs' sound delicious. What says tasty snack more than a premium pouch? If you put an especially big hot dog in it, does it become a posing pouch? We need to be told, Westlers.

Around midday in the late 1970s and early 1980s you would see great herds of these purveyors emerge from a lock-up down by the central station like wildebeest sweeping across the African plains. Well, they were certainly wild beasts.

Some would wear a long white butcher's-style coat as though this represented their dedication to hygiene and food science. However, these coats were always splashed with frightening-looking substances that could have been mustard and tomato sauce but just as easily could have been stomach bile and blood from a recently opened jugular vein. These days Westlers kiosks are nicely branded up and look less like a mobile army surgical facility, but it wasn't always the case.

More usually these wagons were a moveable frappe of bacteria, a bain marie full of boiled-to-oblivion onions and pink, floppy hot dogs that looked like something that had recently starred in a porn movie. And all of it was swimming in water that looked like it had recently been inside of an animal, topped off with a layer of melted fat.

The lads who pushed these little barrows were not chefs; more likely they had recently been in Durham jail for assault with a deadly weapon and, ironically, their new career as a seller of hot tubular slurry in a bun was no less violent when said protein extrusion reached your digestive tract.

How these festering vehicles passed any health code at all is beyond comprehension. Maybe council officials were simply too scared to tell them they were a walking disease trap or perhaps it was all part of a secret government programme to reduce the population of the industrial cities of Britain by killing people with food poisoning.

However, despite the fact that these hot dogs were likely to violently poison you, hundreds of fans with a three-pint hunger on, would buy one, pouring thin, vinegary tomato sauce on it to cover up the taste and chow down. Football seems to do that to us: it suspends all rational thought. No one in their right mind buys warmed-up sausages from a filthy barrow served by a bloke with yellow fingers and 'Insanity Beast' tattooed on his forehead in any other circumstances, but outside of a football ground, mmm, that's good eatin', I'll take three, Mr Beast.

Westlers remain, from their north Yorkshire home of Amotherby, the kings of the football dog and have been for forty-five years, which is a tremendous achievement and proof that it is still a crucial part of match-day lifestyle, not just because of the tasty goodness but also because who among us doesn't laugh out loud when presented with a hot dog resting invitingly in a split finger bun; the sexual imagery is irresistible. Plus, there are few more erotic sights for the twenty-first-century football male than to see a pretty woman wrapping her lips around a hot dog, preferably a foot long. Oh baby, you want sauce with that?

Far less sexy are the burger vans, infinite in number and all emitting that sweet sickly meaty monosodium glutamate odour. Some vans are huge, shiny aluminium-lined mobile cooking facilities serving up a huge menu in clean, spacious surroundings. They're able to serve up enough to feed a frontline battle unit. Others are little more than a caravan full of bacteria serving food that is edible only if you have lost your sense of taste in a terrible parachuting accident and are wearing a colostomy bag.

I knew a lad who worked in such a van on Stockton High Street in the late 1970s. It was his dubious pleasure to dish out burgers and, oddly enough, soup, to people who were drunk on Cameron's Strongarm at chucking-out time, which was 10.30pm for those of you who have grown up with twenty-four-hour drinking. Needless to say, for anyone who gave him a hard time, was aggressive or looked like a 'trendy' – for Lenny was of the poet/hippy/anarchist persuasion – he had his revenge ready and waiting in the shape of a teaspoon of dog shit, collected earlier, into which he would secretly dip a knife tip and smear on to a bap while buttering it for his victim. 'Just enough to poison, not enough to taste' was his motto. You don't want to know what was in the soup.

There's a chip shop at the top of Leith Walk in Edinburgh that proudly boasts of selling a deep-fried Mars bar. This is more of a gimmick aimed at tourists, a self-parody, but one born out of a long Scottish tradition of battering and deep-frying almost every foodstuff possible. Long before it was a post modern ironic icon of the furred-up arteries of the Scottish people, I indulged in the deep-fried Mars bar experience.

At the time, in the mid-1980s, it didn't occur to me that this might be a tad unhealthy; rather I treated it as a luxury item on a chip shop dessert menu. As unfashionable as it might be to say so, I found it a delicious combination of fatty, savoury crunch from the batter, followed by a river of melting chocolate and caramel. Naturally, I had put salt on the batter too, so it was a sweet and savoury experience all at once. I considered this not only to be finger-lickin' good, but also quite sophisticated in the same way that I thought of eating gammon and pineapple as shockingly progressive; after all, it's sweet and savoury all on the same plate. Mother would have been disgusted. Naturally, there was a slight feeling of nausea ten minutes after finishing it, but that was much the same with all food I had consumed while growing up, so I thought nothing of it.

There is much to recommend the deep-fried Mars bar, especially for those who have had enough of life. However, another Scottish delicacy does not come with such a positive endorsement: the deep-fried pizza. Oh yes, I'm serious – serious as a heart attack, appropriately enough.

I'd been drinking in Glasgow and fell into a chippy late at night in Maryhill, catching it just before it closed, and there they were, a small stack of mini-pizzas, covered in batter, deep-fried and looking back at me with come-hither eyes. What's more, the chip shop had run out of everything else. I stared at them, finding them irresistible in the same way a sweaty fat lass with facial hair is irresistible when all the other females have left the club and you've lost the use of your visual and olfactory senses through drinking Stella Artois.

One mouthful was enough. It managed to redefine the word 'greasy'. In fact greasy would have been the low-fat version of this creation. Soggy, oily batter, wrapped around wet cardboard-style pizza base inter laced with the vicious tang of tomato seemingly mixed with some sort of bitter, throat-rotting acid. I skimmed it like a Frisbee into the nearest bin and considered myself lucky to be alive after this brush with extreme Celtic foodstuffs.

As football has become established as a seven-day-a-week TV experience as long as you don't mind watching Europa League games on a Thursday night, many never even go to a live game, preferring the TV coverage instead. However, so strong is football's food culture now that this has not diminished the desire or habit of snacking, drinking beer and eating pies while a big game is on. Thousands of pizzas are baked or delivered in time for the big match. Indeed the connection between football and pizza is now so strong that my local Pizza Hut just has graphics of footballs on its window. There's no attempt to tie it into any specific game or event. The message seems to be, Going to watch some football, why not have a pizza?

Supermarkets do special promotions to tie in with big international games and tournaments; usually this just involves putting images of black-and-white footballs on everything.

I would also wager a few rocket salads are eaten in the privacy of front rooms, safe from the prying eyes of the judgemental food fascists seeking to define you as a middle-class ponce. In your front room, not even Roy Keane can see your sandwich contents.

After reminiscing about the dodgy football food culture we grew up with and which is still present at grounds even if they have expanded their menus to include paninis, wraps and pizza, the idea of going to a game and eating, perhaps, a spicy chickpea curry served with a baby spinach side salad and a chilled bottle of Australian Pinot Gris actually sounds like a bloody good idea to me. It doesn't have to mean you're any less passionate about the game. Ingestion of pies does not inevitably fire up the emotions more than a three-bean salad even though it may raise your blood pressure substantially.

Add to it the chance of some silk-clad cleavage to be spotted and a bit of shelter from inclement weather, and you're making a persuasive argument for the modern football fine dining experience. Maybe I'm one of the new generations of traitors, men who are selling the culture of football down the river in favour of something more gutless and untraditional.

But I like the chance to mix and match these options. Some days you feel in the mood for old-school pie and peas or maybe a cheese toasty. On other days you want to pull a cork on a bottle of Gewürztraminer and enjoy a blushed tomato, basil and mozzarella salad. These days, we can have it all at football. And that's actually quite brilliant. Some might call it fickle; I prefer to think of it as flexible.

The culture of eating before, during and after football games has helped extend the experience and bind it closer to us, so much so that it can be a whole lifestyle in itself.

Food and rock 'n' roll however, have never been happy bedfellows for me. You go out to rock not to dine. As a teenager, the idea of having a meal before a gig was laughable, smacking of some sort of Vegas lounge show. There were very few places where this was even possible. However, one was Redcar's Coatham Bowl, which did chicken and chips in a basket before the bands came on. It didn't make the gig any more enjoyable the time I went there to see Racing Cars supported by Big Jim Sullivan's Tiger.

As much as I love Las Vegas, even I, despite my food ponce tendencies, draw the line at pre-show dining. We had the chance recently to do this prior to Tom Jones' show at the MGM Grand. We declined and got properly boozed-up instead. We felt it was what Tom would have wanted.

Oh, and while I'm talking about eating and rock 'n' roll, I want to know why the Hard Rock Cafe is so called when it plays bloody Madonna and feckin' Kylie. It's totally inappropriate. Keep it 100 per cent rock 100 per cent of the time. Get it right. I wanna rock, I don't want bloody Madonna harshing my buzz. Ahem. Sorry, I just had to get that off my chest; it's been bugging me for twenty years.

I've spent much of my adult life trying to get away from the over-cooked, bland, stodgy, greasy food of my childhood, the kind of food that was on offer in and around football grounds. So the idea of still eating it when there are so many others much better, more tasty options available seems mad to me. That's also why the upmarket version of downmarket eating, such as a £35 fish cake, is so unattractive too. If I'm paying decent money, I want something new and exciting, not just a smaller, better-quality rehash of what I was fed as a kid.

There's a fine line between carrying on traditions and just being reactionary and football fans are not averse to crossing it from time to time, but the fact is football culture has changed and adapted to the new cosmopolitan – some would say bourgeois – lifestyles and ambitions.

The middle-classification of football is rarely thought of as a good thing and is blamed for less atmosphere and passion. But go to any of the restaurants at football grounds and you'll find a mixture of people from all walks of life; it's not just the middle class. The Jeremys and their wives are there, but so is the bloke who runs your local garage, the accountant with a degree from Sunderland Polytechnic or the woman who runs the local hairdressers. It varies from region to region of course. I'm willing to bet there are more financial directors and men called Justin drinking white wine spritzers at Arsenal than at Berwick Rangers.

But still, it is the pie that rules supreme. Not for me, like, but we can't all be food ponces. Unmatched in its popularity, unequalled as football food, even in today's more health-conscious society, going to a game offers people a chance to eat one in an uncritical environment, secure in the knowledge that you are not only satiating your lust for salty, meaty pastry products but also carrying on a noble tradition.

You are the custodian of the flame on Olde Albion's football cuisine and no amount of healthy eating advice can take that away from you. Consuming a pie at every match may knock a few years off your life but given the choice between an early death and a life without pies, many would choose the going brown early option because a life without pies is, in many ways, a living death. Much like watching Hartlepool United play at home in the bitter winter of 1971, while drinking Bovril and fending off a pack of wild dogs with a bag of beef-e crisps.

Eating is so hard-wired into our psyche that anything that can associate itself with it becomes as compulsive as the food itself. It mines the very root of our make-up. So for many fans football without food before or during the game is now unthinkable.

Now, excuse me while I go and make some artichoke dip to spread on rye toast.

5
Television

IMAGINE a world without football on the telly. OK, so your significant, non-football-loving other would be delighted as it would return you to the real world, but any true football fan would be horrified. Football on TV is a way of life now and to imagine being deprived of it is to imagine a less entertaining world. Television expanded and re-energised football's fan base, which was very necessary after the mid- to late-1980s drift away from the game. It's lifeblood for all the football fanatics that keep the football body alive and healthy. The idea that it might be a bad thing is not one that any genuine fan would agree with.

But it hasn't always been like this.

Every summer from 1973 onwards, there was a kids' TV programme called *Why Don't You Just Switch Off Your Television Set and Go and Do Something Less Boring Instead*. It was one of those typical middle-class liberal BBC shows that meant well but was ultimately patronising, assuming as it did that its viewers were too stupid to have thought to do this for themselves or that they were not going to do so right after this programme.

It was essentially an arts and crafts show: how to occupy yourself during the holidays with a tub of Vaseline, a pair of rubber gloves and some amphetamines. Or whatever. The underlying assumption was that TV is a waste of your valuable time and instead of being hypnotised by it, why not go and live life? It's not a bad philosophy really.

This was a common theme when I was a kid. It cropped up in songs, especially counter-culture bands and artists who saw 'staring at the tube' as symbolic of how the straight people had their minds controlled by 'the man'.

'Silent majority still glued to the tube,' moaned Steve Miller in his 'Jackson Kent Blues' in 1970 on his excellent album *Number 5*. The genius that is Todd Rundgren said in 1978, on the *Ooops! Wrong Planet* track 'Gangrene':

> Now think, fifty million kids with nothing better to do
> Than sit around like a zombie and stare at the tube.
> They'll sap your strength and suck your soul and feed you the
> trash
> Till your mind is left blank and your dreams have been smashed'

Both songs also feature stinging guitar solos the like of which could take the top of your head clean off, which, as a disciple of the guitar, naturally got my attention.

So this anti-TV vibe was in the air throughout my upbringing and it was shared by the football authorities too. Football was a live event, not something to sit on your settee and experience with six cans of Budweiser and a pizza.

There was definitely a notion that watching television was somehow a waste of time and possibly morally reprehensible. My parents even introduced class war to TV by insisting that ITV was for 'common' people, in other words the sort of people they had been while growing up. If we had to watch television then the BBC would educate and uplift, they thought. Though I didn't know it at the time, this was a not unusual notion. Subsequently, I've met many people whose parents would not watch ITV at all and wouldn't let the children do so either.

I should say at this point that I'm notoriously anti-BBC. It's nothing to do with the programmes per se, though I do find the corporation institutionally patronising at times, forever trying to tell us how to live as though we're all numskulls and can't work it out for ourselves.

I just can't accept having to pay them money just to own a TV. I vividly recall telling someone this in California. They laughed, 'You need a licence to own a TV? Man, you need a revolution! Do you need a licence to own a vacuum cleaner or a washing machine too?'

I just don't understand what the BBC is for any more and I don't think it does either, because it gives out mixed messages. It tells us it's meant to produce programmes that the market wouldn't produce because they're of niche interest. But they shamelessly chase ratings with downmarket crap. If we have to pay them to own a TV then they should be significantly different from every other channel because any fool can make rubbish TV programmes without a mandated income from the state.

Basically, I want the right to choose to pay them or not. I'll buy the bits I want and ignore the rest. It's not a radical idea, is it, buying what you want to consume? The fact they won't allow us to opt out of the licence fee and add their channels to our digital packages for a fee shows lack of balls and lack of faith in their own product. It'd be so easy now to make that happen.

Right, that's my rant about the BBC over. I know it's a minority opinion and that most people like such institutions as the BBC, along with royalty and marriage. It seems to give people a sense of continuity and comfort. I don't like them exactly because of that, but maybe that's because I was exposed to the likes of Frank Zappa as a boy and thus seem innately to want to take the ornery route; always attracted to the rebel stance and the maverick viewpoint.

Possibly because football was a working-class sport and thus not to be pandered to, a snooty attitude to football on TV prevailed for decades. Although the BBC had shown a game between Arsenal and Arsenal reserves as early as 1937, England vs Scotland in 1938 and the FA Cup Final that year between Huddersfield and Preston featuring a young Bill Shankly, there was little post-war expansion of TV coverage of football. You got the occasional international and FA Cup Final but that was the football fans' lot.

The football authorities were also none too keen on the game being on what was already being called the goggle box; not a term anyone uses now, it seems.

The Football League, led by the pugnacious Yorkshireman Alan Hardaker, were very reluctant to allow live coverage of league games, fearing it would reduce crowds, not just at the match concerned but right across the leagues as people would decide to stay by the fire and watch football rather than venture out into the choking smog of post-war Britain. However when ITV dangled 150,000 English pounds in front of them and asked to cover twenty-six games in the 1960–61 season that did the trick nicely.

But after a terrible opening game between Blackpool and Bolton, which Blackpool won 1-0 in a half-empty ground, other clubs had second thoughts. Arsenal, Spurs, Newcastle and Villa all refused to let cameras in, so ITV pulled out of the deal. Incidentally, that first live league game was a weird transmission starting at 7.30pm, by which time the game was forty minutes old. Presumably, it was thought that missing most of the first half would mean that locals would still want to attend. With this kind of attitude it was doomed from the start.

After this débâcle, live league football would not return to our screens until the 1980s. Highlights were a different matter though. One of the earliest highlights packages was Tyne Tees's *Shoot* programme, which began in 1962. *Shoot* was a constant in the life of any north-eastern football fan until the early 1980s. It would feature matches from Newcastle, Sunderland, Middlesbrough, Darlington and Hartlepool; occasionally they'd venture to York.

Initially it just showed a twenty-five-minute highlight package of a local game but later went on to show highlights of two other games from other regions. Each region had its own football highlights show. Indeed, ITV was a much less homogenised affair than it is today, with a great emphasis on local flavour and culture. *Shoot* went out on Saturday night and then, by the late 1960s, Sunday afternoon.

The BBC launched *Match of the Day* in 1964 with a Liverpool vs Spurs game and with it, a Saturday-night institution. There is no adequate way to describe how thrilling it was at the time for football fans to have these twin packages of football on at a weekend. For a century the only football the population could watch was a game they went to themselves, along with a few Pathé News reels at the pictures. Suddenly, a whole world was opened up. Men would hurry home from the boozer to watch it. This was what some ad exec called Tim would now call 'event TV'.

It illustrated just how hungry the British people were for more football in their lives because as soon as it got on to BBC1 in 1965 and had a nationwide audience it was immediately hugely popular, not just in terms of viewing numbers but in how soon it had become embraced culturally. It soon began to crop up in situation comedies, often referred to disparagingly by ignored wives and girlfriends. By the 1970s it was pulling an audience of over twelve million and was an entrenched British institution. Its introductory music was recently voted the most recognisable theme tune on TV. When one in four people are watching a programme all at the same time – there was no video of course – it is bound to have a huge impact on the nation's consciousness.

Even those who considered watching television a frivolous waste of time could not resist watching football on it if they were fans. It was utterly compulsive.

Match of the Day covered the top-flight games each week so we got to see up close what players who we either never or only rarely saw from the terraces looked like. We also got to see their skill or lack of it up close. We got to see all the goals every week and became experts in our own minds. This was the start of the road to the world of football media we live with today.

In common with thousands of other people, for me *MotD* became synonymous with post-pub groping of girlfriends. 'We're just going to watch the football,' I'd tell my parents, who were already in bed. The door would be closed and the action on the pitch and on the sofa would begin. Millions of men every weekend would try to delay ejaculation by staring at Jimmy Hill. Jim must have been a blind witness to more sex than any other TV presenter of the era; I bet he's rather proud of that.

But even if you were dateless, *MotD* was often followed by a Hammer horror movie, which meant a chance to relieve your teenage lust by seeing Ingrid Pitt's pink-nippled, big breasts in a series of ropey old movies such as *Vampire Lovers* and *Countess Dracula*. So it was the gateway to all manner of flesh-based delights.

The programme was even the title of a track on Genesis's 1977 'Spot the Pigeon' EP. You know you've made it when prog rock embraces you.

So with the big games of the First Division on Saturday nights, and the more local *Shoot* on a Sunday, in common with many of my generation, I got a well-balanced football education as well as a sexual one.

I could watch Leeds vs Arsenal on Saturday night and the next day, Darlington vs Workington. I loved it all and was allowed to stay up late to watch *Match of the Day* and the midweek *Sportsnight with Coleman* (it always annoyed me that 'Sportsnight' was spelled as one word), which featured highlights of league games and European ties too. Add to that the Boro's second division games and I was dining on a veritable smorgasbord of football compared to the previous generation.

I think experiencing football at all levels, be it on TV or live, is crucial to understanding the game. Too many today just watch a top-flight club, often one of the big teams, and don't take in any lower league football either live or on TV. Not to do so is to miss out on the breadth and depth of the game's culture. But the top games are sold to kids with such hyperbole that you'd think nothing else mattered apart from the Premier League. Every Sunday is a Super Sunday apparently; well I'm here to tell you it bloody isn't.

Both *MotD* and *Shoot* were low on production values by today's standards. Indeed, Tyne Tees had only one outside broadcast camera unit, which meant that if it was otherwise engaged on Saturday at the racing or wrestling, on Sunday, they'd show a programme from another region. When this happened we all wanted them to show *The Big Match* from London. London Weekend Television's flagship show was a million miles away from *Shoot*. It had highlights of London club games. It had special guests and interviews. All presented by the great Brian Moore. This was an infinitely more glamorous affair and seemed to be a world away from the north east.

You probably remember Brian Moore. He was one of those rare people on TV who you felt you actually knew and as he was very much part of my growing up, he became a kind of football father figure, my own dad not being that bothered about the game.

Moore was a consummate commentator and presenter, at home in front of the camera and behind the microphone. He was warm without being unctuous, erudite without being elitist, informed without being nerdy and, perhaps above all, just a really good bloke that, who like you and me, loved the game and shared his passion with us.

An omnipresent figure on our screens for nearly forty years, around whom ITV's coverage revolved, when he died in 2001 on the very day that England defeated Germany 5-1, we lost one of football's greatest communicators and loveliest men. I loved him. He was like a kind uncle.

Brian started out as a radio commentator in the early 1960s, even doing the 1966 World Cup Final. The BBC had a radio monopoly pretty much until the 1970s, so if you worked on it, you had the medium's whole audience. Moore was the BBC's first football correspondent in 1963 so, by 1968 when he joined ITV, he was already well known among football fans.

He fronted *The Big Match* for the newly launched London Weekend Television having been offered a contract by the new head of sport, Jimmy Hill. In those distant days, ITV was far more regionally orientated, so LWT broadcast only to London and the Home Counties.

This meant that kids like me on Teesside could see it only when Tyne Tees were not showing a match from the north east, but even then, on such occasions the Sunday-afternoon highlights were usually drawn from Yorkshire TV with the great Keith Macklin, or ATV in Birmingham with Hugh Johns.

It seemed glamorous and exciting. Moore sat in an expensive-looking studio, introduced the games and then discussed action with a studio guest. Back then this was radical because there was no football discussion on TV. Jimmy Hill was often on hand to dissect tactics.

And it wasn't just top-flight action; occasionally you'd get second, third and fourth division games too from places such as Brentford or Orient. I especially liked Orient because the name sounded so exotic; as though the Orient would be a team of opium-smoking Chinamen in silk kimonos.

In those days the TV companies were not allowed to say in

advance what games they were covering for fear of reducing crowds, so we used to play a guessing game all weekend long. As the theme tune started, 'The Young Scene' by The Graham Walker Sound, a tune written by Keith Mansfield, a legendary composer of TV music who also wrote the *Grandstand* and Wimbledon music, it was impossible not to feel a tingle of excitement in your stomach. Whatever happened to great theme tunes? Now it's all an edit from a pop song of the time, whereas they used to be composed specifically for the programme.

Brian was immediately popular. An avuncular figure with balding pate and a Charltonesque comb-over, his first Big Match was a 1-1 draw between QPR and Manchester City.

Around the same time, LWT started to show a midweek game, the *Wednesday Special*. And Brian fronted and commentated for that as well. He was ITV's Mr Football, so it was natural that their 1970 World Cup coverage would rotate around him based in London. He was the ringmaster for what became known as 'The Midnight Special' as Messrs Allison, Dougan et al. dissected the Mexico action in a blizzard of cantankerous rowing and semi-drunk shouting of the odds. More about that legendary programme in a moment.

Brian was the sane one, trying to keep control. Everyone loved it.

He also hosted the essential Saturday-lunchtime preview show *On the Ball*, which was infinitely superior to the stuffy Bob Wilson-fronted *Football Focus*. Brian was utterly inseparable from ITV football. We took him for granted for decades.

Generous to colleagues, when John Motson, new to the BBC, sat down to do his first commentary he found a note from Brian wishing him luck. Typical of the man.

The BBC tried to lure him away with the promise that he could also commentate on cricket, his other passion in life, but he resisted, probably in the knowledge that he was the master of his domain at ITV, and the money was much better.

While he was calm under pressure and was a familiar comfortable figure, he was no mere yes man. In an era which specialised in argumentative, pugnacious pundits, if he felt someone was out of order he would say so.

On the legendary occasion in 1973 when England drew with Poland 1-1 at Wembley and Brian Clough was thoroughly disparaging of Tomaszewski the Polish keeper, calling him a clown, Brian rebuked him, saying the Pole had played magnificently for his side. That took bottle because Cloughie was a fierce, sneering firebrand who could and did shred weaker men with one well-honed sentence.

I remember that night very well as it put another nail into the coffin of England as an international football giant.

Moore developed a long-standing friendship with Clough, sharing his socialist-leaning political worldview. He had been born in a council house to agricultural workers in Kent in 1932. His scholarship to Cranbrook College had given him a step up in society though he was later to say, 'The effect of coming from a working-class background and going to public school was to give me a terrible inferiority complex, and it's something I've never really been able to shed.' Unsurprising then that he should share Cloughie's leftist inclinations.

The BBC's chief commentator throughout this period was David Coleman, a cold, clinical, cliché-drenched automaton prone to gaffes who clearly turned up with a list of phrases that he would shoe-horn into the game by any means possible. Not for Brian gaffes such as 'the Cuban opens his legs and shows his class'.

As live football became the norm in the 1980s and the regionalism which had given ITV much of its diverse flavour was dismantled in favour of a more homogeneous approach, Brian continued to present and commentate. His description of Michael Thomas's title-winning goal for Arsenal at Anfield, 'It's up for grabs now', went down in football folklore. Ten years later he said he'd met cabbies who had memorised the entire last minute of his momentous commentary which just demonstrates the sheer power of television.

He'd reduced some of his work as a presenter in the mid-1980s after a heart scare and by-pass surgery, but was still a regular on the microphone.

His last game was the 1998 World Cup Final. Still hugely popular and barely looking any older than he had back in 1968 , he was gone, perhaps, before we realised fully just what we had.

He had covered nine World Cups and over twenty Cup Finals. So omnipresent had he been that no parody of a football interview was complete without the 'Brian' coda.

A lifelong Gillingham fan, he has a stand in his honour at the Priestfield Stadium and the fanzine there is called 'Brian Moore's Head Looks Uncannily Like London Planetarium'. You know you've made it when Half Man Half Biscuit write you into a song.

Married to Betty since 1955, he was essentially a quiet man, happiest at home with his family. The football world from the boardroom to the terraces mourned him. The fact that he passed on the same day as that historic England win – which he would have loved to see – only heightened our sense of loss.

In an era where football presenters are all too often smug, vacuous heads that talk a lot but say nothing, Brian Moore stands as a shining example of how the gig should be done.

Loved and respected by all who knew him and a giant of the genre he all but created, he left a peerless legacy. I can't imagine that we'll feel the same way about Richard Keys or Ray Stubbs, somehow.

I saw all of Brian's work that it was possible to see in the north east. As an eager student of the game in the 1970s, you just didn't miss any football on TV because it such a rare bird. If you caught it all you'd rarely see more than three hours of football a week on the box. There was *Football Focus* for half an hour on Saturday then turn to ITV for *On the Ball*. Midweek was *Sportsnight,* which didn't always have football highlights on. Most regions had a preview show on Friday nights on ITV.

Starved of coverage of the game we loved, of course, we wanted more, but it did give what was available real status and importance. Live action was even rarer and we craved that with a real hunger. This is why FA Cup Final day was so damn exciting and why, conversely, it's not so special any more for the TV viewer. The only day of the year when football was on TV from 9am to 6pm.

World Cups were exotic beyond a young boy's comprehension. Sitting down to *Good Morning from Mexico* with Frank Bough in 1970 was like peering through the looking glass into a distant world, a world of fuzzy, bright colours. It was magical and attracted huge audiences. The blizzard of West Germany rain that dominated the 1974 World Cup seemed emblematic of the Cold War, the ticker-tape hysteria of Argentina in 1978 brought us kids our first taste of South American passion. In that sense, we began to learn about the world through such events. We lived quite narrow, locally based lives so this was all an amazing broadening of our horizons.

The fear that live TV coverage would reduce crowds for games has not really been proven true. While the Premier League does not attract the same size crowds as football did in the 1940s and 1950s, that's more due to the capacity limits imposed by all-seater stadia than lack of demand. Indeed, the Championship is so popular that it's actually the fourth best attended league in Europe.

If there's a problem with the wall-to-wall coverage we now have, outside of the financial shambles that TV money has helped induce, it's that it's taken the mystery and therefore some of the excitement of the game away. We know so much about the players and see them all so regularly that they've come to resemble actors in an ongoing soap opera. But I'd argue this is a small price to pay for being able to watch dozens of hours of football a week.

However, as the BBC is supposed to lead the way in quality broadcasting, it's shamefully neglectful in its coverage of football as a culture. They ignore the millions of followers of the beautiful game who see it not just as light entertainment but as a deep, rich folk culture, as an art form, as an important part of our civic society. To that end, where are the weekly football documentaries? Where are the explorations of the culture of football? Where are the programmes studying the economics of football? Where are the studies of tactics both past and present? Where are the programmes about fans and their experiences? Where are the explorations of lower league and amateur football? Where is the history? Why is football so ignored? It is a major cultural force in Britain, after all.

Why aren't there a couple of programmes per week on one of their digital channels dedicated to football? On BBC3 they run hours of dross such as *Fuck Off I'm Ginger*, *Dog Borstal* or *Help Me Anthea, I'm Infested*. (These sound made up, I know, but they're real programmes.)

It would certainly attract more viewers than an hour watching someone picking mice out of Anthea Turner's arse or whatever.

The very occasional documentaries Alan Hansen has done come over as little more than televisual coffee-table books. They're welcome but lack weight. Sky has much material at its disposal but seems unable to utilise it in intelligent football programmes. They just don't do documentaries, perhaps fearing their audience is too stupid to watch them. ITV likewise. I suspect those responsible for commissioning programmes consider all football fans to be the same kind of low-life knuckle-dragging idiots and haven't realised that you can like football and not be a moron.

So we're left with a plethora of live action and discussion between pundits, usually ex-players in tight-fitting trousers who seem to speak English as a second language and wrestle their syntax into submission with a series of hoary old clichés and thoughtless assumptions.

With all the football now on TV has come the rise and rise of the pundit. Punditry has been very important in creating the compulsive nature of football on TV. It amplified the debates we all had before, during and after a game, introduced more controversy and therefore allowed us to argue among ourselves more or just shout abuse at the TV, which as everyone knows is tremendous fun.

Punditry was first tried out by Jimmy Hill on *The Big Match* and had proved very popular because it allowed dissection of the play and more opinion about the action. Hill, though an oft-derided figure, was a shrewd man and a canny operator. He knew that one of the things we all love about football is talking about it and shouting our opinions at each other.

Punditry as such had existed only for a couple of years by the time Mexico 1970 rolled around. The whole concept got its biggest boost when ITV employed the likes of Derek Dougan, Paddy Crerand, Bob McNabb and Malcolm Allison to pass judgement on the World Cup action.

There was none of the polite euphemism so common today. No punches were pulled. A spade was called a fucking shit shovel. At times it appeared that they had forgotten they were on TV at all.

This was an era of big characters with egos to match. The rows were legendary, as was the drinks bill. The idea of anyone appearing on a football programme drunk would now be thought unprofessional but you know we'd all really like to see it. Then again, a drunken Jamie Redknapp would be no more riveting than the sober version, though I'd like to see a drunken row between Andy Gray and Graeme Souness, stripped to the waist fighting on the cobbles!

It was the Manchester City coach Malcolm Allison who led the way in this new era of punditry. His Big Mal persona came into its own once the cameras went on. Dressed flash and smoking cigars in the studio – can you imagine such a thing happening today? – he was fierce in his criticism of England after they lost to West Germany and especially of Alan Mullery, who he felt didn't pressurise Beckenbauer enough. Mullery was invited in on his return and ended up throwing one of his international caps at Allison in disgust. Confrontation is avoided these days on football TV; not back then.

It was in-your-face and opinionated, often resembling an informed bar-room argument teetering on the verge of violence. Allison drew complaints for calling Russian and Romanian players 'peasants.' I suspect he'd be banned for life for such a comment today.

If you can find footage of it on YouTube then you really should take a look if you missed it first time round. Allison drank champagne all day before the shows, which went out live, sometimes at 11pm, sometimes during the afternoon. ITV picked up the bar tab, knowing he was great value for money and that the booze was the fuel that lit the fire. Even people who didn't like football tuned in to see the spectacle. Big Mal bloody loved it and so did I. It looked like he was living life to the full. Big Mal was simply extraordinary.

He embraced the fame ITV's show had given him. It was four weeks that changed football on TV and four weeks that changed his life for ever. Malcolm Allison had left the building. Big Mal had moved in.

Off went the tracksuit of the coach, and on came the fedora, the Cuban cigars, the expensive booze and the massive sheepskin coats. He dated Christine Keeler and a Brazilian Bunny Girl stunner called Serena Williams. He drank in Tramps with Michael Caine and other stars. He was a remarkable sight in his pomp: part manager, part playboy. He lived high on the hog. Everything. All the time. Rock 'n' roll football made overt. He was electric. Put him next to some of the managers of today and they would appear clinically dead by comparison.

On the other side at the time, though they were to be united for the 1974 World Cup, was Brian Clough. Born in Middlesbrough, he was bloody-minded, fabulously opinionated, self-regarding, sharp and articulate. He was also fearless. He didn't care who he upset, which was probably the reason he didn't get the England manager's job when Don Revie quit in 1977. He was the best man by a country mile but the FA were shit-scared of him, fearing his force of personality would be overwhelming and that he would end up running the FA, a perception that Brian was happy to confirm the veracity of.

Throughout the 1970s, Brian was always on TV, despite his chairmen at Derby County being unhappy about it. He'd sit in judgement on England games which, when played at Wembley, were often broadcast live. He and Allison were very critical of Sir Alf Ramsey, both thinking they could do a better job and not overly shy of saying so, which to some was as disrespectful as calling the Queen Mother a drunken old slag. Again, contrast this with today's more reverential, polite publicly expressed opinions.

Some reports say that Cloughie, like Allison, was always a couple of drinks in by the time the cameras started rolling which, if true, might explain his loose tongue.

His nasal, cutting drone was a gift to impressionists. Well, I say impressionists; I really just mean Mike Yarwood whose – in hindsight, rather watery impressions – were considered the apex of Saturday-night entertainment.

Unlike Malcolm Allison, who was less than successful as a manager in the 1970s, Cloughie had the managerial chops to back up the loud mouth, winning a tight First Division race in the 1972–73 season with Derby and famously winning two European Cups with Nottingham Forest. He was the Mourinho of his day: always good with a quote and never short on self-belief.

To me Cloughie was a hero. He was from Teesside for a start and you never saw anyone from the region on the national stage. It was easy to see why his sides were fiercely loyal to him and also in fear of him. There is classic footage of him standing on the touchline of a training pitch, barking at his players, 'Oh that's bloody rubbish. Rubbish!' and that was just what was allowed to be broadcast. He was a breath of fresh air, a natural rebel who was keen to take on the establishment – indeed he relished taking on the establishment whether in the form of chairmen, the FA or the media. He routinely insulted chairmen, saying they knew nothing about football, which isn't always a good idea if they are paying your wages, but Cloughie didn't care and his blunt manner gained him thousands of fans. His decline in the later years, ravaged by drink, was a tragedy in the purest sense of a great man brought low.

The flipside of Mal's flamboyance and Cloughie's confrontational style was a tough, articulate Scottish socialist, the Liverpool manager, Bill Shankly. The effect Shankly had on me as a boy was quite profound. In his years at Liverpool he seemed to turn into a guru, holding the fans and the rest of the football community in the palm of his hand. The Beatles had the Maharishi Yogi, the reds had Shanks.

He had principles, ideas, notions about football and how it fitted into life. It was very inspiring to me because I didn't really hear anyone else talking like this. Our house wasn't political. The parents voted Tory because it made them feel more posh. They saw the Labour Party as being for the class they wanted to leave behind. But they had no real notion of the detail behind the policies of the parties.

Shanks was always on *Football Focus*, philosophising, usually dressed in a grey suit and a red shirt. A pugnacious, tough-looking bloke, he was a great role model for a kid looking for a path to take through life.

Liverpool were in the Second Division when Shankly took over. Two third-place finishes were the prelude to a title-winning season in 1962–63. Two seasons later they were First Division champions – such meteoric rises could happen in those days.

He had turned an ailing club into one of England's biggest and best in just a few years. The Liverpool FC we know today was born in this era. From top to bottom he transformed Anfield. He put together a side fitter and stronger than any other. He created what came to be known as the Boot Room.

So fit and strong were his sides that when they won the 1965–66 First Division title they used just fourteen players and two of them were bit-part players.

Shankly delivered the ten most successful years the club had had to date, winning two FA Cups and two more league titles and a UEFA Cup before retiring in 1974 aged sixty. His successor Bob Paisley would build even bigger, more prolonged success on the base that Shanks had created.

Those are the bald facts but, perhaps even more importantly, in that period Shanks became a mythic figure of quite epic proportions, a people's poet and philosopher. At times he seemed to be a father figure to the whole red half of the city and the football world beyond.

How this happened at a time when the fledgling media spent little time focusing on footballers, let alone its managers, is genuinely astonishing and proof of the sheer irrepressible character of the man.

He was aided by the fact that, at the time, the city of Liverpool was at the vortex of popular culture thanks to The Beatles, so anything Liverpool-related caught people's attention.

Hand in hand with the rise of The Beatles was the depiction and celebration of the working class through the plays and novels of Osborne, Delaney, Sillitoe and many others. For perhaps the first time, it was cool to be working-class and more than that it was especially cool to be northern and working-class.

Films like *Billy Liar*, *A Taste of Honey*, *Saturday Night and Sunday Morning* and *This Sporting Life* were played out against a northern backdrop of decaying mills, chimneys and dirt. *Coronation Street* was gritty and full of memorable characters the like of which all northerners had grown up with. Social mobility was at an all-time high as bright kids from deprived backgrounds became successful.

Into this fertile compost of modern culture was planted Bill Shankly. In previous eras his superb west of Scotland accent might have simply made people tune out but now, in the new reality, where the working class had something to say and a ready audience who wanted to listen, he was not only heard, he was appreciated.

'The socialism I believe in is everybody working to the same goal and everybody having a share in the rewards. That's how I see football, that's how I see life.' Born into an industry based on collectivised labour, socialism was in Shankly's DNA.

He even changed Liverpool's strip to all red. The red of revolution made the players seem bigger and fiercer.

He was a proper man of the people and thought it part of his job to write to fans personally and even called on fans at their homes to discuss how the game had gone. This wasn't PR puffery, this was his way. He saw football as pure working-class art; of the people, by the people – and if the team failed then he had failed the people.

He would give tickets away to fans. It's no wonder the fans adored him. He paid them respect and took notice of them. He saw them all as part of the same thing. They all won and all lost together.

This collectivist spirit was infused into the players. They were a team, not a set of individuals. When Tommy Smith once informed him his knee was injured, Shanks insisted that 'it's not your knee, it's Liverpool's knee'.

He possessed a dry wit, once saying that if Everton were playing at his bottom of the garden he'd draw the curtains and telling Tommy Smith he could start a riot in a graveyard. There is an apparently inexhaustible supply of Shanks wit and wisdom, all dispensed in the papers and on local TV news to a public eager to lap it up.

His success as a manager helped cement his legend but regardless of the silverware he was one of those rare individuals who innately commanded respect. It's a nebulous attribute that is impossible to define but it is undoubtedly true of Shanks that both fans and players would have walked on hot coals for him. Even now, ex-players queue up to retell tales they have told hundreds of times previously, seemingly not wanting their memories of the great man to die, still keen to express their affection for him.

Shankly wasn't around in the public eye for long really, little more than fourteen years at Liverpool, probably for ten of which he was in the full glare of the limelight. It feels like much, much longer. His impact was so intense, so stellar that it burned an indelible mark into football. He dominated those early football TV years. His rise mirrored the rise in the coverage of football on TV.

He built two successful sides at Liverpool, the mid–1960s Roger

Hunt and Ron Yeats side and the early-1970s Tommy Smith and Kevin Keegan side. In an era of the long ball they played a pass and move game coupled with an almost brutal aggression. Much like Shankly himself it combined style and precision with physicality.

He was a man of the people to the last, dying – like every good Scotsman – of a heart attack.

Somehow, when you go to Liverpool FC or even just to the city itself, it is possible to still feel Shankly's presence. It's in the atoms, in the molecules, in the dark matter of the place, so deep has his influence soaked.

And if you're in any doubt as to his qualities, search out an interview with him. It's a testament to the fecundity of his words that interviews conducted forty years ago still have wisdom and resonance; they still inspire.

Few can be called great football men; even fewer can be called great men. Shankly was both.

Football on TV in these early decades was loved by all fans. We were largely uncritical viewers, just glad to have any football to watch. We were not media-savvy in the way people are today; there was little cynicism about the coverage. We had nothing to compare it with, after all. This was all there ever had been. This made the programmes all the more impactful and the people on them more memorable and powerful.

I'm convinced that it was the likes of Big Mal, Cloughie and Bill Shankly who, in their regular appearances on TV in the 1970s, showed me that the bloody-minded, rebellious, non-corporate way of going about your life was the best way. I took a lead from them. These men were football's rock 'n' roll rebels – clever and uncompromising, intimidating and scary but totally compulsive, inspiring and thrilling. They're also exactly the sort of men who would not be allowed within a million miles of a TV studio at midnight these days; too radical, too off-message, for our bland modern culture cowed by fear of lawsuits, the diversity of hand-wringers, and the faux outrage of the tabloids, which far too many people buy into.

In the modern football studio everyone is keen not to upset anyone else or to criticise their mates. It's rubbish really and pleases no one. We have sleepy ex-managers like Alan Curbishley droning on about stuff which is perfectly obvious to anyone with eyes and doing it in as tedious a manner as possible. It's not his fault – it's the fault of producers who invite boring people on the shows. Big Mal et al. were performers and entertainers. But there are no people like Mal around any more; they seem to have been genetically or culturally bred out of society by the need to not offend anyone or be sued. This isn't progress.

Today we have wall-to-wall football all year round. I think it's a good thing on the whole but there's no doubt that over-exposure has made people cynical about both the players and the game. Referees are torn to shreds by endless replays of incorrect decisions in a way that simply didn't happen before the camera covered every game from five angles. It leaves people feeling that referees are especially useless today, unable or unwilling, it would seem, to understand that it's always been like this but only now it's on TV every day up-close and personal.

Football being omnipresent on TV is a good thing on the whole. It allows people like me to indulge our passion, but it's not without downsides. The constant exposure on TV has left many disliking, even hating, players. The camera picks up every swear word, every nasty tackle, every bit of dissent. Again, this is nothing new, but when it's on a 42-inch HD telly, it seems worse to those who are easily offended, especially if you don't have the perspective that comes from having watched football for forty years. It gives the impression to some people that they actually know the players; they're life-size in their home, so they have a relationship with them that we couldn't ever have had from the terraces or from a highlights programme on a 16-inch black-and-white TV.

Consequently the hatred and adoration of players is so much more intense and so much more volatile. I see people going bonkers over a player's reaction to a tackle because they've seen it in slow-motion and can tell it wasn't a foul. They get themselves into a foaming lather about the player being a cheat, a wanker and quite possibly a paedophile. I sit in the pub and look at them and think, 'Shut up, you idiot!' This over-focused, over-exposed TV culture has encouraged some to be hysterical girls and I can't stand men who turn into hysterical girls. Get some fucking perspective, I say. It doesn't show your passion for the game, it shows you're emotionally incontinent. But the kind of emotional repression I grew up with seems out of fashion now. It's odd really, I grew up trying to get away from the uptight, repressive culture that was every northern boy's heritage, but now I kind of miss the dour, swallow-it-down mentality. If the alternative is weeping in the streets then I know which I prefer.

Rock 'n' roll has gone through an almost identical experience on TV. It was almost as rare on TV as the football was when I was a kid. Indeed there was so little media coverage, outside of the music press, that if a band didn't put their photos on an album cover you often didn't know what they actually looked like until they walked out on stage. A strange notion given today's 24/7 exposure.

We got by on the meagre diet of *The Old Grey Whistle Test*, the occasional *Sight & Sound in Concert*. After that we had to watch *Top of the Pops* in the hope that some rock bands would be on miming to a hit. All the bands you really wanted to see just didn't appear on TV. Zeppelin, Deep Purple, Sabbath were all huge but the only way to see them, by and large, was to go to their live gigs.

This limited access, as in the football world, gave the whole industry an air of mystique and glamour that you just can't have today with wall-to-wall videos and marketing. It was also a case of: 'Why don't you switch off your TV and go and do something more interesting instead?' – in other words go to gigs, buy albums, go round your mates' houses and listen to their albums or form a band yourself.

But we're raising a generation of kids – well, I'm not, God forbid, but you may be – who have known only opulence in their football and music media. This is making both cultures potentially more plastic and disposable which, if I was prone to worrying about the future (which I'm not), would concern me.

To some, football is just another entertainment purchase, like going to the pictures or buying a DVD. I simply can't get with that programme at all. It's way bigger than that. While I pay to see it all on TV, I still hang on to the notion that football has an important local, civic role as well. It is the hub of communities and has a role in society that no mere entertainment facility will ever fulfil. We're not just customers, we're investors. This may be hopelessly naïve though. Take a trip to Anfield and walk around the half-derelict terraced houses nearby and you can see that, for all the money in football, very little of it leaks out into the communities that the club sprang from.

The trouble is that over-exposure often leads to fatigue. Nothing is as good when you can get it all the time. Not football. Not pies. Not even sex. Now that everyone is having sex and filming themselves for broadcast on the internet, all available at the click of a mouse, the mystique of sex has completely disappeared. Soon you'll be able to watch all your new girlfriend's ex-lovers grinding away on her before you even get to first base. It's a strange state of affairs. I am profoundly glad that, as far as I know, no film exists of me in flagrante. I'd have demanded Equity rates if so.

If I was fifteen today, I would have been a gynaecological expert before any girl had removed her underwear and actually showed me what she'd got. When I was that age, no one knew how anybody else 'did it' – we knew only what we had learned in biology. I still vividly recall my first experience of proper pornography at the Classic cinema in Stockton. I was nearly sixteen and a few of us decided to pluck up enough courage to get into an X-rated film. Funny how the letter X invests something with a dark glamour. So I put on a jacket – a hideous checked brown crimplene affair – naïvely thinking it would make me look older. It worked, not because I looked eighteen but because no one really cared if kids got into X-rated movies. Just like under-age drinking, as long as you didn't cause trouble, they didn't bother you. After all, it was just more money for them.

So we got in to see an *Emmanuelle* film with a shorter Fiona Richmond one in support. The Classic was an early multi-theatre cinema in Stockton and also quite seedy. There really were dirty old men in raincoats in the front row pleasuring themselves.

Fiona was quite the star at the time and was later to be invited into the Crystal Palace bath by Big Mal! Naturally, a photographer was on hand to capture the scene. Again, this is not the sort of behaviour that would be allowed at a football club in today's more sanitised environment.

When Fiona stripped off in this flick and began, for some spurious reason, to brush her substantial pubic hair (now also sadly out of fashion) in front of the camera, it nearly made me pass out through blood loss to the brain. With mouth dry and heart racing, it was quite wonderful. These movies were the softest of soft porn, all soft focus and not a glimpse of an erection in sight. But nonetheless, it seemed an exotic introduction to the world of sex to me. Harmless, really, and any sixteen-year-old would think it tame stuff today.

When I see some of the videos shown on MTV today, half of them are more porny than those movies we saw as teenagers; more thrusting groins certainly. Perhaps knowledge is power but I feel life should be a continuous learning experience. You've got a lot of years to fill, so you don't want to burn out by eighteen after three years of hard core internet porn. I can't believe it acts as a training manual and thus makes everyone incredible, flexible, gymnastic lovers going at it like a steam hammer. I mean, most people are too fat for that these days, aren't they?

Over-exposure, even to the most orgasmic aspects of life, can only ultimately diminish those experiences and send you off in search of ever more outlandish pleasures. Before long you'll be dangling from the lampshade, choking yourself with a dragon fruit while inserting a parsnip up your bottom in search of a more intense orgasm. I mean, who wants to have to do all that after hard day at the office? That's no way to get your five-a-day of fruit and veg.

It's tempting to say less was more, that familiarity breeds contempt in our attitudes to both footballers and rock musicians. Cloughie himself once said about too much football on TV, 'You don't want roast beef and Yorkshire every night and twice on Sunday.'

But I wouldn't want to go back to the old days of a couple of hours of highlights a week, even while recognising the downsides of over-exposure.

You just have to learn to tune out the bullshit and the vapid bollocks that fills so much of the media; that's the art of it. You need an internal filter mechanism that tells you to ignore everything Andy Townsend is saying.

The best football coverage on TV has evolved into an art form all of its own, with slow-motion, impressionistic videos of players, goal, and tackles all played out to a rock 'n' roll soundtrack. There's definitely an overlap between music videos and football. Add to that the new trend for High Definition (which has always sounded to me more like an experience you'd have while smoking home-grown dope) and massive flat screens, and it's more like going to the movies in your front room.

It won't be long before we can put on some sort of electronic suit which will make us feel and see what it's like to play in the game we're watching. All of which is to be welcomed as long as you remember that when you're actually at a match, you're not still in your front room. Sometimes the crowds are so quiet, it's as though they're sitting at home watching. Perhaps every game should begin with a stadium announcement, 'Please, you are not at home, this is not a television show, you are in the real world now, please behave accordingly.'

Football has been cemented as the nation's favourite game by the TV coverage over the last fifty years. It has satisfied the hardcore fan and pulled in the part-time casual tourist too. Has TV made football even more popular? Perhaps. Then again, football has always been massively popular. What it has done is to bring it into our everyday lives and it has also broadened our view of the game – at least if we want it to be broadened – by showing us football from all across the world and football from all divisions. It has evolved into a televisual art form, largely thanks to Sky, who recognised that this was Britain's favourite sport and thus that there was plenty of money to be made from it. They set about treating the game seriously and committing an extensive amount of hours to it and we all flocked to watch it.

The two things have become inseparable and we'll never go back to the days of an occasional live game and only highlights on a weekend. TV may still be an opiate for the masses, keeping them from revolution or serious thought, and it may well be full of absolute rubbish most of the time, but if you're a football fan, these are the best of all times.

A life without football on TV is un-thinkable; how did we ever live without it?

6

Identity

A S The Who once asked, 'Ah who the fuck are you?'
It's not an easy question to answer at the best of times. Who are we really? Well how much time have you got? There are no easy answers. However, football can help us in this. For many people, football is an intrinsic part of their national identity. It helps them define who they are, where they are from and what their values are. Talk to a Brazilian and their national side is the very embodiment of the Brazilian psyche. If the side doesn't play free-flowing, expansive, exciting football, many of the fans see it as a kind of betrayal of their heritage.

The same applies to some degree to Argentina, who like to mix outrageous skill with a touch of brutal physicality. The fluid, unpredictable, creative football of the Dutch has been symbolic of their liberal, expansive, artistic culture. Admittedly the football doesn't reflect their dope culture – it'd be a lot slower and have more snack breaks if it did – but there is nonetheless something quintessentially Dutch about Dutch football.

Similarly a German side that isn't a ruthlessly disciplined collective would be seen by the Germans and by the rest of us as somehow not properly Germanic.

Then we come to England. Being English in the twenty-first century is an elusive, complex thing with many different layers. Time was it meant being the broad-shouldered, honest type, keen on fair play. We were decent sorts who could be relied on.

The more reactionary media still push this idea, if only to then wail about how far we have fallen from this ideal. Indeed, a lot of people see the national side's quality as reflective of our country more broadly, for good or ill. Only football seems to bring this to the surface. Few see anything more broadly telling about English society if we're no good at Rugby League or Union. Even if the cricket team are poor, few seem to see it as part of a great national malaise, but if the football team are poor then somehow, the country is going down the drain and, on the flipside, when we were successful this somehow demonstrated our pre-eminence in the world.

But if Brazil is samba football, what is England? All I can think of is work rate, sweat and err . . . running around a lot. Yup, that's about it. We used to boast about honesty and fair play but I can hear you laughing from here at the very notion of that in the twenty-first century. It's tricky to tie anything down to any greater degree and I think this is actually the very nature of England and the English: hard to pin down, hard to define.

Every time England's football team goes through a dodgy phase – which is pretty often – in some quarters you'd think it was the end of the world. After a couple of poor results early in the 1986 and 1990 World Cup campaigns, this was seen by the loony tabloid press as such a humiliation that we should withdraw from the tournament to save further disgrace being brought upon the nation. 'Bring them home' ran the tabloid headlines. It is unhinged and plain weird, this self-flagellating. It wasn't as if we'd been beaten 10-0 and been chased off the pitch by a group of school girls. There's an audience for this kind of hysteria though. It plays well in England.

Many overseas observers have looked on with bemusement at our tendency to indulge in self-loathing as a nation, to see things as far worse than they are and almost enjoy doing so.

Why do we go bonkers over the national side? More England shirts are sold and England sends more fans to any tournament that England is involved in than is the case anywhere else. I suspect it's because Englishness is so hard to define, that it attracts a broad crowd of people but all of them have differing attitudes and opinions about what England is, both as a country and as a team. This is part of the appeal of the game too. It sets the country in a context against other nations and innately questions who and what we are in relation to them.

I've spent a lot of time in America over the last twenty years and it wasn't until I went there that I really understood how I felt about Britain and England more specifically.

Most great books about an author's home town or country are written from abroad. Joyce wrote much of his work about Dublin while living in Europe, D. H. Lawrence wrote most of *Sons and Lovers* while in Italy. Ezra Pound, T. S. Eliot and Henry James did likewise.

Distance gives perspective and helps you see and feel things about your homeland with greater clarity, uncluttered with distractions of everyday life

Like most people, I had always loved America from afar, primarily through rock music as well as TV and movies. But as I loved bands such as The Grateful Dead, The Allman Brothers, Jefferson Airplane, Quicksilver Messenger Service, Moby Grape, The Doors and many, many others, I had an innately left-field, predominantly West Coast understanding of America, a counter-culture awareness. While this was fantastic in itself, of course, it told me little about the meat and potatoes America that made up the bulk of the country. It was like trying to judge the nature of Britain just by listening to Hawkwind. Nonetheless it was that music which drew me like a magnet to California. And it was a journey which reinformed me about who I was and where I came from.

The shocking thing on arriving in Los Angeles for the first time is just how familiar it is simply through seeing so many films and TV shows. My first time in Beverley Hills was especially striking. Normally the edit for the screen makes things look better and more intense but Beverley Hills was the opposite. It was bigger, better, more dramatic and frankly more beautiful than I had ever believed possible. The same went for much of California. It constantly shocked me with its larger than life reality, at times jaw-dropping in its visual impact, especially when travelling up Pacific Coast Highway from LA to San Francisco with palm trees arcing upwards into an infinite blue sky.

Before going to America, I had never had any pride in being English. I think this was because, growing up on a diet of Rock Against

Racism and the reactionary Thatcher government, nationalist pride seemed too Little England, too right-wing, too bigoted and connected to the old values of Empire, imperialism and xenophobia. Many still feel that way.

Unlike much American music, which gave the listener a sense of the American Experience – the highway, the desert, the cities – as I grew up British music informed my sense of Englishness or Britishness in a far less obvious way. Perhaps because rock 'n' roll is an American art form in origin, until the late 1970s there were few bands that used it to say something about what it meant to come from these islands.

An honourable exception was The Kinks. Ray Davies songs such as 'A Well Respected Man', 'Dedicated Follower of Fashion', 'Sunny Afternoon', 'Dead End Street', 'Autumn Almanac', 'Waterloo Sunset' and a classic album in 1968 called *The Kinks Are The Village Green Preservation Society*, were all quintessentially English songs about England. Lyrically, they stood almost alone as reflecting aspects of English society.

The folk-rock music of Fairport Convention was obviously rooted in the English folk tradition. I loved Fairport and got into them in my later teenage years, but they were inherently about the past, drawing on songs from the traditional songbook. They were not about defining what it was like to be English in the late twentieth century.

The Who brought the Union Jack to the forefront in the 1960s but Pete Townshend's songs were often more sweeping, personal and profound, dealing with universal themes, rather than addressing anything specifically English, even though his viewpoint was that of an Englishman.

The real influence rock 'n' roll had on my awareness of nationality came from the British invasion of America in 1964. With knowledge of that history and later bands like Deep Purple and Led Zeppelin among many others making it big worldwide, it was clear that these small islands had an extraordinary ability to produce music that was loved all over the planet in a way which, say, Italian or French music just couldn't emulate. When it came to rock 'n' roll Britain really was Great and I grew up with both that knowledge and that pride as a given. Even when the English national football side went into decline, we still ruled the world at cock rock and frankly that is a very good thing.

Later, the music of the late 1970s began to address English issues. The Jam, inheriting an updated version of The Kinks' and The Who's tradition, thanks to Paul Weller's brilliance, talked about what our lives were like at that time. Many other punk and new wave bands did likewise, none more so than The Sex Pistols. But by now, I was eighteen and my sense of nationhood was already well formed.

By then, I knew I wanted to grow up in more liberal world where conservative attitudes had dissolved, replaced by open, progressive thinking. The Union Jack and, to a lesser extent, the Cross of St George had become emblems of the National Front and associated values so it was natural to steer away from them.

So I didn't feel that good about being from Britain – Thatcher and her acolytes had killed that – even though I was happy and proud to be a Teesside boy. I can't overstate how crushingly awful that Conservative rule was for me and, I know, for many other people, perhaps especially but not exclusively in the north.

It was the politics of bleak division. It encouraged some of the worst aspects of human nature to come to the fore. It turned people against each other. It denied society even existed. The north–south divide was never more visceral as much of the south prospered while much of the north went to ruin. It was horrible and I fear many of the social problems we have today have their roots in those awful days. There was little to make you feel good about being English, especially when you were living in the north.

However, on arriving in California, I was surprised to be greeted warmly by Californians simply because I was English. This was really surprising. I liked it. It made me feel unusually good about myself, a rare emotion.

Strangers would hear my accent and ask me to say something to them just so they could enjoy my exotic vowels. Indeed one girl's response to the way I said the word avocado was somewhat sexually stimulating. 'Say it again, Johnny,' she said, wriggling in her seat, letting out small orgasmic breaths as I as said the word, my Teesside accent stretching out the vowels. This wasn't the sort of thing that happened in pubs in Newcastle! But who could fail to be flattered by it?

They saw Britain as an old country, full of history and learning. They saw it as a left-field cultural place that gave the world original music, fashion and art. Indeed, it was not uncommon to meet Anglophiles who were obsessed with all things English.

It was also undoubtedly true that many assumed I was cultured and well-mannered just because of my English accent, though it was also mistaken for Australian and Dutch. So I was treated with respect that was either missing or grudging at home. I was also at last freed of the yoke of the class war which I felt very heavily in Britain. In California no one knew what class I was and what's more didn't care. For once in my life I was treated according to the quality of what I said and did rather than being prejudged on a massive set of cultural presumptions based on how I spoke and looked. As the Dormanstown's poet Hunter once said, 'There's no posh cunts telling us what to do out here.' Amen to that.

We all do this in Britain; within a few seconds of meeting someone for the first time, we have assessed and compartmentalised them into Britain's multi-layered, sophisticated class system. We can't help it. It happens naturally and gears our response to them, so much so that many of us even adjust our own accents accordingly.

The freedom from such judgements was very liberating. It made me feel happier – it almost literally did feel as if a monkey was lifted from my back. A very fat, heavy monkey. It was such a relief. I fully acknowledge that I, in common with many others of my background, have a massive chip on my shoulder about being born with sod all and having to fight my whole life to drag myself out of the clarts with little help, few guides and no fucking money at all. It's unforgiving, bloody hard and doing it you get a lot of battle scars that never leave you.

Those born with money and an education that opened horizons from an early age can have no idea what it's like to be born without money and with nothing down for you in life; to be conditioned from an early age to shut up and accept you will never amount to anything; to be the grunt labour.

This inequality of opportunity is something that has always angered me. It's so unfair that a kid born to useless, idiot parents is cursed from the womb and will have everything stacked against them while others will get an easy ride thanks to a pampered childhood.

I recall feeling this bitterness deeply when, on that first trip to California, I was on the balcony of a hotel room fourteen floors up on Ocean Way, Santa Monica, Los Angeles. The balcony faced north west to Malibu, the ocean lapping into the shore as a liquid gold sun melted into a mercury, blue Pacific Ocean. A band was playing somewhere out on Third Street, an occasional riff caught on the breeze. The restless cars moved to and fro like a metal tide; the warm, summer air oozed with that unique heady Californian aroma of eucalyptus, cypress, sagewood and car fumes, a kind of post-modern after-shave. It was staggeringly beautiful and stimulating. I had tears in my eyes born out of appreciation, excitement and bitterness. Bitter that it had taken nearly thirty years of my life to experience this. No one ever told me, when growing up, that I could live in such a place or experience such a thing. Not teachers, not parents, no one. Fuckers. How dare they deny me this? That's how I felt, however irrationally.

Had I been brought up to think anything was possible and any dream could be lived then things could have been much better for longer. I felt angry about that, so much so that even writing about it brings those tears back.

Thank fuck rock 'n' roll, poetry, books and drugs showed me there was another life to live other than the default one I was expected to follow. They had taken me to California; without them, I might never have felt the heartbeat of that fantastic state.

I loved the rootless nature of California. The way that tomorrow mattered much more than yesterday synched in perfectly with where my mind was at, where it's still at. Add in the sun, sea and palm-trees and it was an effortless pleasure to live there. When you've lived your life in the cold, harsh, wet climate of the north of England, no-one with an ounce of joy for life can deny that living in a warm climate, spending your evenings swimming and drinking chilled, crisp Riesling as the sun sinks into the sea is superior. It just is. It takes the load off Annie. It's physically more pleasurable.

But after a few months grooving in the sun, I began to miss something about England – not enough to go back until the money had run out – but nonetheless I was missing the heritage, history and roots of the old country. I also found myself looking back fondly at the stoic, undemonstrative nature of English life; the swallow-it-down and tough-it-out mentality as opposed to California's unhinged, emotional rollercoaster. Meet anyone on the West Coast and within twenty minutes they've told you their life story, their sexual preferences and which areas are their erogenous zones. Even in today's more emotional British society, after twenty minutes we might just have told you our name and how we like our tea, but that's about it.

America is such a young country, driven not by what has happened but what will happen. That is a brilliant way to live your life but it can also mean your life gets shallow and plastic, especially back then. This was all before the internet, so once you were in California it wasn't that easy to find out what was happening back home or indeed anywhere else. When you live in a big country, stuff that happens on the other coast is like international news from 3,000 miles away, let alone anything happening abroad.

There was an international version of the *Daily Express* which came out once or twice a week but that was it. So I quickly became Californicated, divorced from reality, just living in this palm-fringed dream world. Pissed. Stoned. Happy. It was brilliant. But after a few months I started to feel blinkered and intellectually under-nourished. I must say that it couldn't happen today because the internet keeps you in touch with everything. Actually, while that's a good thing, the downside is you lose that feeling of being cut off, of having 'gone away'. That could be a great feeling too, at least for someone like me, keen not to be tied down by the past or by my roots.

Towards the end of that first extended stay, for the first time I fully felt and realised what an old country Britain is; what a weight of history it had and how that had shaped us all. None of this had occurred to me as strongly while on home soil. I began to feel good about coming from this important small country.

And another weird thing happened: my newly discovered pride in being English meant I actively wanted to advertise where I was from. So I had T-shirts with Union Jack themes. Nothing too garish, Nazi or Club 18–30. But it was something I would never have done in the UK or anywhere else in Europe, for sure. Even now, twenty years on, when over there, I still feel being seen to be English is somehow cool.

I'm from the land of The Who, The Beatles and Led Zeppelin and they haven't forgotten it and still dig us because of that. For all the jokes correctly cracked about our teeth, mostly you get treated really well by the natives and it's hard not to feel good about that.

After nearly a year there I began to feel perversely romantic about England's footballers, seeing them as 'one of us', and so I became rabidly more pro-England when in California than I'd ever been while at home, seeking out England games on cable television.

In 2004 I was in Las Vegas, another one of my regular haunts, and was walking through Harrah's one afternoon in search of a drink. I hit on a bar area, deserted except for one bloke sitting in front of a TV screen. On the TV was a football match from the Premier League between Newcastle and West Brom. That he was obviously English was given away by, his body shape and his familiar comfortable position in front of a TV showing football.

I got a massive blue plastic tube full of tequila and fruit juice and went over to watch. He turned to look at me as I sat down. We both knew who we were: English football fans abroad. We nodded, raised eyebrows and turned back to the match. It was all so archetypally English. No words needed. Within ten minutes we had been joined by half a dozen other Brits. The only words spoken were 'What's the score?' and our only other life signs a collective intake of breath followed by a laugh as a reckless tackle went in.

That was an oddly life-affirming hour and a half. Why? It just felt like it was my culture, albeit transposed to the Nevada desert. The sense of English national identity seemed at its most obvious and strong in that bar watching the football.

The truth is, to this day I love aspects of both the American west and British culture; one plays off so well against the other and so, ever since, have gone to and fro to California on a regular basis to try to get the best of both worlds.

It was also on that first Californian trip that I fully realised just how weird the United Kingdom is as a national set-up and how this probably goes a long way to explain the multi-faceted attitude to England's football team.

It took a pool cleaner to open my eyes.

'So you're from England, are you?' he said as I sat poolside at our hotel in Laguna Beach on a white light summer afternoon, while he fished detritus out of the pool.

'Yes, from the north east of England,' I said, keen to make sure he knew I wasn't from London so he wouldn't ask if I knew the guy he met last year called Bob who was also from London. That had happened earlier in the week in a cafe.

He scratched his head. 'England? That's that island off Africa, isn't it?'

I had to laugh. I corrected him and told him where the UK was situated as best I could: up a bit from Africa and then it's the island on the left – small place, funny shape, if you get to Iceland you've gone too far.

He looked suitably embarrassed at his error. 'Oh yeah, silly me. I've heard of the UK. That's the UK flag, right?' he said, pointing to a Ben Sherman T-shirt which had a Union Jack motif.

'Yeah, the colours represent the countries in the Union,' I said, helpfully.

'So it's not a country, it's a union?! Like the Teamsters?'

I laughed again and explained which countries Britain was composed of.

'So it's the British flag, yeah? Not the UK flag?'

'Er, yeah, it is the UK flag as well.'

'So it's two different countries but with the same flag?'

'No, it's the same country.'

'Same country but with two different names?!' he said incredulously. 'Hold on,' he said, seemingly now believing I was misinforming him about my own country, 'how is Scotland part of the same country as England? I thought Scotland was a country . . . and what the hell is Northern Ireland? Ain't there just one Ireland?'

The more I tried to explain the worse it got.

'The UK is also Britain?! Wow!' he said incredulously again, as though I had told him six was nine. 'A country with two names and four countries inside of it? How does a country have other countries inside it?' It was a reasonable question.

Man, I was in trouble. How to explain it when you don't really understand it yourself? Best not to mention the British Isles either.

OK, so he wasn't the finest cut diamond in the necklace of life, but he inadvertently raised an important issue. We live in a uniquely complex political, geo-political mash-up and this informs a myriad of different and confused feelings about our country and our national football teams.

Just try explaining the difference between being British and English to an American who hasn't studied the home country much. It's really hard. I'm English but I'm also British; are they the same thing? Not really . . . but then yes, kind of.

And that's before you get to Scotland, Northern Ireland and Wales. Are they countries? Well yes . . . but kind of no as well.

We take it all for granted, we think we understand, but do we really? Scotland is obviously a country but it's not a country in the same way as say, Australia is because it is part of the Union. Whether that's a good thing – I think it is both culturally and politically – is a matter of opinion.

Like it or not, the United Kingdom is the country we live in, England, Scotland, Wales and Northern Ireland are 'mini' countries with big cultures within it. None of them is independent like 'proper' countries; many would argue they could never be successfully independent. All of them are interrelated but now with some autonomy thanks to devolution. So it's hard to pull the bones out of that and say what being British is.

We're on safer territory, so we think, with cultural or regional identity, especially if you're Scottish, Welsh or Irish. But I live in Scotland and routinely hear the likes of Alex Salmond, the corpulent sack of cholesterol that currently has the job of First Minister of Scotland, referring to 'the Scottish people'. By which he sometimes means the people who live in Scotland, Scottish-born or otherwise, and sometimes means people who are born in Scotland, no matter where they now live, depending on which cause he is trying to twist to his advantage. Such terminology only muddies the waters further.

It was asked after the recent general election, in which 85 per cent of the vote in Scotland was for someone other than the Tories who ended up in government, why the Scots don't vote Tory. But of course, Scotland has many hundreds of thousands of resident 'foreigners' living here, be they English, Croatian, Polish or Australian. Many of them vote too but are not Scots. But for some reason they are all called Scots on such occasions. Words are so casually used and it doesn't help our understanding of the real situation.

This wouldn't happen in America where, once a citizen, you're entitled to call yourself an American. I can't call myself a Scot, even if I wanted to, despite living here for years, because I wasn't born here and Scotland cannot confer citizenship status on anyone; only the United Kingdom government can do that. You can come here from Poland and settle and become a British citizen but you will never be English, Scottish or Welsh or Irish, no matter how successfully you acquire the local accent. Like all of us you will be British, even though the only common aspect of being British is that there is no common aspect. Being a Scot, like being a Teessider, is a cultural and geographical assumption rather than a legal status.

Because of such issues, I reckon few of us think we're British first and foremost, perhaps until we're abroad but, even then, regional identity is often people's strongest sense of self-identity, resulting in their owning up to being a Geordie or a Yorkshireman first, English second and British a distant third.

Most Scots would be happy calling themselves Scottish and nothing else. And the same goes for the Welsh, I'm sure. The Northern Irish situation is even more complicated and, to be honest, I can't work it all out due to being three drinks into a bottle of decent chardonnay.

There seem to be different degrees of Englishness depending on where you live or where you originate from. It often seems to me that the further you get from London, the more regional identity matters. The greater the distance from the capital, the more people set themselves against it.

Personally speaking, I think of myself as a Teessider, Northern, English, and British in that order. Yet my pal Alan, born in the London Borough of Harrow, in what many people still think of as Middlesex, just thinks of himself as English. He has little regional identity at all; no particular affinity, even to the town of his birth. He's a kind of Londoner but not in the same way a boy from the East End is. It's a kind of 'London-lite' condition. Yet go to Bow in the East End and locals are likely to feel equally alien from those who come from, say, Fulham in the west, as a Geordie would. Even English people from those anonymous areas of the south east that do not have a strong regional identity would still think of themselves as English first and foremost. So perhaps that just leaves Rangers fans who like to think of themselves as British!

So being British is a funny business. There's not much to unify us all really, except a love of drink, a passing familiarity with the same language and crippling sexual repression.

There are those who want an English parliament now that Scotland, Wales and Northern Ireland have their own assemblies and some devolved powers. My impression is that this is largely a south-eastern viewpoint. I don't suppose those who propose it would expect it to sit in Kendal or Hexham or even Leeds. An English parliament sitting in Oxford, to someone from Carlisle or York, would sound just like another Southern parliament and thus more of the same diktat from people who are a long way away.

The history behind the evolution of the UK and its regional and cultural identities is confusing but the bottom line is if you scratch the surface you'll find some of us are a bit ambivalent about where our loyalties and affections lie as regards the UK. Those who are not even a bit confused are usually the extremists of one sort or another who, let's be honest, are loopy. A noble British trait is to not be very certain about anything except perhaps the need for another round of drinks.

So it is against this background of multi-layered, multi-faceted aspects to our sense of nationhood that the England football team takes the field.

So let's look at them. The England football team, in some people's eyes, is supposed to somehow represent England the nation, in the world. Our boys. And in a way they do. Look at them lining up and you see a ragbag of ethnic and cultural mixtures that embodies modern England. While some on the extremes try to argue otherwise, I see the English and the British as a mongrel nation, the product of hundreds of different influences both cultural and genetic over thousands of years.

My ancestry has been traced back over a thousand years. Ladies and gentlemen, you are reading a book written by a direct descendant of William the Conqueror. I am a direct relation of many kings and queens of England stretching further back to Charlemagne in France as well as Norse kings. I hope you feel suitably humble and have doffed your cap to me. Now get off my fucking land, you peasants!

Actually it was all the De Nevilles' fault that I lost my inheritance. My ancestors once owned large tracts of Yorkshire and the north of England – Raby Castle among others was their gaff – then they backed the wrong side in the Civil War and within a few generations the whole lineage was skint and surviving as agricultural workers in god-forsaken places in the east of Yorkshire. Bugger. It probably means Gary Neville is a relation too. An unsettling thought.

My blood is thick with the DNA of all manner of people from all across Europe and beyond. My partner Dawn is an exotic mixture of Caribbean, Scottish, African and Geordie.

Perhaps it's not so odd that a country so used to absorbing people from elsewhere should have a bit of an identity crisis. I would suggest it's actually one of our major assets and not the weakness that some want to paint it as. I think the fact that we've always been a destination for people to come to, work, live and occasionally plunder has made us stronger. Diversity is a trendy word these days, but I like it, reasoning: Why paint with one colour when you can have 101? Cultures that don't change atrophy – trouble is, a lot of people hate change and want to pull up the drawbridge.

The England supporters reflect the country's mixed view of our own identity. There's a minority of England fans who would not agree with diversity. There's a minority of England fans who are still fighting illusory battles. They're the ones that still sing 'no surrender to the IRA' and 'I'd rather be a Paki than a Turk.'

They used to see every England game as some sort of re-enactment of a historical battle. They haven't gone abroad and wrecked a pretty little town in Europe for a while but I bet they do again at some point. These people never go away for good. These are the hooligans so recognisable to our European neighbours. The thick-necked, beer-gutted England fan in an ill-fitting England shirt is a cliché but only because it's been so typical for so many years.

They are one of the reasons some feel reluctant to be too pro-England, knowing it provokes the worst type of reaction in some people. We shouldn't let them take the flag and our team from us, but they're so boorish it's often easier to keep your head down and walk away.

If you look at the flags and banners at England games, they tend to hail from the likes of Rochdale, Carlisle or Maidstone. Fans of the biggest clubs are much less visible. Supporting England seems to be something you're free to do if your club isn't competing at the highest level. For a fan of Arsenal, for example, it's harder for some to cheer on Rooney or Lampard because they are your enemies through the season.

You've spent all season booing them and they are emblematic of your closest rivals so it's hard, if not impossible, to shed that feeling overnight just because they pull on the England shirt. Yet a Rochdale fan has no such inhibitions because these players do not inhabit their football universe on a weekly basis. It's how I've always felt as a Boro fan. As soon as anyone pulls on the England shirt I want them to do well and I still see England as the ultimate.

International football is the pinnacle of the game. I don't buy the idea that the Champions League has superseded it; there is something special about competing as a nation. Most countries' fans don't seem to share our tendency to self-loathing and inward critique. They get behind their country with gusto and are shamelessly patriotic. Not for them the stupid attitudes some English have. I recall one witless cretin saying that he didn't want England to win the World Cup when Sven was manager because we played such boring football! Arse. Such self-importance and pomposity is very much a part of some Englishmen's and -women's souls.

This makes it hard for the national team. They are required by some to be nationalist role models, by others to be more talented than they are and by others asked to live up to a team forty-four years ago who were victorious in an entirely different era. I feel sorry for England players. They're lauded so highly and slated like lazy dogs by the tabloid press and the suckers who take their lead from them.

As a bit of an idealist, because our country is the United Kingdom I think it should be represented as such at tournaments. That is my firm opinion. Why? Because I think it would help, in time, to cement some unity and help pull and keep us together as a nation. I feel differences are good but divisions are dangerous and would point to the Balkans to illustrate how quickly those who had lived in peace for many years can quickly fall out, with devastating consequences.

It has been tried in the past, primarily for the Olympics from 1908 to 1972, when Great Britain fielded an essentially amateur team, though it was largely Englishmen. There have also been a couple of friendlies, one at Hampden Park in 1947 which saw GB, captained by Middlesbrough's legendary George Hardwick, whip the Rest of Europe 6-1, . This was a commemorative game to mark the return of the English, Scottish, Irish and Welsh FAs to FIFA, having left in 1920 and thus denying themselves the chance of playing in the early World Cup competitions. It was marketed as the Game of the Century and pulled a big crowd. The game was repeated seven years later on the seventh anniversary of the Irish FA. Sadly, it was GB who got their backsides kicked this time, losing 4-1. And that was about it for team GB.

There's a proposal to bring it back for the 2012 London Olympics with Sir Alec Ferguson or maybe Roy Hodgson managing but, despite FIFA stating in writing that a United Kingdom side will not affect the status of the home nations' FAs, everyone is still too obsessed with maintaining their independence to risk it setting a precedent. It will be the triumph of narrow politics over sport if this prevents there being a British team at the British Olympics.

There is no UK side and there probably will never be one because the sport grew up with separate associations who now all want to protect their power-bases and level of influence on the international scene. I would still love to have England, Scotland, Wales, Northern

Ireland national sides as well, perhaps for a 'Commonwealth'-type competition in the same way athletics works. We used to have the end of season Home Nations tournament, which I recall most people enjoyed but which all would say there'd be no room in the fixture list for any more, despite the fact that clubs played forty-two games back then, not thirty-eight.

But this is fantasy; a UK side will never happen and the vast majority of fans of each country disagree with my view. I know that from the volume of abuse I've had when proposing such a change.

I think most English like to see the other three principalities doing well, while most of the principalities are anti-English and are glad if England loses. This makes some English rather annoyed; they feel we deserve their support. I don't care either way. Why would I? Basically, to the rest, England is the big bully and the rest are the brave underdog. Such is inevitably the lot of the largest country in this weird union.

I always support all UK national teams and love to see Scotland doing well, though this often involves a long wait. The anti-English sentiment in Scotland amuses me as its mostly good-natured ribbing rather than outright xenophobia. Some English are way too sensitive about it; look at the fuss over Andy Murray's off-hand quip about supporting anyone but England. You'd have thought he'd put an army together and was about to storm Berwick-on-Tweed and take it back for the Scots. It's still used by the more prissy English people as a stick to beat the lad with. Most Scots I know are nowhere near as anti-English as the English often make out; they just enjoy baiting those types of English people and I totally understand that.

The English fans and even more so the media have been insufferably arrogant – with little reason to be so – over the years. Though, England having been a bit rubbish for years, this has never been less the case than it is today.

I sense the real hatred that was around – especially when Thatcher was in power and using Scotland largely as an experimental region for her politics - has declined In all but the most nationalist areas. Maybe devolution has reduced it too.

It's also true that England, a nation of over 50 million, punches well below its weight at international football. Other small countries like Holland, Bulgaria and Sweden have gone further than England in World Cups and European Championships and that rightly attracts mockery from its smaller relations, especially in the 1970s when Scotland's national side was much the superior of its bigger neighbour.

This, over the decades, seems to have actually informed the collective English psyche. I often think it's the root of so much of the bipolar manic behaviour so many England fans display, forever torn between wanting success and feeling cheated out of it, between the notion that we should be great but plainly are not.

There are those who are distraught and angry if the side loses and others who don't take it too harshly. England has the most fans at any tournament no matter where it is in the world. We're mad keen to follow our football team. As I mentioned in the chapter on shirts, more England replica shirts are sold than any other countries' shirt on earth. This must reflect the desire to show off being an England fan and thus being English among its citizens.

Some seem to invest an awful lot in their national side and feel it's almost a personal insult if they play poorly, an insult to their national pride. You can hear them on any football phone-in after a game, whining like someone had humped their wife. Their pride is wounded, though quite where they got this pride from, given England's long history of failure, I don't know. It's like getting upset because your three-legged horse keeps failing to win the race.

Others – and I'd include myself in this – just shrug and get on with life without seeing how England have performed as indicative of anything more about the country than the skill of some of its players. The idea that it insults and debases the country as a whole seems lunatic to me. It's just football, not war.

Interestingly, the Scotland fans, as their quality of football has declined, have become more good-humoured and less prone to break your stadium into pieces in a drunken rage. The Tartan Army expect little from their side except effort and commitment and are consequently happy with little victories. Wales and Northern Ireland are similarly less demanding.

England is a different matter. Winning the World Cup in 1966 has turned out to be a curse and one generation after another has been crushed by the weight of expectation that win has created. It has been crippling. For forty years I've seen it inhibit and terrify one team after another and I've no doubt that it will be the same in South Africa 2010.

I'm writing this before the 2010 World Cup and, not being a prophet, have no idea what will have happened by the time this book comes out, but if I had to bet, I'd say we'll play poorly for two out of three of the group stages and do well enough in one to give easily fooled fans false hope that this is a new dawn. Then we'll struggle in the knock-out round and get knocked out in a close game on or before the quarter-finals.

Now, if we've gone on and won it I shall be delighted but after all these years I can't let myself believe it will happen. I want to believe but I just can't any more. But I shall still fervently support them. Some claim not to follow the English national side, saying it's club football and nothing else for them. I never really believe them. I think this is a defensive strategy born out of our long history of losing. You watch, as soon as it looks like England might do well, all those who have shunned the side suddenly jump back on the bandwagon.

The curse of the Empire has been woven through the English fans' attitude to England even without most of us realising it. Most of the worst xenophobic, defensive chants and attitudes stem from that sense of loss of power, of being a once great nation now left with nothing except a chip on our shoulder.

Those old English notions of superiority to the natives are also in the mix. Who are these foreigners anyway? Don't they know we invented the game and gave it to the world? I also believe the arrogance many England fans have had until recently, and which, even now, lies dormant underneath the surface awaiting a revival, stemmed from this notion of English superiority. And for those people, England's failure is all the more disgraceful because it undermines this assumption and attacks their sense of self-worth.

This was my father's take on it. As England failed in the 1970s he very much saw it as a decrease in England's greatness as a country, an irreversible decline from a pinnacle. Had he fought the war for these long-haired losers?

On the flipside, others who are more self-conscious about the legacy of Empire have always veered away from a sense of national pride, fearing it is part of that imperialist tradition. This was my inheritance and it's a shame really because feeling pride in your country shouldn't have to mean you're a xenophobe, thug or Nazi. Talking of which, for decades, England's performances against Germany have often seemed like an extension of the two world wars.

It was West Germany that first brought me to tears over a football match as a boy. It was West Germany that made me grow up and stop being deluded about England.

West Germany 3, England 2 in the Mexico 1970 World Cup was heartbreaking. We were 2–0 up and threw it away. That 1970 side was superior to the 1966 side: the addition of the likes of Francis Lee and Colin Bell made us faster and more of a goal threat. We should have got to the final of that tournament, where Brazil would surely have beaten us. The shock of defeat by West Germany after we had been so on top was too much for me. I sat on our stairs weeping at the injustice of it. The pain that goes hand in hand with the pleasure of football had bitten me for the first time and it hit me again in 1972 when they beat us 3–1 at Wembley. It was shown live on TV on Wednesday night. It was a European qualifier. We didn't just get beaten, we were crushed. The Germans were in green that night and were far superior even though it took them till the last ten minutes to score the winning goals. It was the end for England; 1970 had been bad but this was the nadir and it wouldn't get better for ten long years as one side after another struggled and failed to make it to a tournament. English clubs ruled Europe but England's players were well short of the standard needed and the curse of '66 has remained like a ghost in the England machine.

Those two results burst my England bubble. My early years had all been about England's glory. It was our game; we were the champions, my friend. Even after 1970 it felt like it was a blip and we would reassert our supremacy soon enough. By 1972 this was clearly delusion and throughout the 1970s I learned that what I had been told, and what I am still being told, about England was a lie or at best delusion, in the same way that the history I was taught about the British Empire was at best selective and at worst downright false.

When I was at school we had yet to really pull free of the notion that we went about the world civilising the natives who, had we not done so, would have been living a godless life in the trees. While this was never explicitly said, it provided the under-current of many history lessons. British/English good, Foreigners bad.

This has soaked into football and has been slow to be expunged. You'll still hear people saying things such as 'the foreign lads go down easily', as though the British player is the upstanding decent gentleman and not a diving cheat, despite all evidence to the contrary. Such attitudes are a hangover from the years of delusion which painted foreigners as swarthy and untrustworthy.

Since 1970 England have not been good enough to win anything, nowhere near good enough. For years we played old-fashioned football and were out-thought and out-played by better organised teams with greater skill. Yet for decades we have fooled ourselves into thinking we were much better than we really were.

I remember going to Wembley to see England beat Cyprus 5-0 in a 1975 European Championship qualifier; Malcolm MacDonald scored them all. Cyprus were terrible and stood off us all night. Even though I was only about fourteen, I knew Cyprus were no great shakes in international football and beating them was no guarantee of a side's quality, but those around us in north London that night took this as an indication of certain victory in the upcoming tournament. There was no perspective. Only, 5-0! Get in! We're magic! But of course we didn't even qualify, losing to Czechoslovakia and drawing with Portugal subsequently. It was a typical overrated England performance, one of many false dawns.

My balls hadn't even dropped before I realised that England were overrated by their own fans so why the hell so many people have taken until the last couple of years to realise the same truth is beyond me. It must be just the triumph of hope over experience. The belief in England's abilities and expectations has a very, very deep taproot, like some sort of mega-parsnip, and it has taken forty-four years of failure to finally uproot it and throw it on the compost heap.

However, given the slightest encouragement it will revive itself and once again assume enormous proportions, giving rise to demands based on virtually nothing other than 'We are England and we should be beating sides like' this no matter who sides like this are. Then when we once again fail to do so, we will beat ourselves up as a country, find some poor sod as scapegoat and give it to him with both barrels in order to assuage the sub-conscious guilt of having gone down this stupid road again, not having learned the lessons of the past.

As much as I share the joy, the pain and occasional despair of watching England over the years, it's not a worthy form of patriotism to get yourself into a fat-bellied, beered-up rage about England's football team. It doesn't show your passion for your country, as many would say. It shows lack of perspective and understanding about where England is in world football. It's like getting angry that your McDonald's Happy Meal isn't Michelin-standard cooking.

We are and have been since 1970 in the second tier of international teams, significantly adrift of the best but not hopeless. More fans than ever recognise this now, but it doesn't take much for that jingoistic British Bulldog spirit to come out; one good win over Argentina, or whoever, will do it.

A cry of 'We're gonna win the bloody thing!' will go up. The media drag out the 'England Expects' rubbish before every big game or every tournament just to keep the pressure on. They say it's all about getting behind the team, but it's always felt more loaded than that to me. It's more about setting players up too high, in order to cut them down to size when they don't achieve the level set for them by the slavering tabloid media.

This disparity of attitudes to the England team is illustrative of the disparity of attitudes to English society. Some feel it is in terminal decline, others that it's capable of great things. What we used to call football played the 'English way' is no longer effective at international level where more than sweat and work rate is needed. Most have realised this now, which leaves us with no national football identity as such. Others used to consider the English way also embodied fair play, but that has long since been proved untrue by many a slow-motion replay of England players diving.

I like being a member of a mixed-up nation, uneasy about what it is, a constantly shifting sand of influences. Indeed, that is our national identity: messy, confused and imprecise, much like our passing game.

It means it doesn't stand still long and constantly challenges itself as new cultures and influences get absorbed into the body politic of the nation. There will never be a settled, constant view and those who want one are probably going against the grain of the nature of the beast that is the United Kingdom.

We're a messy, slightly self-conscious amalgam, open to many influences; a mongrel nation with a lot of history. We're not fantastic; we have a lot of problems, but underneath, some really good qualities. And personally, I really rather like that and I suspect the more comfortable we become with this reality, the more successful as a team and as a country we'll be.

Supporting the national side gives us all a rare chance to come together en masse and shout 'Come on England!' Even though our responses to the outcome of the games may vary, that unifying national desire to see England do well, may, if only briefly, be one of the last single unifying elements in our culture and for that, if for no other reason, it should be cherished.

7

Collectibles

WHEN looking at just how massive and widespread football is in this country, it isn't just down to the nature of the game itself, it's also because it's enhanced and supported by a myriad of different strands of culture, none stronger than the culture of collecting and of gambling. These have helped tie us into the games every week. None more so, until relatively recently, than the football pools

For nearly seventy years the football pools have used the game to encourage people to gamble small amounts of money in the hope of winning a life-changing pile of cash.

I was actually a pools collector for Littlewoods for over two years from 1977–79. In return for a 12.5 per cent commission of the total money I took each week, all I had to do was collect everyone's coupons and money every Thursday. It was a big round and I took a lot of money and earned anything from five to fifteen quid a week, which was a lot of cash for a kid of sixteen; the dole at the time was £11 a week.

I also collected Spot the Ball coupons, one or two of which could easily 'accidentally' go missing without any repercussions because essentially no-one could ever prove that they had got the X in the right place as they didn't have a copy of what they had submitted. I'm also sure it didn't matter how accurate you were; if you were in the roughly correct area one would be chosen at random regardless. So that was a handy financial supplement too.

People loved doing the pools. Like the lottery today it was people's one big chance to change their lives, though to my knowledge not one person ever won anything for the two years I was doing it.

The great thing about doing them was that it flattered your

football knowledge. Surely you knew enough about football to pick eight score draws out of Saturday's games, right? I would sit and do my dad's coupon agonising over which looked like even games. The most I ever got was six. It was a compulsive thing though and missing a week meant you felt you'd missed your chance to win, so people did it for fifty-two weeks a year, every year for decades. It was a ritual.

There was the big boy, Littlewoods, the smaller Vernons, the obscure Zetters and, in my experience, never-seen Brittens. Littlewoods started them back in 1923 and by 1994 there were 10 million pools entries per week. Then came the National Lottery and knackered it. The companies were all eventually sold to Sportech Ltd. You can still do the pools but the vibe has died. It used to be so important.

Old lads would sit in my regular boozer the Tav and do their coupon, shouting to the barman, 'Do you fancy Carlisle vs Rochdale for a draw, George?'

'I don't fucking know, Alf. Shurrup, will you?'

'What about Blackpool vs Preston?'

'Aye, aye, that's a draw. Local derby, isn't it?'

Then someone else would pitch in. 'Nah, Preston will walk it; they're on good form, them.'

'Are they, like?'

'Oh aye, won 4-0 last week. You want to go for Brentford vs Reading.'

'What the fuck do you know about Brentford, Jack?'

'I know what I'm talking about.'

'Oh aye, well how come you've never won nowt?'

''Cos it's all fixed, man . . .'

And so it would go.

In the summer it was even more amusing as the British games were replaced by the Australian games, about which no one knew anything. They could have made up a whole host of teams and we wouldn't have known.

'Do you fancy a draw between Brisbane Wolves and Pine Hills, Sid?'

'Nah. I'm going for Taringa Rovers vs Beenleigh FC.'

'Taringa are rubbish, son, they lost 5-0 last week to Albany Creek Excelsior.'

'Shut it, son. I'm a big Taringa fan. Who the fuck is Albany Creek Excelsior anyway?!'

'Haven't a fuckin' clue. Who's Taringa, like?'

'Haven't a fuckin' clue.'

You can still do the pools; the New Football Pools was relaunched in 2008 along with Spot the Ball and you can play online. But it's not the same as it was. It used to be a unifying football tradition.

It was a great thing to do a pools round. It opened my eyes to how other people lived.

It was also a great round to do because you got to meet the daughters of all the blokes who were putting the money on. They'd answer the door and shout 'Pools lad's here' and then stand and smile at you and make small talk while the old fella came to the door.

Many a brief relationship was fired up by that pools round. I went out with one girl, Bev, briefly. When we'd split up, the next time I went to collect their coupon, her dad Big Jack came to the door grinning from ear to ear.

'I hear you're not good enough for my daughter, young Nic,' he laughed.

'Apparently not, Mr Davis,' I said apologetically.

'Never mind, son, you'd get nowt off her anyway, she's as tight as a duck's arse, takes after her mother like that.'

This was absolutely true. All my groping advances had been rejected.

'You want to be asking that Mandy out across at twenty-four; she'll give you a good time and she's built to last, that kid, if you know what I mean.'

He held his hands up to his chest to indicate Mandy's sizeable breasts, of which I was already only too aware. They had soothed my teenage dreams for many months.

'If I was twenty years younger I'd be sniffing round 'er like a dog round the sausages.' He laughed again.

This kind of talk from adults was totally alien to me, but I really enjoyed it and it showed me that not everyone in the world was uptight and stuck-up like at home.

At Christmas I'd get invited into some houses for a drink, which I naturally loved. This only ever happened in council houses. None of the nice middle-class homes up The Avenue, one of Stockton's prime bits of leafy real estate (yes, there is some), ever invited you in. The people in those houses were nice enough but you didn't get into a relationship with them.

Like my parents, they were stand-offish and kept themselves to themselves and were a bit cold. However, many of them were trusting enough to leave their coupon on a table along with a pile of money in the porch or foyer; the front door was left open for me to enter, take the money and leave without having to disturb anyone.

But on the nearby estate Bishopton Court, a big circle of council houses surrounding a green, it was very different. They'd never leave money out for me, clearly worried it would be nicked. But ironically they were much more friendly and generous.

'Howee in son, you'll have a drink won't you?' they'd say and there'd be a sideboard groaning with ale, sherry and whisky.

As this pre-dates the working-class obsession with lager, the beer was served at room temperature and opened on one occasion by Mr Rodgers taking off the cap of the bottle with his teeth.

'There you go son, get it down yer neck,' he'd say with relish. It seemed to me that they got as much pleasure from sharing a drink as I did from consuming it.

I'd have a Double Maxim or two and talk about the Boro. Some of the blokes I met in those days were, in their own way, great philosophers. This was still the era when there were a lot of wise but uneducated people who hadn't had the opportunity for a formal schooling. So you'd learn a bit about local history and maybe politics too.

These houses seemed warm, messy and friendly. They didn't stand on ceremony and were open-hearted. A drink in return for fifty-two weeks of knocking on their door and providing them with a chance to win a lot of money seemed only fair to them. They were much more generous places than my own home, which seemed cold by comparison. My mam and dad would never have thought to invite someone in for a drink even if they did see them every week. They didn't even have drink in the house except for an ancient bottle of Bell's which stood in a dusty cupboard for years untouched.

While the pools were an institution that unified the football world in pursuit of eight score draws for a brief moment around five o'clock every Saturday, as we didn't have much football available to us on TV and just one match every other week to watch live, the young football-obsessed boy or girl in the 1960s and 1970s, filled up our football lovin' cup with as many comics, annuals, programmes and memorabilia as possible.

I had got the collecting bug aged seven in 1968 by becoming obsessed with Batman bubble-gum cards and at the same time Monkees bubblegum cards. These were stills from the TV show printed on to card and came in colourful wax wrappers which I would smooth out and keep in an envelope for years like some kind of autistic hoarder. A startlingly pink slab of bubblegum, often brittle and inedible, wasn't really of much interest to me (just as well as it was sometimes made out of a form of plastic, apparently). No, I just wanted to see the six cards in each packet.

It was an early form of blind gambling. As you collected the set, it became a regular occurrence to go weeks and weeks simply buying ones you already had. It drove me insane. I bought more and more to try and get over a fruitless period, manically attempting to get the whole set.

This occurred to me last year when gambling on black jack in Las Vegas. It's strange how you can reconnect with childhood emotions. I was on a bad run on a blackjack machine, not having won for ten or eleven spins and haemorrhaging money. I should have stopped and walked away, but instead I gambled more on the basis that the bad luck had to end soon and I would win back all my losses. Of course, the big win didn't happen and I ended up further in the hole. On such emotions is Las Vegas built. It was exactly the same in 1968 with bubblegum cards as I spent all my pocket money trying to get the last cards in each collection.

The Monkees cards featured stills from the TV series on one side and a small part of a big picture of the band on the back which, when you had the whole set, made one big picture. For months I tried in vain to get Peter Tork's left eye. It was all I needed to complete the picture. It drove me to tears, in fact so much so that I was banned by my mam from collecting them any more. Instead you could send off a postal order to the company for the missing card. That's how I completed the collection, but it felt like cheating and I wasn't happy about it. But the collecting bug had got under my skin.

I began collecting Land of the Giants cards, also just stills from the TV series which made a big picture once flipped over. At the same time, judging by what's left with me today, I seem to have dabbled with collecting sixties pop group cards and Beatles cards too. There were also Dr Who cards that came with Zoom ice lollies and then there was the magnificent PG Tips range. Each year they brought out new collections with a book to stick them in.

My first was 1965's Wild Birds of Britain, followed by Transport Through the Ages, Trees in Britain, Flags and Emblems of the World, British Costumes, History of the Motor Car, Famous People, The Saga of Ships and the last ones I collected, 1971's The Race into Space. All came with a little bit of information and to this day, I owe the fact that I can identify all European flags to the PG Tips cards. The smell of tea still puts me in mind of those cards as I'm sure it does many of my generation.

So when 1970 arrived and along with it a plethora of World Cup collectibles, including World Cup Soccer Stickers and Esso's World Cup coins which were given away with petrol, I was already indoctrinated into the concept of collecting stuff and I couldn't resist. I bought the sticker album and began collecting all the players of each participating country. These were just a small glossy paper 'stamp' of a headshot of the player, hardly that thrilling really but compulsive nonetheless.

The Esso coins were fantastic, made from some alloy and stamped with a head profile of each England player. You got one for every four gallons bought and better still they were quick and easy to get the whole set and came with a presentation booklet. Texaco had done the same thing a year earlier with the twenty Famous Footballer set of coins but we didn't have a Texaco station near us so I never got hold of any of them despite craving them badly like some kind of junk junkie.

Soccer stickers came in yellow packets of seven for sixpence and were made by a company called FKS. No gum involved, just a thick packet full of hidden potential glories. Brilliant. It was easy at first. I had the album 80 per cent full within a few months. Then the torture began again. The full England squad was on the first two pages and was the most important and crucial to collect. I could have just about tolerated not collecting an obscure Peruvian goalie but not one of the England players. The manufacturers surely knew this and fixed it so there was a shortage of some players. By the time the tournament kicked off I had got all thirty England players except Nottingham Forest's Ian Storey-Moore. Ian fucking Storey-Moore – the name still haunts me, probably the only double-barrelled named footballer of his generation. No matter how many packets I bought I couldn't get him. We stood in playgrounds with our wedge of 'swaps' going through the time-honoured 'got, got, got, haven't got' routine. One kid had actually got Storey-Moore but didn't have any duplicates and wouldn't give me his only one, not even for the entire El Salvador squad, an especially weird-looking group of men as their shirts had been painted on and the photos clumsily retouched. Who even knew where El Salvador was before the 1970 World Cup? See, football is a geographical education too.

By the time Brazil lifted the Jules Rimet Trophy, I had the entire collection except the Forest player and once again I was banned from accruing more swaps in the vain pursuit of him for fear I would fritter my pocket money away all year instead of spending it on endless sweets and brightly coloured bottles of 'It's frothy, man' Cresta, which bent your brain with chemicals and sugar.

Once again, the postal order was sent off and he duly arrived in the post. It still felt like cheating but the shock of having him in my hand after nearly a year of trying, during which I had got over 350 duplicates, stays with me.

Panini stickers soon took over this market and continue to dominate today. They began long before Panini became the artisanal bread of choice. That would have been rather confusing. Am I collecting stickers or bread buns?

There was an explosion of collectable football-themed cards from the mid-1960s onwards in everything from iced-lollies, newspapers, comics and the ubiquitous bubblegum. I kept on collecting domestic cards but there was a problem. Once you had collected a full set of domestic cards of First Division players for one season, the next season was almost identical. So you had collect a different brand, perhaps featuring action shots rather than the head portraits. But I'd wager most lads collected one or two full sets and then drifted away from it.

But help was at hand because by 1972, I had started collecting records and this passion has stayed with me ever since. All those years of PG Tips cards and Soccer Stars had primed me for a life of hunting down dusty slabs of vinyl and it became all-consuming. No Saturday was complete without a trip on the bus to Alan Fearnley's Records in Middlesbrough; an emporium dedicated to second-hand records sold cheap. I was like a junkie in a pharmacy, carefully going through literally thousands of albums searching for stuff I'd heard about or just liked the look of.

I was lucky to have cash to burn. My parents gave me £5 a week pocket money by late 1976. This was serious bread. You could buy anything up to ten second-hand albums for that or even fifteen pints of bitter. But on top of this fiver I had the 12.5 per cent commission from the Littlewoods Pools round. This gave me anything from ten to twenty quid a week to spend on albums and going out . . . and spend it I did. It was how the album collection grew so quickly and how I could afford to go out most nights of the week drinking.

And I still have my Ian Story-Moores and Peter Tork eyes issues with records. I have the entire collection of Steve Miller Band singles, both USA and UK versions, except his debut UK single 'Sittin' in Circles'. I have looked for it for thirty years and have never seen a copy. Even today, when buying records online from anywhere in the world has made getting rare records infinitely easier (and some would say, somewhat less exciting), still it's failed to emerge. There can't be many copies but someone must have one.

It was around 1970 that companies woke up and realised that hey, this football business, it's rather popular isn't it? I bet people would like to buy more football stuff. That same year was the first time the Buckyball was used in a World Cup. It was named after Buckminster Fuller, who was a brilliant and fascinating fella.

We take the ball for granted, don't we? Without the ball football is merely, well, foot. And when we think of a football most of us think of the classic black-and-white panelled ball. There's a new fashion for that sphere with sanitary towels wrapped around it but it's a fad that will pass.

A proper football is twenty hexagons and twelve pentagrams in black-and-white. It was FIFA's official ball of choice for thirty-four years. Indeed, it was the first standardised ball and it remains the most popular at all levels of the game to this day. It's an icon of the sport.

And that ball was effectively invented by Buckminster Fuller and is still known to this day as the Buckyball in his honour. There have been many colour variations made of leather, part or wholly synthetic but the Buckyball set a standard so definitive that it remains as valid today as fifty years ago.

If you're new to Bucky, he was a truly astonishing man. His books might change your life.

He was an American who among many other things was an architect, an inventor, a designer, a poet, a futurist and radical thinker. Perhaps most importantly, as you may well know if you've ever lived in an eco-pod or been to the Eden Project, he was responsible for the invention of the geodesic dome.

Had I paid attention in physics and chemistry classes instead of reading the sleevenotes on the latest Deep Purple album, trying to understand Yes lyrics and dropping pencils on the floor so I could look up Shuna Yeaman's skirt, I wouldn't have a CSE Grade 4 to my name and I would already know that there is a family of complex carbon structures named after him called buckminsterfullerenes, which are also known as Buckyballs. And it was from this concept that he produced the idea of the thirty-two panelled football.

The first thirty-two-panelled ball, which makes a near-perfect sphere when inflated, was marketed in Denmark in the 1950s and was eventually adopted as the first 'official' World Cup ball by FIFA in 1970.

The classic Buckyball was the Adidas Telstar that Pele and his mob kicked around in Mexico and that Cruyff did his 'turn' with in 1974. Today, the Buckyball is still the most kicked ball worldwide.

Earlier balls were a bladder in a casing that was sewn up. You could split your head open if you headed the laced-up part but no one was bothered because it was thought a large gaping forehead wound made a man of you.

Balls came in all styles and constructions, leather, rubber or plastic; there was no standard ball. They were often rectangles of leather, more ridged and less round, much like your head after a game. The Buckyball changed all that.

But the ball was merely a spin-off invention in Mr Fuller's long and distinguished life. As a radical thinker he was instrumental in developing the concept of synergy as the basic principle of all interactive systems. Quite simply he was one of the most important and profound thinkers of the twentieth century.

In the 1960s his notions of existence, earth, environment, space and other far-out and cosmic matters were embraced by many a hippy and bearded student through books such as *Nine Chains to the Moon, Utopia or Oblivion* and *Operating Manual for Spaceship Earth* all of which sound like the titles of very good progressive rock albums and are well worth reading while high on drugs.

He developed the Dymaxion (dynamic and maximum efficiency in case you're wondering) House in 1927, and the Dymaxion streamlined, omnidirectional car in 1932, as you do if you're a genius with a bit of time on your hands. Whatever happened to the omnidirectional car? Can you still buy one?

If you find yourself in Santa Barbara, California – and I recommend you do at some point in your life because it's bloody lovely – you can toddle along to the Buckminster Fuller Institute to discover more about this amazing man. Interestingly, Ted Turner who was a guitarist in one of my favourite 1970s bands Wishbone Ash, left the band in 1974 and a year later went into a project called World Man Band to raise global consciousness based on the writing of Buckminster Fuller. As ever, rock 'n' roll and football seem to fuse together in my life.

One of his mottos was 'Dare to Be Naïve', which of course was adopted by Spurs when managed by Ossie Ardiles.

He also said, 'Truth is cosmically total: synergetic. Verities are generalised principles stated in semi-metaphorical terms. Verities are differentiable. But love is omni-embracing, omni-coherent, and omni-inclusive, *with no exceptions*. Love, like synergetics, is non-differentiable, i.e., is integral.'

Aye, well that's just what I was thinking, Bucky, while drinking Bucky, ironically enough. No not really, I'm not a Glaswegian.

So you could now buy your official World Cup Buckyball. The Buckyball was an innovation much needed because most footballs we played with fell into two categories, lightweight plastic ones often called floaters, or heavy-duty leather balls which we called casers, because they had a leather case around a pink rubber bladder.

My caser was a Christmas present in 1971; typically it wasn't a new Bucky-style one, it was the old school head-splitter. It was my pride and joy for many years. However, you couldn't just play with it; you need to look after it as well. If the leather ball was left out in the rain or got wet, it would stiffen up when dry and become rock-hard. So you needed to rub dubbin into it. I still don't know what dubbin was, but I bought it from the sports shop. I suspect it was some kind of wax and oil combo that kept leather supple.

For a kid to strike a ball like this with any power required a well-developed thigh and it more usually got a puncture from a rose bush and was condemned, deflated to a dusty corner of the garage. Soon enough though, leather balls began to be coated with a plastic polyurethane to stop them becoming waterlogged. There was clearly money in balls and by the mid-1970s there was a wide range available.

Great, so you've got a ball; now, what else do you fancy? How about some swivel boots? What were swivel boots I hear you ask? Ha! That, my, friend is a good question.

For a time in the early to mid-1970s there was a peculiar football boot in the shops with the studs embedded on to a rotating plate. This was sold as an aid to quick, tricky movement which would also prevent you from twisting ligaments in your foot or ankle. Not that twisting those ligaments was a problem for anyone, certainly not compared to being kicked in the neck by a brutal centre-half. How does that sound to you? A rotating stud plate? It's mad isn't it? Surely, we have evolved to do this as animals without the aid of a rotating disc on our feet. I did wonder if they would allow you to pirouette around on the spot, spinning like a ballerina but sadly, no, they didn't.

I knew a kid who had a pair of these boots. The plate got stuck with mud and meant that at times, when he tried to turn, he would twist his ankle, as the boot refused to budge. Then it would free itself and turn at the slightest provocation, causing him on more than one occasion to lose his balance. Turns out they were far more likely to cause you to snap your foot than if you played in slippers, but then the 1970s was a dangerous era for toys.

The best-selling items of the early 1970s were Clackers. In these more sanitised times, they would never have got to market because they caused kids severe bruising. All you had was a piece of string with two heavy plastic or glass balls on the end. Your task, Jim, should you choose to accept it, was to lift them up sharply to 'clack' above your wrist. When done properly they would bounce off each other and . . . err . . . well . . . Christ, I have no idea what the bloody point of them was, but every kid had them. To add to potential wrist bruising, some of them would shatter into a million shards and put a small boy's eye out. Local news was filled with tales of woe as sorry-looking children with ballooned-up wrists stood in A&E next to the simple kids who had got their head stuck in a pan. Between that, blue Cresta and nylon Y-fronts it's a wonder any of us survived the 1970s childhood at all.

After the 1970 World Cup suddenly there was more football merchandise in the sport shops. Now, when I say more, there still wasn't much, but these things are relative; compared to the barren desert that preceded it was a veritable plethora.

Plastic sports bags in club colours with the club's name printed on the side began to appear. Interestingly, by contrast with today's world, these were not, nor needed to be 'authorised' or 'licensed', the twin words of lawyerly oppression in the twenty-first century. Most clubs names were not trademarked until the 1990s and so anyone could produce, say, a sports bag with Chelsea printed on it. Similarly, the club crests were not seen as an emblem to exploit so anyone could and did reproduce them on woven badges which could be sewn on to a shirt.

Other football stuff to collect included a range of six-inch-high plastic football figures in an action pose. You couldn't get them in Boro red-and-white colours, more usually in all blue or all red. They were not meant to resemble anyone in particular; they were just an action figure but were somehow great. So I got all of them plus the goalkeeper and they stood on my bedroom drawers as though they were my own personal football team.

Then there were pennants, sometimes with a club crest printed on. These were made of soft plastic and had the honours of the club listed too. I was bought an Everton one for some reason. It was of absolutely no use to me and lay in a drawer for ten years before being junked when I left home. But then again, what use is a pennant anyway? Hardly exciting.

As I discussed in a previous chapter, football shirts were still made out of cotton in the early to mid-1970s, as were shorts. Socks, however, were a different matter. They seemed to be made out of wool or a wool/cotton mix which, when it had got wet with sweat or rain, set into a brittle platform. Your socks could stand up on their own if you didn't wash them immediately after use. And even if you did, after repeated wearing the stiff, board-like foot became a permanent feature.

By the mid-1970s we were rescued from getting trench foot from these creations by the 100 per cent nylon sock which kept your foot sweating badly in the summer and freezing cold in the winter; 1970s nylon should have been illegal under some sort of United Nations World Health Organisation edict. It was good for nothing but was all the rage. Indeed a shop opened up nationwide called Brentford Nylons, advertised by Alan 'Fluff' Freeman on TV, which sold only things made from nylon, so proud of the substance were they. This led to the hideous introduction of nylon bed sheets which after a while went all bobbly and disgusting. They also made you sweat because the fabric didn't breathe. In short it had no redeeming factors at all except for the fact that the static the nylon sheets produced from the friction of a decent masturbation session could make your hair literally stand on end and turn your entire bedroom into a Van Der Graaf generator. It's all probably still in landfill good as new because the bloody stuff was absolutely indestructible.

What manufacturers nor the FA nor anyone else in football seemed to have realised until the early 1970s was that not only was there profit in selling people football merchandise but that it would also bind people more closely to their clubs and to the game itself. There was a tremendous unquenched thirst for all things football related. Hell, I even bought the game blow football.

In today's more cynical world, you may think blow football was some kind of oral sex game played by fake blonde women in Holiday Inns with reserve team strikers, but it was in fact two small goals, two plastic tubes and a small lightweight ball. The aim was to blow the ball in to the other person's goal. Try doing that on your X-Box! See, these were more innocent times or, some would say, more boring.

But it wasn't just a time of great expansion of merchandise. There were also lots of comics to be devoured.

One of the few truly excellent things my parents did for me was to encourage me to read from an early age. By the time I went to junior school I was already reading books meant for ten-year-olds. I was the best reader in junior school for three years running, perhaps the only academic achievement that gave me any pleasure at all.

So it was natural that along with many other boys I asked for football annuals for Christmas and birthdays. The Roy of the Rovers annuals were a favourite among many and stretched back to 1958. But here's the thing, I never liked Roy of the Rovers. I did read the stories occasionally in the *Tiger* comic but I always thought he was too straight for me, too clean cut, too much of a goody-goody. As the emergent rock 'n' roll spirit was growing in me, I seem to have learned from an early age to spot allies.

Roy was like a strict teacher to me. I wasn't a fan. His thighs also seemed alarmingly thick and granite-like, which offended me for some reason. My favourite comic strip football story was Jack of United and Jimmy of City in the excellent Score 'n' Roar which hit the newsagents' shelves in 1970. It was a tale of brothers who played for Castleburn United and City. Jimmy was my hero – a long-haired, creative goal scorer – whereas Jack was the short-haired, solid dependable defender. In my eyes Jack was a boring bastard and Jimmy was the man. Usually they ended up playing each other in some outlandishly implausible situation. Jimmy was the younger brother so perhaps I identified with him because I was one too.

The Jack and Jimmy stories lasted only about three or four years and ended just as I was going through puberty, but their work was done: I was Jimmy. I realised decades later that this was another brick in the wall, a piece in the jigsaw, another colour on my palette that formed the person I was to become.

However, there were other options for your football literature hit. *Scorcher* featured real-life football info as well as stories, including 'Billy's Boots', featuring a pair of haunted boots which when Billy pulled them on turned him into a football genius. That was fantastic and somehow not laughably stupid.

As well as the comic-based annuals were other player-endorsed affairs such as *Alan Ball's Football Annual*, *Denis Law's Book of Soccer* (soccer was an oft used word in those days before anti-American snobbery made it unfashionable) and any amount of newspaper-sponsored books of football. The best thing about most of these annuals was the photos, usually of muddy footballers in mid-air and of goalkeepers leaping to collect a ball. It always looked cold and wet and decidedly unglamorous.

I would get biographies of footballers like Dave Mackay or Danny Blanchflower out of the library but they were boring affairs and seemed to speak of an era many moons ago in the 1950s. Rock 'n' roll had the upper hand in that regard. Inspiring books such as Ian Hunter's *Diary of a Rock 'n' Roll* star, published in 1974, was a thrilling read and has remained in print ever since. It's tales of ordinary madness – touring with Mott The Hoople even though they were often far from glamorous – really provoked my imagination. Travelling around playing music seemed so brilliant a way to make a living. Hunter's wit and wisdom make it as relevant and entertaining a read today as they did in 1974.

That same year I also devoured *S.T.P.: A Journey Through America with The Rolling Stones*, Bob Greenfield's legendary document of the Stones' 1972 summer tour of North America. The debauched decadence, along with the teetering anarchy that the book describes, was magical even though aged thirteen I really didn't fully comprehend what all the plates of white powder were.

It was a life filled with groupies, more groupies and then some more groupies all keen to fuck anyone even vaguely connected with the S.T.P. What thirteen-year-old boy in the grip of puberty wouldn't want a piece of that? Of course, I wasn't to know that The Stones were a remarkable set-up and that most bands didn't tour on this scale nor attract such a coterie of weirdos, winos and lunatics. Most bands sat in cramped vans with no heater and lived off cold baked beans as they drove up and down the M1. But it was inspiring to me. Hedonism and rock 'n' roll is a thrilling mixture.

I had already read Hunter Davies's 1968 book about The Beatles which by modern standards is quite a tame affair but which perfectly captured the feeling of the world changing in 1964 and of an industry being born before the participants' very own eyes. There were always cheaply produced paperback books on groups of the moment to read too. These were little more than propaganda written by publicists but obviously, I wasn't knowing or cynical enough aged thirteen or fourteen to realise that. So I ate up books on T.Rex, Slade, The Sweet and to name just a few.

So the world of rock 'n' roll was being painted in my juvenile brain and the picture it made looked pretty bloody great and largely populated with sexually available girls, which didn't sound like the sort of life that was likely to be available on Teesside at all.

Back on the football shelves for the serious student of contemporary football there was only one book that really mattered. *The Rothmans Yearbook*. As I'm sure you're aware, it had all the stats of every side, every game and much more from the previous season. It was statto heaven. It was where you learned all the clubs' nicknames, colours and ground names. My first one was bought for me in 1970 – the first year it was published in fact – and for ten years I had every copy. Oddly enough it never made me want to smoke the sponsor's fags, and it didn't seem to infiltrate my mother's smoking preferences either, as she stuck resolutely with Silk Cut. So much for advertising, eh.

Around the same time I also bought *Wisden* because it scratched the same nerdy statistic itch. There's no point in trying to make anyone who doesn't love these tomes understand why they are so thrilling; it's not something you can logically reason away. But to those of us who get it, we know.

It was in the same spirit that later I would buy *Record Collector*, *Billboard* and *Goldmine* books of collectible records charts and valuations, thus once again drawing together the strands of football and rock 'n' roll.

But as I grew out of comics, magazines became much more important. There was *Charles Buchan's Football Monthly*, but I always found that a dry affair aimed at older boys. This was where *Shoot* came in. *Shoot* was brilliant because it had pictures in it which you could tear out and use as posters. The articles were rubbish; even aged ten I knew that. There were silly questionnaires about what Terry Conroy's favourite food was or how many hats he had or whatever; hardly stimulating reading, but the full-colour portraits and action shots were highly prized as bedroom wall adornments.

So as ever, once I started collecting *Shoot* from 1973, I had to get every copy, including back issues. Around the same time I was, oddly enough, buying *Popswop*, a teenage pop magazine/comic which was largely about David Cassidy and Donny Osmond every week, and also the *NME*, which most certainly wasn't. *Popswop* had teenage cartoon strip stories, usually about some plain-looking girl falling in love with Gary Glitter; worst move you ever made, darling. Oh yeah, Gary was quite the thing back then. Who knew? I liked the cartoon strips best of all, probably because I was emerging from the culture of 'Billy's Boots' and other such graphic stories.

But quickly, it was the *NME* and to a lesser extent the *Melody Maker* and later still *Sounds* that became more and more important to me and *Popswop* more irrelevant. The *NME* was inky and made your hands filthy, which seemed appropriate for the music it talked about. It used vocabulary I didn't really understand. It used the American 'ass' for arse. This was entirely new to me and naturally I thought it mean 'ass' as in the animal. But the context it was used in clearly indicated otherwise.

It too had its own cartoon strips. The Lone Groover cartoon was a particular favourite, Tony Benyon's classic cartoon of a masked hipster who called everyone 'dude' long before Bill and Ted. It was full of references to 'nasal talc', 'stash' and other narco talk that no thirteen-year-old boy in the north east of England could hope to be familiar with. It wasn't the sort of stuff you learned at your mother's knee – not unless your mother was a groupie on a Rolling Stones tour.

It was but a short step from the Lone Groover to the Fabulous Furry Freak Brothers, another teenage favourite, this time, much more deeply rooted in the West Coast counter-culture. By the time I knew what the likes of Fat Freddie's Cat were talking about in the FFFB comics I was already playing guitar, drinking every night and easing myself into a life of dissolution. Freewheelin' Franklin's motto *'Dope will get you through times of no money better than money will get you through times of no dope'* had started to make perfect sense.

I managed to get hold of a copy of *Zap Comix* from a market stall in Stockton. How it had ended up there is anyone's guess. *Zap* was an underground, subversive publication started in 1968 in San Francisco which came with 'Fair Warning: For Adult Intellectuals Only' emblazoned on the cover. As it was issue three and they published only sixteen, this copy could well have been sold by cartoonist Robert Crumb himself on the streets of Haight-Ashbury. It was his legendary drawings of characters such as Mr Natural and the horny feline, Fritz the Cat, that filled *Zap Comix*. I already knew his work from the front cover of my copy of Big Brother and The Holding Company's *Cheap Thrills* album. It was anti-establishment, alternative and radical for 1968 and seemed every bit as radical when I got my paws on it in 1976, presumably as life on Teesside was still some way behind that of San Francisco.

I especially adored Mr Natural, a guru type who was above and beyond space and time. Clearly, with the FFFB in one eye and Mr Natural in the other, it wasn't going to be long before I began to consume those substances of which they spoke and which had inspired Robert Crumb in the first place. But therein lies another story for another day.

By now I was heavily into poetry, beat poetry especially, and knew that *Zap Comix* was all part of that late-1960s scene that was so attractive to me. You were not supposed to like football *and* poetry at school. Those two things were mutually exclusive for the northern male in the 1970s, and still today, I would wager, so it was imperative to keep such matters private. A slim volume of poetry by Ginsberg, Snyder or my favourite, Ferlinghetti, was a bigger taboo than pornography, indicated you were quite probably a homosexual, and could guarantee a kicking even at my relatively tame secondary school. But I suppose that was part of the attraction of it too. It was certainly dangerous. You had to be careful who you told about 'Coney Island of the Mind' or 'Howl'.

Another cool read was the American *Creem* magazine, which was also hard to get unless you subscribed to it, but occasionally I got a copy on trips to Newcastle at Virgin Records. Reading Lester Bangs's pieces was like looking into another world. I didn't really understand them much of the time as they were stuffed full of hipster talk, phonetically spelled words and analogies to things I knew nothing of. But that was all good. It felt more important precisely because I couldn't quite understand every word. It was challenging and spoke of a worldview as far away from what I had grown up with as was possible. Bangs was, it appeared to me anyway, quite possibly insane. His paean to Lou Reed 'Let Us Now Praise Famous Death Dwarves' was all the proof I needed; a whacked-out interview that was an unhinged work of genius.

Looking at it now, all this literature both high- and low-brow formed the building blocks of my character. There's a direct progression from those early football comics of *Score 'n' Roar*, *Popswap*, *NME* right through to the Freak Brothers.

In the twenty-first century it seems entirely normal that kids' and indeed adults' passion for football is exploited in as many ways as possible by their club. There's more product than anyone could buy in six lifetimes. You can still buy pennants; I note that even lowly clubs such as Berwick Rangers – one of the bleaker and more fantastic outposts of football in the UK – has them for a mere £4.99.

Go to any Premier League club shop and you'll find everything from coloured wigs, cufflinks, 'art' prints which look like they've been done by the kid in junior school who is good at drawing, wallpaper, footballs, golf bags, douche bags and duvets all with the club logo on or featuring one of the star players. You can buy a life-size, six-foot-high plastic transfer of your favourite player and stick it on the wall, but it's essentially doing the same thing as when we used to cut out pictures from *Shoot* and put them on *our* wall, only for a lot more money.

In thirty years it's gone from famine to feast but if you look at most clubs' stuff, it's rubbish really.

Tacky is the look *du jour* and cheap the default quality. Most of it looks like the kind of stuff you'd find on a market stall. I mean, who wants a mirror with the club crest on? No one; it's rubbish as a mirror because it's got the bloody club crest on it! I can't see what people get out of smothering their lives in club's shitty merchandise. Scarfs maybe, OK a shirt but not pyjamas or a money box in the shape of a football boot full of chocolates for fuck's sake. Just because it exists is no reason to buy it.

It would seem that the fans who buy this crappola have fallen for the idea that the more official club merchandise you buy, the bigger fan it shows you to be, which has always been a spurious notion at best. An interesting development at Manchester United, one of the biggest purveyors of merchandise, is the wearing of the green-and-yellow scarves as a protest against the club's current owners. Green and yellow being the original colours of Newton Heath, the club United grew from. So it seems in the twenty-first century merchandise can even be used to make political statements. What next? The Man. Utd urban guerrilla outfit? Club-sponsored petrol bombs maybe? Hurry, buy your club Armalite rifle while stocks last!

In the twenty-first century, football merchandise, magazines and the rest is a huge global industry, rising from being a cottage industry forty years ago; just think, without the income it provides your club could never have afforded to buy that Dutch lad who had scored a lot of goals in the Erevidise but who has put the ball in the net just four times this season.

Football stuff is important cultural clutter and it wouldn't be such a huge market if generation after generation didn't crave it so badly. However, it's long overdue for an upgrade in quality. It needn't be so downmarket and tatty. It could strive to be a more artistic, quality expression of love for the club. As it is it more usually looks like over-priced market stall crap. And that, I reckon, is taking the piss out of fans' loyalty.

8

Language

THE English language is a rubbery, flexible animal and football offers an opportunity to test and enjoy it to the fullest extent. There is a cryptic glory to the football lexicon; it's a secret language for the acolytes to love and it fell on to fertile soil with me.

Many everyday football expressions are specific to the game and don't feature in life in any other context. Only in football parlance is someone said to issue 'a come and get me plea' when they want to be transferred. As much as we'd like to do that to get a girl- or boyfriend, your mate doesn't go up to an attractive stranger and say, 'See him over there, he's issued a come and get me plea.'

If someone wants to leave the company you work for, no one refers to them as a 'want-away worker'. These expressions are found only in the football press.

The language has expanded purely to better express aspects of the game. Players are not just beaten, they are 'skinned' or, more controversially and inaccurately, 'raped'. Players are 'tapped up' to join another club, a beautifully concise term which seems to owe its origins more to the plumbing trade than to sport.

A side will be accused of 'parking the bus', which is a superbly graphic image to describe a very defensive strategy. An aggressive tackle will 'go right through him', and a manager will be said to have 'lost the dressing room'.

We all know what these obtuse expressions mean, so much so that we rarely stop to consider their unique nature. Even such a familiar term as a 'bicycle kick' is a fantastically graphic, precise expression.

It is often the more dull, obvious terminologies that become clichés, such as 'a game of two halves', 'he'll be disappointed with that', 'good feet for a big man', 'give it 110 per cent' and the most hated and most entrenched of all, 'at the end of the day'.

Regular purveyors of these expressions attract the ire of the more word-conscious members of football's cognoscenti. Well they attract my ire anyway. But then I am word-mad.

I was an early learner when it came to reading and one of my earliest memories is making a list of words that began with Z when I was little more than four years old. Even the shape of letters fascinated me. I loved the sturdy symmetry of a capital A and the fluid expressive look of a cursive *f*. I also began 'collecting' phrases I liked. I would write down colloquial expressions that I heard on television in a little book and would try to work out what the more obscure ones meant. How are you to know what, 'Well I'll go to the foot of our stairs', really means when you're a kid? It's not immediately obvious.

When I was about six I realised that Middlesbrough, though abbreviated to the Boro, wasn't spelled Middlesborough, as many mistakenly think. That first 'o' is missing and I used to ask teachers why this was. If we called Middlesbrough the Boro it should be spelled borough, surely. Naturally, they had no idea why and told me to shut up and stop asking stupid questions. Being intellectually inquisitive wasn't encouraged in my junior school; digging holes in sand with a spade was. Even at that early age we were being indoctrinated to be quiet, stop thinking and just do something menial.

Hand in hand with enjoying strange local phrases was a love of accents. As I was born in Hull I grew up with a Hull accent. On arriving on Teesside aged eight I was immediately mocked for having a voice that was unlike that of the local kids.

They emphasised the Yorkshire element to it, as though I spoke like Geoff Boycott, which I clearly didn't, as his is a south Yorkshire accent, quite different from the East Riding's. I'm sure it was more likely to have been a high-pitched version of ex-Hull and Boro striker Dean Windass myself, but of course, as we had no recording devices at the time, I've no evidence. As we got to 1973 or 1974, we did get a tape recorder. By then I'd been on Teesside for four years – a lifetime for a kid – and had lost all traces of the Hull accent. Those tapes reveal a classic slurred Teesside voice, often running words into each other like a drunk. This, like a Glaswegian accent, is most useful when you actually are drunk because it doesn't sound any different and thus you can pass for sober in polite company.

As kids do, I set about adapting to the local vernacular better to fit in. Because of that I became very aware of accents, mimicking ones I heard on the TV. Even now, when talking to someone with a strong burr, I have to resist the temptation to copy it in my responses, because it does sound like you're taking the piss really. It's not that; I just love accents, even the much derided Brummy and Black Country accents, voices which sound innately melancholic, ever so slightly pitiful and a little surprised.

It is one of the most distinctive aspects of British culture that our accents and colloquial expressions change so much over such short distances. They blur, merge and alter from one place to another. Listen to how a Geordie accent blends north and west of Newcastle into a Northumbrian burr and as it reaches Berwick it fades seamlessly into borders Scottish. The Berwick accent rather magnificently seems to be both Geordie and lowland Scottish all at once.

In the town of my birth, Hull, the East Riding of Yorkshire accent shares some of Teesside's open, stretched vowels but is nothing like the classical west Yorkshire accent of Castleford just twenty miles west.

Most people from outside the region think my accent is Geordie when obviously it is the more elite, rare Teesside. To the uneducated they may sound the same but they're actually very different. But then again, we live in such a linguistic, dialect-rich country that most accents change with a few miles. Even within the few miles of the smallish area which comprises Teesside there are variations. Your classic Middlesbrough accent is Chris Rea's or Chubby Brown's. Comedian Bob Mortimer has a diluted version, as does Paul Daniels. But as you shift west It softens and becomes like Vic Reeves's Darlington voice. In those few miles it starts to become a more recognisable County Durham accent. There are those who will say Darlington is not Teesside, and they're technically right, but I've always thought of it as an honorary member of the rare Teesside clan.

Hartlepool on the coast has another variation of Teesside, perhaps a dash more Mackem in it as the accent begins its change as it travels the twenty miles north to Sunderland.

Middlesbrough was a northern outpost of Yorkshire until the boundary changes in 1974 pulled it into Cleveland, but there's nothing recognisably Yorkshire about the Boro voice. By the time it's left Northallerton or Whitby, it manages to alter completely. Similarly Richmond in north Yorkshire lies just less than thirty miles from Middlesbrough but its accent has only the merest hint of the elided Teesside vowels.

The Teesside accent has it roots in Irish. In the early nineteenth century, Middlesbrough had the third biggest Irish population in England after London and Liverpool. When combined with the local accent, it elongated the vowels of words. A Geordie would say 'shirt' as 'shurt' or even 'shawt', but we'd say sheerrt drawing out the 'er' part of the word. The same thing happened when Irish met the Lancashire accent in Liverpool.

But it's not just the accent that is interesting, it's the local slang and how it's used. When we thought something was good, as kids we'd say it was 'beauty', as in 'Aw man, that goal was beauty.'

The expression 'nick off' was used to express going somewhere as in, 'We'll nick off in a minute.' Many, instead of saying 'anyway', would say, 'any road', as in, 'That's my opinion any road.' It's an off-beat word with 'way' being replaced by the much more prosaic 'road'.

Down in west Yorkshire, my granddad Fred from Castleford would greet me with the words, 'Nah then our John, is thee winnin'?' This, if you don't know, is a version of 'How do you do?' What a brilliantly poetic expression.

My old favourite, 'Well I'll go to the foot of our stairs', I've always thought of as a Lancastrian expression simply because I first heard it in the 1960s on *Coronation Street*. It's a tangential and totally wonderful way to express disbelief.

Go anywhere in the country and you'll find such expressions; some remain local, others become widely used.

'Gone for a Burton' began as a London expression to say someone was dead and had its origins in a wartime advertisement for Burton

Ales which featured an absent man. It went on to be used widely, though seems to have now fallen by the linguistic wayside a bit.

My parents, presumably in the attempt to become more middle-class, seemed to have consciously dropped most of their original Hull-isms and expressions and often encouraged me to do so too. I'd be chided for dropping an 'h', which is a characteristic of the Hull accent, because it was 'common'.

While I didn't develop as strong an accent as many of my contemporaries, you just can't help it rubbing off on you, no matter how your socially aspirant parents wish it otherwise. And anyway, growing up in an out-of-the-way part of the country that many couldn't even point to on a map (indeed you won't find Teesside on any contemporary map) made regional identity via accent and colloquialisms an important part of my self-identity and remains so.

But from an equally early age, that self-identity was also wrapped up in the language of football and rock 'n' roll. Jargon in both helps keeps the culture a mystery to the non-informed. Like all jargon it helps keep the tourists at bay and deny access to the casual browser.

If you hear a guitarist talking about his truss rod or whammy bar, unless you too are a guitarist, you will likely have no idea what they are on about. They sound like some sort of orthopaedic support. Similarly, if the uneducated hear about two footballers indulging in a bit of handbags, they may think it is all part of some fashion accessory shopping outing.

And if you hear a man on the television describing another man dribbling and opening his legs, don't worry, it's not the naked channel.

To those of us who spend our lives absorbed by football, the language of the game is second nature, however lateral or obscure the imagery is. We all know what being nutmegged means, or to shorten it to the players' vernacular, just plain 'megs', but there's no reason for anyone else to. To the rest of society nutmeg is what you might grate on to a rice pudding or, as an amateur druggie, try to consume a lot of to get high, in obedience to the popular rumour. It doesn't work any better than smoking banana skins; it's much easier and cheaper just to buy proper drugs.

We're so used to the language of football that we rarely stop to think about it, but let's take that word 'handbags' and look at it a bit more closely. In case you don't know, it's used to describe a puffed-up bit of lightweight aggression between two players. Often it's little more than a bit of pushing and shoving. Not enough to get either of them sent off; like cats fighting, it's all wind and piss really. It's only evolved as a term over the last ten or fifteen years.

I don't recall handbags being used in the 1980s because on-pitch aggression was more tolerated then, so there was no need for players to indulge in some aggro-lite nor any word needed to describe it. As the rules tightened up and outlawed most of the exciting physical aspects of football, it became more necessary for players to express their annoyance at another player physically enough to show they are serious but not physically enough to get sent off.

This behaviour was first referred to be commentators and pundits as, 'That was all handbags at forty paces', a clever adaptation of pistols, or guns, at forty paces as it clearly suggests the harmless nature of the incident. But it's actually a very complex analogy. The idea that a lightweight tussle is like two women – the handbag being a female accessory (don't get me started on man bags) – trying at distance to clout each other is a strange but effective one.

Mind, if you've ever seen two Geordie women fighting it's no lightweight duel, it can be a blood and snot tear-up, and have you seen the size and weight of some handbags? They could render a rhino unconscious! Nonetheless, we know instinctively what it means and why it works.

As it became more entrenched it began to get shortened to, 'It was just a bit of handbags' and now the word can be used in any sentence without introduction, as in, 'There was some handbags between Terry and Defoe.'

It will probably leak out of football into wider society to be used to describe such behaviour. It may also evolve further to describe verbal jostling and not just physical behaviour as in, 'Nicholson's argument with the tax inspector was just a bit of handbags.'

The growth of the media, especially TV, has increased the speed with which words and phrases can catch on, be hip, become clichéd and then dropped.

A good example of this was Iain Dowie's expression 'bouncebackability', an entirely made-up word to describe his side's powers to recover from a setback. This went from zero to hero within a few weeks, being picked up by the media and reused by other pundits in 2008. Briefly it was a cool word. But perhaps because it was so distinctive, like a catchy pop song it quickly became tired and over-used and by 2010 was rarely used at all.

Others are more durable. Take 'the mixer', for example. The mixer is where you put the ball when time is running out and you're desperate for a goal. 'Stick it in the mixer,' comes the cry. In other words put the ball into the penalty area and hope that something happens.

I think the mixer was invented by ex-WBA, Man. Utd and Villa manager Big Ron Atkinson. I don't recall it being used even twenty years ago. However Big Ron's language has survived longer than his career as a pundit, which was tragically cut short by his infamous racist outburst at Marcel Desailly, albeit one he thought no one could hear. Despite doing programmes to 'prove' he isn't a racist, he's never been let near a commentary again.

However his great legacy to the game lives on in a series of expression, in a language that came to be known as Ronglish. Along with 'the mixer', 'early doors' has also stuck with us and I use it myself all the time outside of a football context. Early doors is a weird one because the crucial word in the phrase is early and that would do fine on its own to describe the situation because early doors just means it's early in the game. The 'doors' is essentially superfluous, but they add so much somehow. He claims he didn't invent it but he most certainly popularised it.

'The keeper has gone down in instalments there' is another magnificent expression that is still trotted out when someone goes to ground slowly, often in a rather arthritic manner. The 'Hollywood ball' has many great days ahead of it too as possibly the finest way to describe a flashy, outrageously difficult pass. This is already mutating in to he's gone Hollywood' as, like many of these expressions, it gets abbreviated and compressed.

Any player who has boundless energy and can run without tiring will at some point be said to have 'a good engine on him' which again was, if not Ron's own invention, one he made widespread. How else could that attribute be expressed other than with that term? It is perfect.

And someone giving a tackle, or a shot or anything else on the pitch his total commitment, will be said to have given it 'the full gun', which is more Ronglish.

However, some were so quintessentially his expressions that no one else seems to dare use them. They're like sacred songs that no one dares to do a version of. Only Ron can use 'spotter's badge' as a compliment to a player who sees a pass or movement before anyone else does. Similarly, 'The Reducer' is off limits. The Reducer is the hard tackle a defender puts in on a player, usually a creative player, early in the game. What a stunning expression, succinctly suggesting that the ferocity of the tackle reduces that player's ability to influence the game. The Reducer. Its genius shorthand is so innately Ronglish that it cannot be used by anyone else. It stands in splendid isolation, hermetically sealed in Ron's world. It lives out there with other classics such as 'lollipop', his word for a step-over, and giving it the 'little eyebrows', meaning a near-post glancing header.

Ron's influence in football language is unrivalled. In a few years, by constant exposure on TV, his phrases became embedded in the football nation's consciousness and dictionary. No one has invented so many expressions to better express what are often complex moves or action on a football pitch and he added so much enjoyment to the game on TV.

His originality was a welcome counter-weight to football's long-running love affair with what, after decades of repeated use, became football clichés. The 'boy done good' has been used for as long as I've watched football but lately seems to have finally fallen out of favour. The same can be said for 'a game of two halves'.

No one except American TV commentator Tommy Smyth refers to the goal as 'the onion bag' any more, though it was very common in comics when I was a boy.

As a kid, the cliché I liked best, often said by a player or a manager after a bad game was, 'I'm as sick as a parrot.'

No one says it any more – the sick parrot died in the early 1990s – but it was very common in the 1970s and 1980s. Origins of the phrase are, as ever, many and varied. Some say it dates back to a seventeenth-century play, others to an outbreak of bird flu in the 1920s, or a corruption of 'sick as a pierrot', referring to the pale and miserable face of that French pantomime character.

I always thought that it was at least revived in the 1970s through Monty Python's dead parrot sketch, though on reflection, I can't imagine many footballers were fans of the surreal, educated Python humour. Sick as a parrot's cousin at the time was 'over the moon' – almost everyone was over the moon after a good result. While not as extinct as the parrot it has nonetheless also waned.

These phrases emerge from a kind of primordial swamp of words and become common currency for many years and then, just as mysteriously, they fade away again. It's interesting how some terms become entrenched regardless of how times change. Substitutes are still said to be on the bench even though the days of there being a bench to sit on are long gone. Today they should really be described as 'on the silly racing car seats'. Managers are still said to sit in the 'dug out'. But there aren't any old-school hole-in-the-ground dug outs any more; more usually they sit in what appears to be a glorified bus shelter.

As tactics have changed so has the terminology used to describe positions. Such terms as 'inside right' and 'left half' have died out but centre-forward, full back and centre-half have all remained. It's an illustration of the shifting sands that the language of football is based on. A recently invented positional term has been the 'Makelele role' which is essentially a defensive midfielder.

Playing 'a man in the hole' is also a recent creation, dating back maybe less than ten years, even though sides have always played with a man in the hole, a slightly withdrawn striker who floats between midfield and forwards.

Perhaps the most interesting positional expression is that of 'sweeper', a player who sweeps up behind the defence as though his boots are metaphorical brushes.

As a teenager I found the world of football was a rich linguistic feast, an education in simile, metaphor, euphemism and imagery. So much so that when, in an English class, we had to write a project to read out to the class, I did mine on the unique language of football. This was a naked excuse to swear in class while pretending it was an analysis of the lingo of the game.

In fairness to the teacher, she played along with it. However, while somewhat juvenile, it nonetheless hints at just how unique a place a football ground is when it comes to words. Here's an extract from it. Bear in mind this was written in 1975.

'If you go to see Middlesbrough play football, you will hear some expressions that you will not hear anywhere else, such as 'Get right up his arse!' This is a term, always delivered at high volume, which expresses a desire for your teams' player to mark an opposition player very closely. It does not literally mean the fans want the player to get up the other player's arse in anyway whatsoever. It is not to be taken literally.

'Similarly, when the fans chant 'The referee's a wanker' after he has made what they consider to be a bad decision, they are not actually making a comment about his predilection to masturbate. It is an insult used to express displeasure with the quality of the official. However, many have pointed out that this is a confusing insult as most of those using it as a term of abuse will actually indulge in masturbation too. They are quite literally wankers themselves.'

I imagine the teacher thought I was a little smart arse but it went down well with my contemporaries. While I'd primarily been motivated by finding a way to be rude in class, I was genuinely interested in the language of crowds and continued to be so.

Banter between fans can verge on the surreal. I once went to see Barnsley play and the south Yorkshire crowd, a bluff, dour bunch at the best of time, delivered extended metaphors with a dry, unflinching wit. In a piece I wrote, I called them the Barnsley Surrealist Collective.

As one of the home team players failed to control a ball, an old fella piped up, 'Ey up lads they're playing with the rubber ball again!' As a striker, with only the goalkeeper to beat, knocked it wide of the post, another fan shouted, "He couldn't put the fuckin' kettle on in our house, that lad.' And as if to encourage the Barnsley team to play better, another Yorkshire wag bellowed, 'Come on lads, give it double giro.'

Double giro? Rubber ball? Kettles? Where did all this banter come from? It seemed to have grown organically out of the local football community. I'd never heard those expressions anywhere else before or since. No one seemed to think this was odd language. In its own way it is a form of poetry, illustrating the action with a tangential metaphor or analogy.

My pal Harry recounts a story of being at Middlesbrough in the early 1970s and looking out at the fabulous green sward of Ayresome Park at half time with the Boro 2–0 down.

'At least the pitch looks great,' he said to an old bloke beside him.

'Bloody should do the amount of shit that's been on it,' was the crisp, sour, instant response.

It's that clever, funny and yet totally unforced humour that you can only get from being at a football match. It's an attractive, rich, very local culture.

At least as rich was the world of rock music that I had also fallen in love with. There was so much to learn and understand, starting with the basics. We now routinely call rock music rock 'n' roll. It's become a catch-all term that includes all variations of the genre. However, in the 1960s and 1970s rock 'n' roll meant the music of the 1950s: Bill Haley, Little Richard, Chuck Berry, Jerry Lee Lewis and the rest of them. Rock 'n' roll was for Teddy Boys and not the music of the long hairs, which was more usually called heavy rock back then.

The term heavy metal, now commonly used for much guitar music, was rarely if ever deployed in the 1970s to describe bands like Sabbath that were subsequently labelled with it. If it was used it was a bit of an insult, suggesting a lack of subtlety. It wasn't until the early 1980s and the rise of NWOBHM (New Wave of British Heavy Metal) that the term gained credibility and fans.

Progressive rock is an interesting term designed to describe the more complex, extended music being made in the late 1960s by groups such as The Nice and The Moody Blues. It soon got abbreviated to just 'prog rock' and then simply 'prog'.

Prog was the beast meant to be slain by punk; except it wasn't.

It just hung around and then evolved into the modern format that is prog metal, a more muscular, less pastoral version of the original prog.

Being into 'prog' said much about you in the 1970s. It really divided people every bit as much as punk did. Those like me who loved it and would seek out even the most obscure purveyors of it such as Jade Warrior and Fruupp, found it filled up our imaginations like nothing else. Those who hated it found it to be self-important hippy wank. This meant the word 'prog' had power, because it was so divisive by the mid- to late-1970s and ever since.

The expression 'rhythm and blues' has had an equally interesting etymology. It was originated by future Atlantic Records man, Jerry Wexler, in the 1940s. He worked at the time for *Billboard*, the legendary American chart and music industry magazine. At the time it was used to describe almost any music that was being made by black people. Previously, this had been called race music, though surely all music is race music as everyone belongs to some race or other? By the 1960s it was the music on labels such as Stax Records that best embodied it, played by people like Carla Thomas, Sam Cooke, Wilson Pickett and many more. R&B became a style that anybody of any race could play, even white boys like the excellent Frankie Miller, in my view one of the best R&B singers we ever produced here.

But somewhere in the 1980s it began to mutate to mean a more polished, pop/soul-orientated music and today it is embodied by the likes of such booty shakers as Beyoncé. The marketeers, especially in the States, ever keen to invent a category to pigeonhole everything, have now created the Urban Contemporary chart for R&B. When and why did 'Urban' come to mean black? Urban people are of all races, surely? But there you have it, the English language is there to be used and abused.

All such terms were important as a kid growing up because you allied yourself to them and were consequently defensive about them. I spent later teenage years avoiding getting my head kicked in by Mods and punks, the latest Mod revival producing a new breed that looked down upon hairy rockers like me and mine.

These terms had so much more than an image associated with

them, they were a by-word for a whole set of cultural assumptions. As though being a rocker involved signing up for a manifesto so that everyone in denim with long hair believed and thought the same things. As a teenager I actually thought this was true, but this was obviously ridiculous and was proved to be so when time and again, people who liked the same bands as me turned out to be absolute twats and others who liked punk and new wave were lovely. So that was a good lesson to learn: not to judge a book or a sub-cult by its cover.

Once I picked up guitar though there was a whole new set of jargon to learn. Hurrah! There is much underrated pleasure in the jargon of your hobby or passion. It binds it to you; it makes it yours because it excludes those who are not interested and gives you a secret language. So with gusto I began learning about truss rods, big muffs, headstocks, compression units, noise gates, attack, and decay and sustain.

The place to go to educate yourself in these matters was a guitar shop, but a guitar shop for the non-player or the recently started player is an intimidating place. In the 1970s on Teesside it was full of men who looked like Gordon Giltrap: mid-thirties, lots of hair and a pallid complexion that suggests going outdoors was only a rare event for them. They were serious musicians, or rather they thought of themselves as serious musicians. When punk came along they absolutely hated it because it was three chords or fewer and none of them a diminished seventh. They had invested so much in being serious musicians that the sudden popularity of music played by amateurs was an insult. These were the people that punk loved to tweak the nose of.

Personally, I thought of the best punk rock as little different to non-punk rock. I loved The Stranglers, Elvis Costello, Penetration, Siouxsie and the Banshees, The Sex Pistols and The Clash. I wasn't supposed to, of course, being also mad for UFO, Thin Lizzy, Zep etc. at the time. This may have been a sign of my open-mindedness but also an acknowledgement of the fact that a lot of the punk and new wave girls looked fantastic in their tight, drainpipe jeans and ripped tops and so it was worth keeping your hand in, as it were, with other forms of music, to give yourself the maximum chance of pulling a lass. Lust is perhaps the most powerful cultural motivator.

I drew the line at disco though. Disco was the prime music of the late 1970s. It was the music of the masses and you had the best chance of pulling on a Friday night if you went to discos and liked disco girls. I just didn't though. It didn't hit my buttons. I needed loud guitars like I needed food.

So growing up in the arms of both music and football provides their followers with a whole lexicon of expressions to use and continues to do so. It gives everyone a kind of literary education even without your being aware it's going on; it is an exercise in euphuism, imagery, simile, metaphor, consonance, synaesthesia, metonymy, periphrasis, synecdoche and, if you're especially lucky, a bit of polysyndeton; inducting you into a world of clever and vivid expressions. It gives us access to a private club and keeps all those who do not share the passion outside and everyone, at least sub-consciously, loves that feeling; it binds us to the culture. It makes it ours.

Now I must go and watch a WAG play with her big muff.

9
Travel

IN the last twelve months I've flown to Las Vegas, Los Angeles, San Francisco, Amsterdam, Copenhagen, London, Manchester and, er, Bristol. I'm not exactly part of the International Jet Set; does the Jet Set even exist any more? It sounds very 1960s doesn't it? Well I guess we're all in the Jet Set now because a lot of us fly around the world in a way which was unimaginable thirty years ago.

Until I was in my mid-twenties I had been outside of the UK only once, to Switzerland with the school when I was eleven. This wasn't as unusual as it now would seem.

As you'll know if you're of a certain age, the working and lower-middle classes didn't travel that much until the 1980s, often never going abroad. While the Spanish package holiday had taken off in the late 1960s and early 1970s, it wasn't the kind of thing my mam and dad would do. The idea of being surrounded by bluff miners and their thick-forearmed wives from Barnsley on the piss for two weeks filled them with horror. That was too much like the world they had grown up in. They had spent their lives struggling in vain to become lower-middle-class to get away from it.

Add to that some innate xenophobia and the idea that foreign food was essentially inedible poison and their impulse to travel overseas was quite stunted. As kids we went on holiday to glamorous places like Scarborough, Whitby or Flamborough Head (it's not an actual head) and in the summer these places were packed with lots of people, many of whom had travelled fewer miles than the fifty we'd travelled from Hull.

They were simply not that adventurous. My dad had spent the war in Africa and since being demobbed didn't seem to feel the need to go abroad again; indeed, to my knowledge he didn't go further afield than Yorkshire or County Durham for twenty-five years until a 1970 week's holiday in Torquay. He was following in a family tradition as my granddad Fred didn't leave Yorkshire for over sixty years and, as far as I could tell, had absolutely no desire to do so.

Again, while this might seem plain weird to the modern mind, it wasn't so at the time. We live in a faster, more mobile society where travel is cheap and we are all much, much more wealthy, have more leisure time and have access to credit to allow us to fly 6,000 miles for less than £300. This, to my mind, is brilliant even if some middle-class people wring their hands and pretend we're killing the planet by doing so. Usually the people who are so concerned are the ones who have been doing it all their lives and have, if anyone has, caused the problem in the first place, and now seek to deny others the lavish pleasures they have enjoyed for their whole lives, seemingly oblivious to the fact that it is bloody easy to do without something when you've had your fill of it.

There are few worse sights in Britain than the middle class in full liberal moralising mode, lecturing us scummers on how to live. Fuck you. It makes me want to do the exact opposite of what they say just to spite the bastards and I'm sure I'm not alone in that.

Of course, if my parents had been football fans of a successful club, we might have been a little more adventurous in our travel because following football was traditionally one of the few ways in which many of the labouring classes managed to see parts of the country that were more than a few miles away.

I didn't go to away games until I was older but in junior school I knew a kid who did, along with his dad, uncle and other assorted Middlesbrough fans. They hired a noisy diesel mini-bus which sounded like it was permanently on the verge of breaking down and would go to all away games they could get to and from without missing work. He came back with tales of distant exotic lands such as Birmingham, Nottingham and – most glamorous of all – London.

In the mid-1970s London was a long way from the north east. Obviously, it's still as far now, but it feels much nearer. The city had a mythic quality. If you wanted something rare, unusual or just not available on Stockton High Street, shopkeepers would shake their heads and say, 'You'll have to go to London for that.'

It was an odd relationship because London, as well as being the capital and repository of any material desire you could wish for, was also, well, The South. And The South was not a good thing when you were northern. The South was weak, untrustworthy and flashy compared to The North, which saw itself as strong, dependable and honest.

Now, if you're a Southerner, don't take offence at this. It was always a very flawed notion.

But I grew up with The South being used by everyone from friends, neighbours and teachers and – later in the 1980s – even my bank manager, as a derogatory term to describe anything soft, insubstantial, flighty or jumped-up.

Indeed, Alan – a bank manager who worked for the NatWest on Grainger Street in Newcastle in the mid-1980s – once said to me, 'Long may there be a north–south divide.' He was suspicious of the yuppie, wide-boy element creeping into City banking and twenty-odd years on, all his worst fears have come true.

He was the last of the generation of bank managers that treated you as a person, not a customer or a computer reference number. He had no annoying jargon, didn't look twenty-three and wear a cheap suit. He hadn't been on a course to learn how to deal with the public. Instead, radically, he sat there, listened and made up his own mind. I don't even know if bank managers exist any more, do they? They've probably been reinvented as Customer Unifying Numerical Transaction Servers and assigned an appropriate acronym.

But all this anti-southern bias was rather odd because as kids we didn't know any southerners nor had we ever spent time in the south. Consequently, I gained an early impression that The South was a different land, a through-the-wardrobe kind of Narnia.

'Down South' was sold to me as a place to define yourself against, but it was a confused concept from the start. Sheffield was 120 miles south of where I lived but wasn't Down South. It was still The North. But Watford or Bromley definitely were. Yet Exeter or Bristol wasn't. That was the West Country, which though down south wasn't Down South the way London and the Home Counties were.

This makes no logical sense at all and confused a small, quizzical boy like me. When my granddad would tut at someone on the TV who was saying something he didn't agree with, if he didn't have a broad northern accent, he'd make a clicking noise with his tongue and witheringly say 'bloody southerners'. As I say, I hadn't actually met any southerners so when very small I thought of them as a different race of people, like Hobbits perhaps, or some kind of web-footed tribe.

This regional apartheid has diminished somewhat in these days of greater travel and less insular local communities. Our horizons have expanded, in part thanks to travelling to see away games, and thank the lord for that. However, I like to take pride in my roots in the north east but without it being a stick to beat people born in places such as Watford and Bromley with. That being said, after eighteen years of north–south divide indoctrination, I do occasionally find myself thinking 'typical southerner' when the latest fashion victim, Danny Dyer-type cockney gob-shite or blinged-up nancy-boy footballer prances on to the TV screen; some things go too deep.

It's hard not to admire those fans who follow their sides home and away, especially if you live in the north east or Carlisle, because you will have some round trips of over 600 miles. That's dedication – and being the most dedicated they're also usually the most vocal, supportive fans too.

It's not unusual these days to only hear the away fans singing at a football game, especially at some of the big clubs who attract glory hunters, business suits on a freebie, and others just there to witness the spectacle rather than support the home side.

When I began to go to away games, usually with a group of other fans, I loved the bond and excitement in venturing to other clubs to support your side. The dedicated away fan is a different breed to the home fan, with a tougher mentality and psyche, having been hardened by travelling into the belly of the beast.

You have to get there, find a pub you won't get beaten to a pulp in, preferably one selling toasties; find your way to the ground and the right turnstiles, all the while being surrounded by the opposition. It raises the blood pressure and it binds you all together in adversity.

This was especially true in the 1970s and 1980s when violence was at its worst and you really took your life into your hands outside of an opposition ground.

These days the policing around grounds is strict and the organisation to get away fans in and out of the ground more rigorous, sometimes unnecessarily so. Most away fans these days are not hardcore nutters looking for trouble and there's often no reason at all to keep them penned in the ground for half an hour after the game like dangerous wild animals. For anyone who grew up going to the game in the 1970s and 1980s, the atmosphere in and outside of grounds today is like a vicar's tea party in comparison (without the kiddie fiddling). While there are occasional resurgences of old-school hooliganism with running fights in the streets, these are very much the exception.

The cost of both tickets and petrol may be some of the reasons behind a decline in away support numbers in recent years. Some clubs have also restricted tickets for away fans to reduce the chance of trouble.

There was a time until the mid-1960s when the authorities assumed people could behave themselves well enough without turning a city centre into a military state for the afternoon. This was because during the pre- and post-war years there was little, if any hooliganism. Fans of each side could stand side-by-side on the terraces without having an urge to kill each other. Who knew humans could be so civilised? Presumably, having been at war for six years, people were ready for a little peace.

There was no trouble even though people turned up at games with wooden rattles heavy enough to render someone unconscious with one finely timed blow. Wooden rattles always struck me as a bizarre tool to express support. How does the clacking sound of wood on wood express your support any more than, say, clapping? In fact, such instruments of pleasure have a long history dating back at least to the 1490s when they were used as bird-scarers. Later there are accounts of farm boys making themselves wooden rattles to keep amused during the long dark winter months when there was little to do except stare at the fire and pick an orifice or two. Quite how and when people thought, 'I know: I'll take that bird-scarer to the football', is not certain but I'm sure it was early on in the game's development. We should just be glad they didn't pick up a scythe or some sort of whittling tool or we'd have had mass slaughter at some grounds.

Anyway, this lightly policed post-war peace was shattered in the 1960s and the tabloid press created the word 'hooliganism' to describe the running battles outside and inside football grounds. It all plugged into the outrage at the Mods vs Rockers fights on Brighton beach. The word itself had emerged in the 1890s to describe London street gangs and may have an Irish origin. By 1904 Conan Doyle was already using it, so it had entered the lexicon quickly. Had it existed fifty years earlier it may well have been used to describe outbreaks of violence at football games, because hooliganism is not a modern invention by any stretch of the imagination.

In Derby in 1846 a football match erupted into such violence that it caused the Riot Act to be read and soldiers sent in to quell a rebellious crowd. There are numerous reports of pitch invasions at the end of the nineteenth century. So while the tabloid press and the knee-jerk reactionaries will always want you to believe that we currently live in a uniquely awful, lawless era, this is, as the vernacular would have it, utter shite. People have been kicking lumps out of each other on and off the pitch since football began and indeed well before.

As hooliganism grew throughout the 1970s, as usual, some blamed the media, others blamed the drink; others still thought it was symptomatic of a wider decline in morality. You'll see these arguments still being used for most of society's problems by reactionaries. But there's been an awful lot of research conducted by academics with beards and thick glasses into football hooliganism, possibly just because they liked sitting in dark rooms watching video footage of men kicking seven bells out of each other, and there are few firm conclusions to explain exactly why and when it happens. People can be absolute twats. It's in our nature as creatures. That's probably the closest you'll get to the truth.

Post-war, when crowds were at their biggest, supporters would travel on trains to games. Hull City's ground Boothferry Park actually had its own railway station; steam trains pulled in to bring fans right beside the ground. While long-distance ventures were less common, a Middlesbrough fan would often travel to places such as Leeds, Manchester, Liverpool, Nottingham and Sheffield, all of which were little more than an hour or two's train ride away. It got you out and about, away from the wife, kids, mother, father and everything else. It gave you a chance to get pissed as a fart too of course.

This great tradition was abused in the 1970s when it was a rite of passage for many an aspirant hooligan to break a British Rail 'football special' train into tiny pieces and drench it in piss and cover it in shit, all as part of the awayday experience. Contemporary reports detail how fixtures and fittings were not just smashed but were dismantled. Presumably fans turned up with a tool kit specifically to unscrew tables and rip out toilets and throw them from the moving train. This was serious deconstruction.

For a decade or two the football special train, chartered by British Rail to ferry supporters to and from games, was a regular thing. However, instead of becoming a cheap form of mass transport for people, they ended up being host to violent, destructive lunatics. West Ham's band of hooligans even got the name the Inter City Firm.

Mind, it wasn't all dirty protest and Doc Martens to the head; in the early 1970s the Football League actually owned a train called the *League Liner*. It was loaned out to clubs to use to take fans to and from a game, was kitted out with a disco, dining car and bar, even dancing girls and music pumped throughout the carriages. The players sometimes travelled with the fans too. What a fantastic idea. Very classy. That should be resurrected.

But with much of BR's old stock being broken into pieces by rampant hooligans, it was no wonder then that rail companies wanted nothing to do with them any more once the railways were shamefully privatised, though as recently as 2007 the deputy head of British Transport Police called for their reintroduction to better utilise his resources. Some clubs do lay on trains for their fans, more usually coaches, but the 'glory' days of the British Rail awayday is surely a thing of the past, much to the relief of everyone except train carriage repairers.

I never went on a football special. Their reputation went before them. They were guaranteed to host an orgy of destruction and violence. Instead we went packed six or seven to a car or on coaches and minibuses hired for the occasion. Many fans were moved around the country by these coaches. Travel the motorways of this country on a weekend and you'll pass a variety of coaches of all shapes and sizes crammed full of half-inebriated fans, scarves flying out of the windows and a pair of naked buttocks pressed to the back window. The coach trip is an ideal opportunity, free of the responsibility of driving, for a boozy day out. Back in the 1960s, crates of ale would be bought from the local pub – it was literally a wooden crate. In the 1970s we had Watneys Party Seven cans, which came with a little tap on. This was considered an amazing breakthrough; you could have a bar in your house. OK, no you couldn't, it was just a big can of beer with a tap on, but they were ideal for long coach trips.

We would line them up on the back seats and appoint a barman for the journey who would dispense drink into plastic glasses, coffee mugs or pop bottles. So much more civilised than a carrier bag of cans from Kwik Save.

Of course there are lunatics who do not wish to get drunk on the way to an away game and they tend to use a thing called a car.

With the growth of car ownership the need to use the train or the bus diminished. Add to that the fact that you could travel without having a toilet thrown at your head by a psychotic jail bird or being forced to bare your arse in a minibus just outside of Scotch Corner, and this made it all the more appealing for some.

However, it created other problems, primarily where to park. Many football clubs were set in the heart of the community and were built when the idea that almost everyone would own a car would have been thought of as fantasy. Indeed, even as a kid in the 1970s, only the middle-class kids' parents had cars. My dad was given one as a perk of his job, ironically at British Rail offshoot Freightliners. Well, I suppose they couldn't give him his own train.

He and my mother saw the mustard-coloured Austin 1100 as very much confirmation of their newly elevated status in society. Personally, though I like old classic cars, driving has never interested me, possibly because to do it would involve sobering up and thus feeling the pain of existence all too brutally. So I never learned and never regretted it. I'd be a danger to you if I had. The roads are full of people who are too useless, stupid or uncoordinated to drive and I know I'd have been one of them. So next time you see me, thank me for not passing a driving test. I probably saved a few lives.

Since so many football grounds were set in the backstreets of our towns and cities, parking was severely limited. When new grounds were built, they were invariably on the edge of town surrounded by car parks. This gives them an especially soulless feel. Places like Bolton and Derby, both of which used to have tremendous, small, exciting grounds in the city centre, are now set on windswept, out-of-town concrete deserts. It really doesn't feel like progress.

Go to Newcastle and the whole city is dominated by the physical presence of St James' Park. It sits atop Gallowgate like a giant spaceship, bearing down on you as you go about your daily business. Even before it was developed, it was still a powerful force in the town. On match days it was impossible to be unaware of it as the noise would reverberate across the whole city. Whether you are a fan or not, there's no avoiding football in Newcastle, it literally affects everyone in a way that it just wouldn't if the ground was set out of town.

While the imperative to have modern stadia is understandable, taking clubs away from the communities that they sprang from has always seemed regressive to me, no matter how necessary it is for economic and safety reasons. It hints at the move of football away from being part of community culture and towards being another branch of the entertainment industry.

Here in Edinburgh, I often walk up Calton Hill which sits at the north end of Princes Street, sporting Nelson's monument on top. From there you can get a breathtaking 360-degree view of the city. To the north east sits Easter Road, Hibernian's ground, right in the heart of Leith. The panorama shows just how integrated the club is into the community, surrounded by Georgian, Victorian and post-war housing. If it were transplanted to an out-of-town development, it would leave a big cultural hole in Leith and it would disconnect the club from the local people who still turn up in their thousands to see them play. It'd be a lose-lose.

The early grounds of my football life are both no more: Hull's Boothferry Park and Boro's Ayresome Park. Both grounds were once considered so important, so good, that they hosted international games. Ayresome Park was even one of the grounds used in the 1966 World Cup. Thirty years later the gates were closed. Both have been replaced by out-of-the-box flat-pack stadiums which have none of the atmosphere or feel of the old grounds. The Riverside is at least 10,000 seats too big for the size of crowd the club can reasonably attract. This makes it quiet and a bit soulless as acres of unoccupied red plastic seats glare back at you.

Newcastle United is a great example of how developing a ground from its original location offers the possibility of modernisation while keeping it connected to the roots of the club. It's important also for the local economy and for away fans to have a ground in the city because it allows them to have a good time and spend money in the city centre before going to the match. Stick it on the edge of town and they tend to just go to the game and then leave.

When Middlesbrough fans travelled to away games, we didn't provoke much hostile emotion among many football fans. Even supposed local rivals Sunderland and Newcastle are, in my book, just trying to hate us, they don't really mean it. Thirty miles is way too far to sustain a proper rivalry, especially when you're never challenging for the same trophy. This meant that, compared with some clubs such as Leeds, Manchester United and Chelsea, home fans didn't seem too provoked by a few hundred Boro fans in their midst. However, by the mid-1980s this had changed and any fan was seemingly a target.

Thus it was that I found myself outside of Cold Blow Lane, home to Millwall. They had the crème de la crème of nutters called the Bushwackers. In 1985, an almighty battle against Luton fans at Kenilworth Road during a cup game left thirty-one policemen injured and one poor sod had been struck with a concrete block! I presume the concrete was liberated from the stadium walls rather than brought in to use in random acts of violence.

Seats were torn up and used as weapons. Only the appearance of Millwall boss George Graham, managed to quell fans for long enough for the game to kick off. Presumably, they were all scared of George.

In the late 1970s a similar incident at Ipswich led Tractor Boys boss Bobby Robson to say that Millwall fans should have had flamethrowers turned on them, which could actually be turned into a sport itself and one which many would pay to see. *Burn a Hooligan*. It's the next reality show.

So we'd gone down to see Boro play Millwall in 1985. Such is the nature of these incidents, it's impossible to know how or why they occur; all I knew was one minute we were walking away from the ground after the final whistle and the next, the six of us were surrounded by Millwall fans chanting in our faces. This despite my life-long practice of not wearing any football colours; maybe we just exuded a Teesside vibe or had a northern stench about us.

All of us were experienced football fans and knew that a bit of laughter and banter is the way to usually defuse these situations. This was something else though. This was like being surrounded by a pack of hyenas circling for a kill. The nominal leader of these men screamed at a girl in our party, 'We're going rape you and kill this black bastard', pointing at Hunter, the biggest and most black among us. Presumably they wanted the scalp of the big man as a kind of trophy.

This was genuinely, pant-shittingly terrifying. There are moments in life when with a cold certainty you know your life is in danger. The only other time I experienced anything so frightening was one night in Los Angeles when, during a stoned argument about music, a lad went to a cupboard and produced a large gun, better to express himself, and pointed it at me.

Hunter was the product of the loins of a West Indian sailor and a Middlesbrough barmaid. At six foot three, seventeen stone and with a hair style that can only be described as kind of collapsed afro, he was an intimidating sight. He was also totally fearless, having grown up in Dormanstown, a place rougher than most maximum-security jails. As well as being fearless, he was as hard as the iron that was mined out of the nearby Cleveland Hills.

So as this Millwallian screams he's going to rape his girlfriend and kill him, Hunter didn't bother to try and negotiate his way out of the situation instead he roared with mock laughter and in one move grabbed the Millwall lad with both hands around his head, bringing his knee up as he did so at great speed. The consequent high-velocity impact was bloody and rendered his assailant semi-conscious and howling in pain. A few backed off on seeing this, but it was too late, Hunter's blood was up. He whacked another lad, who was shoving me in the chest, in the face using only the hard part of his palm. That broke the bloke's nose open and sent him flying. Somehow, two more were on his back, with us, including Sandy, the girl, trying to drag them off. But there was no need because Hunter despatched one with an elbow to the eye socket that Alan Shearer would have been proud of, while wrestling another to the floor.

What had been a crowd surrounding us just melted away, leaving the first Millwall fan still coming in and out of consciousness on the ground and Hunter kneeling on the chest of a skinhead, slapping him in the face shouting, 'I thought you were going to kill me! Come on, give us a smile you cockney cunt.'

It had lasted no more than perhaps ninety seconds. The police rolled up, some were arrested, some detained, we all managed to slip away. As impressive as Hunter's performance had been – and I've no doubt it saved us from a kicking or worse – it was all too much for me. What was the point in all this? I like football, but I didn't like it enough for all this. So, like many people around that time, I stopped going. I'd had enough. If I'd wanted to fight a guerrilla war I'd have joined the army. This period was the apex of the hooligan pyramid.

It was a sign of the times. In rock 'n' roll things went a similar way, at least at festivals. If you went to Reading Rock Festival to see any number of NWOBHM bands in the early 1980s, bands and MCs faced a tsunami of cans filled with piss. In 1983 Steel Pulse were bottled off within minutes of taking the stage, their crime being to try to play reggae to a crowd of rockers and punks. Five years later, Meatloaf suffered the same treatment. Similarly, the Monsters of Rock festival as Castle Donington was going down the same road. The

MC, the much-missed Tommy Vance, used to conduct proceedings from inside an American football-style crash helmet to avoid being rendered unconscious by the tidal wave of bottles and cans. During Motorhead's set in 1986, someone let off a firework rocket at the stage. Two years later, two people were killed at the front of the stage while Guns n Roses performed, trampled underfoot in the mud. Oh the 1980s under Thatcher, those were the days, eh. Bliss.

Going to festivals is something you're supposed to enjoy; it's always been cool and groovy. But the reality, especially in Britain's climate, is that you are more than likely to suffer trench foot and could have more fun jabbing a sharp stick into your buttocks for three days. So apart from Knebworth, which was a one-day festival in the summer sun, the bucolic Fairport Convention festival at Cropredy and one quickly aborted Reading Festival, they've never held much attraction for me. You only need to visit one mile-long trench of 100,000 people's piss and shit to know you don't want to do it again.

My experience going on the road to see Middlesbrough play was occasionally combined with seeing bands to capitalise on the effort you'd made sitting cramped up in the back of someone's van or car. One such occasion was a visit to London for an Arsenal game. Neil Young was playing Earls Court so we arranged a doss with a Teesside ex-pat who was now living in Kings Cross. In what you might recognise as a bit of a theme, I got into an argument with our host about music. He, having previously enjoyed his rock 'n' roll had been 'converted' to the new synth pop of Depeche Mode. This was akin to madness in my eyes at the time. How could you trade in UFO for Depeche Mode? It was wrong. And I told him so. Luckily, he didn't have a big, fuck-off gun. But when you're essentially arguing, as I was, that not only was UFO musically better than Depeche Mode, it was actually morally superior music to the mincing, baggy-trousered Essex synth boys', it's really only fair enough to be told to fuck off, which is exactly what happened, leaving us without a doss for the night.

This meant that after Neil had left the stage, we had to spend the night on Kings Cross station; something you were allowed to do at the time without too much interference from the coppers.

Interference from whack-jobs was something else. The place seemed full of mentally deranged people who would wander up to you and start talking their own strange language.

However, as at the time I lived in Newcastle, this was entirely normal to me; indeed, one famous tramp spent most of his days in the Grainger Market holding an empty jar and approaching strangers with it, holding it up to your face as though showing you an exotic fish or insect. It was, of course, empty. But even though I was familiar with lunatics a night in the freezing cold was a bad outcome to a stupid argument.

The best part of thirty years later, I can see what an arse I was. But when you're young, your own taste is somehow definitive. However, while I can see the logical flaws with what I was saying, there's still a small part of me that thinks I was actually right. Depeche Mode became interesting only when they embraced the theatre and dynamics of rock 'n' roll. The difference is these days I'd never lose the chance of a free doss over an argument about that.

As for many of my generation, football and rock 'n' roll were the first cultural things to take me away from the home and down to London but also to such places as Sheffield, Edinburgh, Manchester, Leeds, Birmingham and many, many more towns. Had I supported a successful club I would have ventured into Europe.

So at a time when people from my background really didn't do a lot of travelling, football and music had taken me to parts of the country I would never have been to by the time I was eighteen or nineteen.

Football has in a very real sense expanded working-class horizons. It set an example that we later followed when going to gigs to see our favourite bands and helped progress the idea of a mobile, flexible northern workforce that was unafraid to travel to find a job and get on in life. This became essential as the old industries closed in the north to be superseded by service and IT industries, largely located in the south.

We think nothing of travelling these days. Want to go to Munich to see your team play in the Champions League? No problem, just hop on a plane at your local airport. Want to see Joe Satriani playing in Las Vegas? No problem, there's a flight leaving every day. But while we take all this for granted now, many of us have football to thank for getting us out and about in the world.

10

Relationships

YOU'RE sitting watching the game on TV and you're vaguely aware that someone has just come into the room and is talking about something . . . something about flour maybe but you're too engrossed in the action to pay it any attention. Bloody hell how did he miss that?!

When there's a break in play, you turn to see what the noise is all about and fall headlong into a row.

'You've not been listening to a word I said, have you?'

'Err, yes of course I have.'

'What did I say then?'

Your mind races; what was it now, flour . . . baking bread maybe. Say something, anything.

'You were saying you needed some flour. Are you doing some baking?'

Their face is like thunder. 'I need flowers! For my mothers' grave!'

They scream at you but out of the corner of your eye you can see someone has scored; however, to turn and look at it now would be fatal so you have to resist with all your willpower.

'You love football more than you love me!' they shout and storm out of the room, slamming the door.

You are now in deep doo-doo and all because you were preoccupied with the match. It's really not fair. You didn't mean any harm, you were sitting there quietly, minding your own business but now you have to miss the rest of the game to apologise and make it up. This is the sort of incident we football-focused people encounter to one degree or another all the time. No one gets so upset with someone who is distracted because they're reading Tolstoy or Dickens, now do they? No, they're lauded as intelligent, academics with their minds on higher things. Whereas your football fan is sneered at for shutting out the world while there's an important free-kick on.

At least in these days of multi-channels and TVs in every room, you don't have to worry about hogging the TV. It's the isolation that's the problem. Few people want to sit in the room with you while you're whining about John Terry's positional sense to no one in particular. So they get up and do something else, leaving you in splendid isolation.

Football and relationships is a complex often volatile subject. It starts with your parents. My dad would watch it if it was on TV, but then he'd watch underwater taxidermy if it was on the telly. He rarely took me to the game, doing so only after repeated nagging from me and long-winded orchestrated campaigns of brown-nosing my mother to get her to put pressure him. He'd watched Hull City in the post-war years but didn't seem to know much about them so I assumed he didn't go very often.

This wasn't untypical of aspirant lower-middle-class people in the 1970s. I think they saw football as belonging to the culture of the common folk that they were trying to get away from.

However, others are brought into the world by parents who are football-crazy and who indoctrinate their kids in the same traditions. This brings its own pressures because it means you are obliged to follow their side as well, which in turn means that when you go through your rebellious stage you can go against them by supporting someone else, preferably your local rivals, which can bring a lot of heartache for them but which will please the angry teenage soul.

Or maybe you don't like football – it is possible – and thus you are letting the family tradition down by your lack of interest which can also put a rift between you and them.

'What's wrong with you? Why don't you like footy? Are you gay?' You know the sort of thing.

As you grow up you face difficult choices: do you make friends only with other football fans? Many do because it's simply a lot easier. You're among sympathetic people. However, I can't recommend that way of life. We all need some outside perspective on our football lives to keep us the right side of sanity, but it's true that trying to explain and justify your utter obsession with the game is hard to do and it doesn't really stand up to logical scrutiny.

It can put a barrier between you and other non-football people. Sometimes I think it's a kind of autism, so incredibly focused are football people on the game, sometimes, – though not in my case – to the exclusion of almost everything else.

Andy, my pal who I worked with on the *Daily Record*, tells me there are Celtic and Rangers fans who count the number of words in an article on either of the clubs and if one team has more than the other, will write or call in to complain of the coverage being biased against their club. That is surely a sign of madness. But it does seem to completely fill some people's lives; they name their children after favourite players, they even tattoo themselves with the name of a player even though sometimes that player will be transferred not long after the ink is dry.

But those of us who are at least moderately aware that our sporting passion might appear slightly odd to the outsider try to present ourselves in a more favourable light.

You know what it's like: you meet a nice girl, she's great-looking and great fun but she doesn't like football. What the hell do you do? Do you hide your thirty-volume collection of Rothmans football annuals? Do you hide all the Panini sticker collections? How about your collection of football boots going back to 1976? How to explain the lucky pair of unwashed underpants? You know that if you admit how much your life revolves around football it will make you look bad. It will make you look a bit sad, a bit of a nerd and certainly not cool.

There's only one thing for it: you will have to pretend that you are much less interested in the game than you are. This will be very difficult because she'll inevitably want to go out on a date on the night of some really important game.

Early on in the relationship you'll tolerate having to miss the match because you are driven by a possibly greater passion than football. Sex.

But that will last only so long and you'll soon get caught in the pub being distracted by the scores on Sky Sports News. And the first time you ask her to be quiet as a match report comes in will be the make-or-break moment. If you've proved yourself to be a more fully rounded individual by now, then maybe she'll just accept it as part of your character. If you've not then you're screwed.

Growing up as a football-loving rock 'n' roll obsessive wasn't guaranteed to get you a lot of women. Most girls at school liked neither, so you had to cultivate at least a veneer of interest in other matters. I was lucky because I liked books and poetry and that was a bit of an in to the Eng. Lit. Girls and others, who were open to the idea that the male of species didn't have to be a macho monster, get into fights and use his own shit as hair gel.

But there was no doubt that you had to tone down your passion for both football and rock 'n' roll. To reveal the depth and extent of your obsession was a passion killer. The really cool kids did not pay attention to football – I knew that, so I kept it all a bit quiet in certain company. For a year or two it was like living a double life. I'd go out on a Saturday for a few drinks and then on to the football along with the rest of the working-class adult world, but outside of that I was apparently a slightly fey, bookish boy with an armful of albums and slim volumes of poetry. I've always enjoyed the dichotomy of the two worlds, actually.

But this isn't an exclusively male issue. Girls who grow up loving football face accusations of being too butch or even of being a lesbian, as though that would be a bad thing. Just as some lads are keen to express their macho credentials, equally some girls are keen to show how girly they are and this doesn't include liking sport. I call them macho girls and they are every bit as much a pain in the arse as macho men, forever wanting to wear pink, be 'addicted' to chocolate and witter on about self-appointed 'girly' matters.

Being a woman who likes football can also mean you get into terrible rows with insecure men who have such low self-esteem that they can't bear a woman knowing more than they do. It will almost certainly mean you are regularly patronised by men who will assume you're there only because you fancy the players or something equally facile. They'll also assume you know nothing about the game and probably try to explain the offside rule to you, which in turn may make you want to punch the stupid twat in the face.

Even now if I meet someone for the first time at a party, I breathe a sigh of relief if they're into football because it guarantees I can talk to them for pretty much the whole evening if necessary. It really takes the pressure off. You can't talk politics because unless they're on the same side as you, it's an instant hackles-up argument. Music can divide people in a similar way. If they can't bear heavy rock, what am I going to talk about? Rap? Nah. I don't think so. But we can all discuss what we think of football, players, teams and history. OK, you might end up rowing about something, but in my experience this is less likely, usually because they're also relieved to have found someone they can talk to and thus can avoid talking about interior decor or bloody soap operas with their partner's boring friend.

The non-football person has to learn to accommodate the football-obsessed and the football obsessed has to be aware of how demanding their passion for the game can be.

I was once best man at a wedding in Liverpool and as you'd imagine many of those attending were big Liverpool fans. Thus it was that during the wedding ceremony, someone was delegated to wear a radio earpiece to listen to the game and report the score. This led to muffled 'get ins' when they scored just as the bride was agreeing to honour and obey. This wasn't a new thing to the priest who seemed to take it all in good humour; maybe all his services were punctuated by such behaviour on Saturdays.

The problem we all face is trying to justify exactly why we need to spend so much time watching and mulling over football. It's one thing to enjoy the occasional game but another thing altogether to watch the Erevidise league coverage on a Sunday night or sit through six hours of *Soccer Saturday* on Sky which, when all is said and done, is just four men watching a television that you cannot see, an existential programme if ever there was one.

The question will inevitably come: 'Do you really enjoy this?' And nothing you can say will make enough sense to justify it. If you're like me and will watch any football wherever or whenever I come across it in life, you need a very patient partner, especially as you sit through a four-hour football discussion on the radio. You need to realise that you are being very over-focused on it and that it can make you incredibly selfish.

As I say, football is a broad church and holds all its acolytes under the same banner, but some are more on the fringes than others.

Gay football fans and gay footballers occupy one of the more distant outreaches. I knew a couple of gay blokes who went to the Boro for years, both of them in the closet at the time except to each other. At the time – this was late 1970s – your typical football fan thought that gay blokes would wear pink and ponce around in frilly panties. Seriously.

They couldn't have imagined that two blokes in jeans and T-shirts standing next to them were of that persuasion at all. Asking them both now, thirty years later, what their experiences were, they were both agreed that sexuality was never raised at all. There was no homophobic chanting and indeed, that had started in their experience only in recent years. I don't think it ever crossed anybody's mind that a footballer or a football fan might be gay when I was growing up. It wasn't in the forefront of people's minds. It was all a mystery to us, a hidden world that we'd sort of heard about but only in a kind of mythic way, like the lost city of Atlantis.

Even in the unprogressive 1970s, being gay didn't seem much of a big deal to me. This wasn't because I was some young hip cat, it was just that I couldn't see how it affected anyone who wasn't gay. So some lads like other lads. So what? I couldn't see the problem. I knew you were supposed to be offended but I couldn't see why I would be. It was no more offensive than finding out someone preferred the colour red over the colour blue to me.

The idea that we were surrounded by lesbians never occurred to us as teenagers. They were even more exotic and distant and mythical. Homosexuality was a male preserve, it seemed. There was never a female equivalent of a mincing poofter in 1970s sit-coms. The 1970s were a homophobic decade and for anyone growing up who wasn't straight life must have been incredibly difficult. Of course, in hindsight, I can now see that I went to school and was friends with lads who were actually gay, whether they knew it themselves or not at the time. Had I known I still wouldn't have been bothered, even though, as a 'proper' bloke, you were supposed to be appalled by such a thing.

I think it was Rod Stewart's 'The Killing of Georgie' hit single in 1976 that was responsible as much as anything for my relatively unusual attitude. It was the first song to use the word 'gay', and in very sympathetic terms. I loved Rod Stewart from The Faces, the epitome of the lads' night out good time rock 'n' roll band. But even without that example, I'd always thought that whatever way anyone is inclined is their own business and it didn't affect me one way or the other.

Of all the threats you faced as a lad, most of which involved being kicked in head or bollocks or being humiliated by older, more experienced girls, being turned gay against your will was not one you had to worry about. Not even when you shared a bed with the current Chairman of the Arts Council, which I once did, albeit in a non-sexual fashion. So I never understood the anti-gay vitriol which was commonplace in the 1970s even if you didn't experience it on the terraces.

It was just as well Rod had been open about such matters because football was and still seems to be in denial about gay footballers. There must be some. There are some. But in the macho environment of football, it's a big no-no. It's pathetic really, the last great taboo that the alpha male of the species just can't seem to accept with an open heart. Do they really fear getting a blow job in the showers or something? Would it really destroy team morale, as some claim? It's just sex after all, it's not nuclear war. It seems to be an unnecessary hang-up.

While your relationships will intersect with your football life for good or bad there's one relationship that is a forever bond, a marriage which you cannot divorce from: your relationship with your club.

Unless you are a promiscuous fan who flits from club to club, in which case you won't have a fan-to-club relationship, the bond between you and your team is like no other in life.

It's not like loving a band. It's not like loving another human. It's not like loving a pet.

It's strong and yet very nebulous. When you think about your club you feel affectionate, warm, protective, defensive and even nauseous perhaps. You recall all the good times and some of the sad times too. You have a personal history with the place. It has given you such pleasure, such love and such bitter disappointment.

Virtually the only thing you haven't felt for your club is sheer unadulterated lust, though there have been players down the years who, you know . . . if you had to . . . well, maybe.

The only way to describe a fan's life with the club is as a relationship. It's not like being loyal to a store, like always buying your knickers in Marks & Spencer. It's not like your admiration for a writer or for an actor. It's much more personal and intimate than that and this has always been part of football's great pulling power.

It's not being like being obsessed with a band, because it's much more prolific and public than that. No one would go and see their favourite band play thirty-eight times in nine months or forty-six times if you're in the Championship. The club is part of who you are. It's not divorced from you in any way; it is in your DNA almost. This was certainly the case for me.

As soon as I landed on Teesside as an eight-year-old and realised that I was to be a Middlesbrough FC fan, I set about researching the club. In the first half of the twentieth century, Boro were usually in the top flight, finishing third in 1914 and fourth in 1939. There seemed to be something about impending world war that brought the best out of the club, as they remain the two peak positions they have ever achieved. Presumably if we ever get into the top four, we can expect the breakout of conflict within weeks.

From the mid-1950s we were in the second division – never lower than fourteenth never higher than fourth – ticking along quite nicely if undramatically. In 1973–74 we won the second division with a record points total and began an eight-season run in the top flight mid-table. Since then we've gone down to the third tier, nearly gone out of business, got promoted to the Premier League, got relegated from the Premier League, got promoted again and . . . err . . . well . . . relegated again.

It's an unpretentious club to support. I always loved its location set in the terraced backstreets of the town. Ayresome Park seemed to grow organically out of the streets that surrounded it. It was physically exciting in a way that the Riverside, no matter how superior it is in terms of facilities, simply isn't. This may be because I'm older. I can imagine that being eight and going to the Riverside for the first time is a thrilling new experience, if only because it would be like no place you'd ever been before. The sound of several thousand people cheering is a thrilling thing. The sound of the same thousands sitting in silence or yawning is equally impressive but in a different kind of way.

The way I see it, the Boro are a lovely plain girl who doesn't dress herself up fancy, who occasionally bangs like a shit-house door in a gale. She never going to be flashy or glamorous but she's reliable.

The Boro doesn't go in for many grand gestures or have especially high ambitions at any time. I rather like this. Cynics will say it's just a coping strategy for a fan of a club that doesn't win anything very often but I genuinely like supporting a club that isn't a high achiever but isn't a major loser either. We've never been in the fourth tier and that's surprising really because it's a small club in a small town which has consistently punched well above its weight.

We'd spent fourteen out of fifteen years in the Premier League before getting relegated last year, which was a pretty impressive run really and it was probably time for a spell in the Championship. No one else agrees with this but I think it does a club good to be relegated occasionally. It's a chance to reboot the whole place and rejuvenate it. People worry it can be the start of a long-term decline, but if the club is run sensibly, that shouldn't happen and under the steady, guiding hand of Chairman Steve Gibson, Boro seems to be a stable, well-run place.

The great thing about relegation is that it means that the next season, more than likely, you'll win a load more games. This should not be discounted. Even in a weaker league winning games counts big on the fan pleasure index. Personally, I have no interest or passion in hanging on to seventeenth place, winning six out of thirty-eight games and just surviving in the Premier League. I'd much rather win sixteen games and finish mid-table in the Championship. Why?

Because winning is more fun and because in the second tier you have the chance to push for promotion, whereas a club like Boro is never going to get in the higher reaches of the Premier League; we've peaked at seventh and I think that was a massive over-achievement which cost the club a lot of money too, money we didn't have and subsequently had to tighten belts to recover from.

Mere survival after a few seasons is just plain dull. I'd much rather be a yo-yo club; that's the best of all worlds to me. But I know I'm very much in a minority of about one on this, as usual.

As all fans of clubs who rarely achieve much know – and that's most fans – it gives us a perspective on football that people who have always supported a successful club can never have. When you hear fans of Arsenal or Chelsea or Manchester United whining that their club has lost five or six games this season and what a disgrace it is, we can see it more easily as over-reaction. Maybe lower league fans are a calmer, less hysterical bunch. We don't expect much and are happy with smaller victories.

I suspect this is why I don't care what non-Boro fans think of the club, pro- or anti-. You'll hear many fans of big clubs arguing with vitriol in defence of attacks on their club. They seem overly concerned about what complete strangers think of their club – often to the point of paranoia. This is quite amusing for us dispassionate observers.

Whether the club's character affects your own character I'm not sure, but I do think it is one of the colours in the rainbow; or perhaps you adjust to fit in with the fortunes and culture of the club. I do know that many long-time Boro fans share similar characteristics: a certain world-weariness, an air of pessimism, an ability to laugh in adversity, chronic self-deprecation, and a bleak sense of humour. I simply can't imagine supporting a successful club and I actually think it would make me feel uncomfortable. I never feel more comfortable and happy with the Boro than when they're a bit mediocre. It seems natural.

While some of the media and the more alpha male pundits and fans will tell you that winning is everything and second is nowhere, I would counter that notion by saying having a good time is the be all and end all of football. Shanks always did have his tongue in his cheek when he said football was more important than life and death;

an ex-miner who had grown up with the fatal dangers of the pit would never be so flippant about such matters.

Football offers us a personal, private relationship. It can be with a club or with the game itself. It is a living, breathing entity. OK so you can't dress it up in leather, kiss it, put your hands down its trousers, ride it till it screams or call it darling, but it will provide you with support, comfort, passion and humour in a way that many relationships in your life simply can't or won't ever match.

So is it any wonder that the game has become so embedded into so many people's lives for so many generations? We're in love with it, man.

11

Future

JUST after the Second World War, football crowds were at an all-time high with a total attendance figure of over 41 million. Football had never been more popular. Yet if you didn't like football, you could easily ignore it. Apart from the crowds around the ground and the match reports on the back pages, there were few other means by which the game would intrude in your life. There may have been a Pathé news reel at the cinema with a few minutes' report on a Cup Final but that's all.

Spin forward sixty years and football is less popular in terms of crowd numbers but it is all-pervasive. You can't get away from the game. It's all over TV and radio, it's on the news, it's on the newsstands, it's in the shops. It's gone from being a sport people watched and played locally, to being played out to a global audience. Even non-football fans can tell you half the England side simply because they're exposed in the mainstream media so often.

It's been a massive change, not so much in the amount of people who are interested in football but more in how they express and enjoy that interest.

So what does the future hold? Will it continue to be the great love of the British people; or is it an affair that is on the wane? It's hard to think it's going to get even more exposure or become even more popular. The top flight is on maximum exposure at the moment. I suspect at some point in the future clubs will be able to negotiate their own TV rights and in return for a subscription you'll be able to watch every game your club plays on the internet. In that sense, any increase in exposure will be very 'niche' and targeted. It's less likely to be an increase of big TV events. But equally, the popularity of the game is not likely to drop if only because, if you tire of your local club, or the league they play in, there's always so many other alternatives to watch.

There is talk of changing how football's covered on TV, such as letting cameras in dressing rooms and interviewing managers pitchside during the game. This was done very well by Rebecca Lowe on Setanta during their short period covering the Blue Square Premier. It's a lot of extra fun, for sure, but such changes are just cosmetic. Even if they instal on-pitch cameras in players' heads, it'd just be a superficial dalliance and while it might entertain us briefly, it wouldn't make anyone watch who wasn't already interested.

While top-flight football dominates as the national sport, there are those who would argue it's driving young people away from the game due to high prices and that without the addiction of the live game to go to, their interest is more shallow and thus more likely to wane as other distractions come along. I tend to sympathise with this view. There were few other distractions for us as kids so we were thrown into the arms of football from an early age and it went deep into our cultural DNA.

While the popularity of the game is obvious for everyone to see, there are nonetheless many issues that are alienating people from the game. The level of wages paid to players has sickened many who can't stomach seeing someone – especially a less than stellar player – earning twice as much in a week as they would in three years. Whatever the arguments of supply and demand you might want to throw at this attitude by way of defence, the fact remains that these inflated wage levels just feel fundamentally wrong; they are simply against natural justice.

Many argue that rock and movie stars earn huge money, so why not footballers? This is to make a fundamental error. Footballers are paid a wage regardless of their performance, whereas performers' income is related to sales. You can be on a three-year contract, play like a drain and get the same money.

It's also the attitudes which go with this wealth – best expressed by Ashley Cole's infamous explosion at being offered 'only' £55,000 a week – which alienate many. When you hear that a player such as Shaun Wright-Phillips is hustling for an improved deal on his 70k a week with two years still to go on his contract, despite not even being a first-team regular, it looks a lot like greed and it's certainly not edifying.

However, fans who tire of this tend not to reject football as a whole, they just go and watch lower league football instead.

The local tribal element, so strong for so many years, has never been weaker at grounds such as the Emirates, Old Trafford or Stamford Bridge, all of which have become 'leisure break' destinations. People from all over the country will plan a weekend away around the one or two games they can get tickets for. Football tourism might be good for the box office but it keep prices high and thus excludes many more dedicated fans from being able to go. But money talks and that's all that counts in today's market.

The grounds themselves have never been quieter, partly as a result of football tourism. This again has been a huge cultural shift. Fans used to see it as their duty to inspire their team; now it's the other way around. Games at many grounds are quiet until something happens. Through a life spent watching television and other media, we have become a reactive culture as opposed to a proactive one. We are, in effect, saying, I've paid my money, now entertain me. You'd think today's spectators were at the theatre rather than at a football match; indeed, fans are sometimes told to sit down by other fans and stewards.

If I was a kid growing up with the current football culture would it be so inspiring as it was to me when I was young? Well, there's no doubt it is still capable of stirring the soul like few other things in life. That hasn't changed. And the urge to collect memorabilia and wear shirts etc. seems as strong too.

Yet, while the visceral power of football still exists, there are so many other cultural distractions that simply didn't exist in the 1960s and 1970s. It's also true that kids experience the game in a different way these days, especially through television and other media.

There's more of everything. Much, much more. Everything is more instant You can download any music you want for little money. You can stream music or exchange files with anyone anywhere in the world. All we could do was tape our mates' albums and that tape would inevitably unravel or play with a disturbing amount of wow and flutter. Whether this makes everything more disposable, less precious, is open to question but I'd assume that to some extent it does. A download doesn't cause the same ripples of social interaction that carrying Humble Pie's classic double live album *Rockin' the Fillmore* did in my youth. It defined you in public. It was like carrying a personal expression of art around with you. It was part of my identity. Nothing digital can do that so blatantly.

Rock music was being invented as we grew up – there was little history – so it was intrinsically our culture, by and for us. That's how I saw it. Today, we can all dine at the groaning table of fifty years of popular music and feast on it to our hearts' content without any effort at all. I doubt kids feel quite so close to it as a culture as I did, even accepting that bands like the Foo Fighters and White Stripes are every bit as powerful and compulsive as anything I grew up listening to.

And football can claim to have experienced the same overload, as it's become a seven-days-a-week event. There are hundreds of websites to visit and you can express your opinion on them and be sworn at by complete strangers. What fun. You can see clips from football all over the world on YouTube and research the history of the game if you are so inclined. There's never been more information available at our fingertips. The question is, has this proliferation bound people more closely to football or is it making the ties looser?

The average age of a Premier League crowd is now in the early forties. As I said earlier, kids don't go in the large numbers they once did because it's too expensive and, perhaps, some parents don't want them in what they might perceive as a dangerous environment. It's often said that parents are over-protective of children because dangers, however remote, are amplified by our tabloid culture and many can't distinguish between media hyperbole and reality. We didn't have any such inhibitions. The fact that if you were not careful you'd get a kicking was a given in everyday life. It might also be true that some kids experience life through the TV more than we ever had a chance to.

Football at the highest level, though not further down the pyramid, is sold to the public in a way it never used to be. In fact, when I was growing up, football wasn't marketed at all. You had to get a season ticket or look in the paper to see what games were on and that was about it. There was no hype.

I suspect this makes many kids and young adults treat football as less of a personal, local cultural thing and more as a part of the entertainment industry. Every big game is advertised like a new movie, complete with high-octane trailer. There's no doubt that the sense of loyalty to your local team has been diminished, though far from erased – not yet anyway.

Personally I've always been hardline about the club you should support. This is how it should work. You support the nearest club to where you were born or where you are growing up. If, like me, you were born in Hull and grew up on Teesside, then there should be no supporting of more successful sides such as Arsenal or Manchester United. No. You're stuck with Hull or Middlesbrough and you should be proud of it. When I arrived on Teesside aged eight, I measured the distance from my house to Ayresome Park and to Darlington's ground, Feethams. Boro was four miles away, Darlo seven, so that was it, I had to support Middlesbrough: it never even occurred to me to be a fan of some distant team in Manchester, Merseyside or London.

These things should be set in your personal culture before you are a teenager. If you subsequently move, you take your original allegiance with you. Even if your parents support another club, perhaps the one of their birthplace, it should make no difference to you as a kid. You support the side local to you when growing up.

Even when I moved to Edinburgh the way I worked out who to go and watch was decided entirely by the distance between my flat and Hibs' and Hearts' grounds. Hibs' was nearer, so I chose them. Simple.

This is a hopelessly old-fashioned notion, of course, and even in my youth, some kids would support Leeds just because they were more successful, but they were always sneered at as plastic fans by the rest of us. The reason I feel this local element is important is that I don't see football as a leisure activity purchase. I see it as part of the local civic structure and thus the fans as part of that culture. If everyone just supports anyone, the game as a whole becomes more homogeneous and less interesting. It also makes it very hard for many smaller clubs to survive if the bigger clubs suck in all the support and the money.

Society is going that way, though. Every High Street in the country looks pretty similar today, with small independent shops being pushed out by the big multi-nationals who are the only companies that can afford the ludicrously high rents. Even the advertising at games has become part of this. Whereas it used to be signs for the local butcher or garage, now it's all Budweiser, Ford or some other huge company, at least in the Premier League. Individuality is being replaced with corporate conformity and pretty much everyone seems happy enough to go along with it, even though, if you asked them, they'd say it was a bad thing.

However, the urge to do anything about it is very weak or non-existent. In just the same way, fans will not boycott their club if it's being run badly or by people they don't like. If Manchester United fans don't like the Glazers running their club, they could close it down within weeks by staying away en masse. The people have the power, but only as a collective and, for some reason, people are loath to act en masse in the UK, which is probably why we've never had a revolution. The British will moan on about how crap things are rather than actually go out of their way to do something about it. It's not one of our most attractive national characteristics.

However, as you get down the leagues, things revert to what I like to think of as normal. Go to a place such as Hartlepool United or York City and this big-business culture is almost wholly absent. And these clubs still get reasonable crowds of several thousand. This is the roots of football, the bedrock upon which all the insanity of the Premier League is built. If and when the Premier League implodes due to debt, bankruptcy or corruption, it will be these roots and those that support them with their ticket money which will sustain the game in the long run.

I think many of my age feel that football is now at least two different games. There's the Premier League and Champions League game and then there's the rest. In some ways this is the best of both worlds. We can have the old-school culture of local football as we have always known it but on top of that we can have the hyper-ventilating, over-the-top money soap opera of the top flight.

The more reactionary people in society see modern footballers as setting an awful example to kids, pointing to those who seem to see sex as a team sport to be played in a five-star hotel room with some damaged bimbo. They see the flash lifestyle and the ego that goes with it and think it sets a bad example. I think this is far too simplistic a way of seeing the world.

You can't foist being a role model on to a player and say, sorry pal, everyone looks up to you now so you'd better behave. If you take money from the media or advertising for being a family man, all the while getting blown by hookers in your local Harvester, then fair enough, you'll deserve a savaging for being a hypocrite. But most footballers are just regular blokes who never expected to have to be looked up to and it's unfair to dump that on them. Most of them also do a lot of work in local communities with kids and raise money for charities too. You never see that in the papers. Most of them are regular, if often culturally narrow, under-educated people.

I also don't buy the idea that kids are so hypnotised by players that if one of them is caught roasting a woman in a Marriott hotel with five of his mates the kid will go out and do the same. The only thing kids copy is stuff like goal celebrations, which is harmless enough, as long as it doesn't involve exploitative sexual practices with a corner flag.

And anyway, if your kids are taking their lead in life from Steven Gerrard or David Beckham or whoever, then surely you're not doing your parenting job properly. But even if that is the case, as it was in my life, it still doesn't mean a kid will ape the worst of players' behaviour any more than they will inevitably copy the best. The human psyche is more complex than that and as a kid you're influenced by a myriad of things for both good and bad. You're like a beer mat soaking up the spillage of life.

Kids seek out those who inspire them, they're not inspired by anyone just because they're on TV. Going back to my own history, when I saw Cloughie, he inspired me, but Derek Dougan, who was often on with him, didn't. You take your influences where and when you find them. You can't prescribe them. Just because a footballer is on TV flogging a product won't make kids buy it if they don't already have a bond with the player in some way and, even then, kids, unlike most adults, are not sheep. They often question stuff more than their parents do. I certainly did.

I was inspired by the mercurial genius of the likes of George Best, Alan Hudson, Denis Law, Rodney Marsh, Stan Bowles and Charlie George. I knew from an early age that these men were different. They were the players who illuminated the dark winter afternoons. While the meat-and-potatoes journeymen were important, they were not my inspiration. The solid, dependable types didn't seem attractive at all to me. While others got frustrated at the creative players when they tried outrageous tricks which didn't come off, early on, I spotted that it was the very lifeblood of the game and of life itself. Trying to do things differently was obviously not the easy path – Bestie proved that – but it looked and felt much the more satisfying route to take. If I was ten years old now, would I feel the same way? There are simply not those kinds of characters around these days. Brilliant unpredictable individuality has been sacrificed for seven-out-of-ten consistency. Intense exposure has made the flash, egotistic players such as Ronaldo seem unbearable whereas, in a previous generation, he'd just be judged much more by his football. In this era he's judged by everything else as well, up to and including his facial expressions, attitudes and the colour of his boots.

The game has fewer characters than it ever did previously, perhaps because the need for intense collective conformity has never been greater in football and in society as a whole. The intense scrutiny of the modern world makes people cautious and conservative. Players can't hide anywhere any more. Wherever you go and whatever you do, some sod will be taking a photo of you on their phone or filming you and flogging it to the tabloids for a couple of hundred quid. Everyone is a grass these days. Everyone is part of the paparazzi. Time was no one would grass up a footballer who was out on the lash or seen with his hand up a blonde's dress. These days it'd be a headline news with comments on his hand technique from a sex therapist.

It forces players to retreat even further from the public gaze in order to get some privacy. If only the public could stop wetting themselves, pandering, fawning or wanting to fight someone just because they're famous, it would be a saner world. But with the current trend for adults to behave like hysterical teenagers, that doesn't seem likely.

The imperative in modern broadcast media and football is not to offend anyone. It's childish. So what if someone expresses a view in a manner you don't like? Deal with it. No fucking swearing, no harsh criticism, everything tame; why is that a good thing? Some people are way too precious and seem to think being offended is some sort of infringement of their civil liberties and ought to be outlawed. Worse still, too many in positions of power agree with them.

But surely the important human right, if there is one here, is the right to be offensive; it's the basic right of free speech. Outside of incitement to hatred and outright libel, you should be able to say stuff that annoys, aggravates and offends in the media without worrying that some greasy lawyer is going to sue you on behalf of an individual or pressure group with wounded pride. In this environment the likes of Big Mal and Cloughie would never be out of the courts.

I see this as all essentially part of the infantilisation of modern British culture. In all walks of life, but especially on the TV and radio, we're talked down to as if we're stupid, simple or six years old.

The FA stops managers from talking about the game their teams have just played in too critical a fashion, calling it bringing the game into disrepute if they say a referee was wrong or officiated poorly. This is nonsense and, in a bitter irony, actually does bring the game into disrepute. Let people say what they want and we'll be the judge of the veracity of their words. If they're wrong or silly, so be it, but why the denial of free speech?

So everyone has to keep their head down for fear of being painted as a monster in the press. I'm not fan of John Terry but the acres of press coverage of what, if we are to believe the stories, was a bog-standard affair, were out of all proportion. The way it was covered, you'd have thought he had been caught selling enriched uranium to Iran.

Such characters as Shankly and Clough, I now realise, were vicarious authority figures to me. That might sound quite fanciful but it was how I looked at them. I often used to wish that Shanks was my dad. He seemed so thoughtful, so organised and sure about what was the best path to take through life and how to conduct yourself. He had an innate morality and purpose, guided by a political outlook.

By contrast I looked up to no authority figures at home or at school, which is why Shanks and Cloughie were so important to me. They were adults I could somehow trust for advice when I was most adrift on the ocean of life – along with the lyrics and music that I was obsessed with.

From my early teens I was largely left to get on with my life the best I could. There was no guidance, little advice from my parents. I suspected then, and am sure now, that they were out of their depth with a modern teenage boy. They didn't know what to do with me or how to handle me. Understandable really; I was a smart-arse teenager, full of myself, certain I was always right, convinced by the time I was fourteen that I was already more educated and wiser than they were and not shy of telling them that.

At the time I thought the freedom I had was good thing. I could stay out as long as I wanted, go to pubs from fifteen onwards and there was no one saying I couldn't. But of course, all kids need some guidance, some sort of help to understand what's going on. It's such a volatile, crazy time of life as you change from being a boy to a man, though some would say I've not quite made that change yet.

As in many 1970s comprehensive schools teachers were more concerned with getting through the day than with educating us. It wasn't the worse schooling you could have, but it was a long way from being good. You were pretty much left to educate and motivate yourself with little help from those paid to teach you. I bet it's not changed that much.

In among the disaffected and the lazy teachers were a few psychos who ruled classes by fear and intimidation. Our deputy headmaster was like that. He would stalk the corridors looking for children to pick on and preferably to viciously cane. In hindsight I believe he got his kicks from hurting children and he got away with it for years. We didn't know about such things at the time and saw it all as part of normal life.

Any sentient creature would have realised how pointless caning children was after a few short months because it was the same kids who got caned every week. Caned for smoking, or running in the corridors, cheeking a teacher or whatever it was. The same hard core returned to take their punishment. So obviously, the caning wasn't working. It wasn't a deterrent from errant behaviour, which was surely the point. It became a punishment that the kids grew accustomed to. You could do what you wanted as long as you were prepared to take the beatings from the deputy head. Thus the rule of law was totally undermined by the very discipline which was supposed to control behaviour.

By my fifth year, those who took the canings not only didn't respect him, they laughed at him and it all came to a head one early-summer day. One lad, a big bastard who had a beard by the time he was fifteen and had been a target of this bloke's cane for fully five years, was called into the deputy head's office. When he produced the cane, the kid, now much bigger and stronger than his erstwhile assailant, grabbed it off him, snapped the willow into two pieces and proceeded to whack the bloke about the head with it. Sadly, none of us got to see this as it all happened behind closed doors, but for that day, possibly for the only time in his life as he was later to go to jail, the lad was a hero to us all.

Aggression, both between kids and between the teachers and kids, was daily routine. We had a teacher who threw blackboard rubbers at your head; if they connected they would split your head open. Another would pick you up by your hair. We had a French teacher who was assaulted with a dildo. Not sexually assaulted, just plain assaulted, beaten around the head with a twelve-inch veiny rubber cock by a kid who must have been out his mind one way or another.

We even had a Rural Science teacher – always a doss job who pinned boys to the ground with a two-pronged fork across the neck for being cheeky. Actually that was very funny.

As I witnessed this kind of daily drip drip drip of brutality, it instilled, in me at least, an innate mistrust of authority. It made me suspicious of anyone who wanted power and ultimately it made me want to live a life where no one had authority over me. Hence, I never wanted to get a job working for anyone else. Naturally, when you grow up with the only authority figures in your life being people with no innate authority but who use their position to exert power over those who otherwise would not respect them, you search out others to fill that role, which was where the culture of football and rock 'n' roll came in.

For kids who are going through similar experiences in the twenty-first century, I wonder where they find the positive influences they need to drag themselves upwards to a better life. Is it from some vaguely ludicrous rapper called, quite possibly, Ludicrous? Is it from the wit and wisdom of the magnificent Mourinho? The trouble is, TV has elevated everyone to such heights of glamour that they do not seem to live a life that is in any way connected to regular life. Shankly looked and talked like a regular working-class man. He didn't seem aloof in the way Mourinho does. He wasn't super-rich and led a life similar to those who went to see his teams play. We can't say this any more so it wouldn't be surprising if this meant kids do not have a direct connection to them the way we did to our heroes. They might admire their fame, talent and money, but that's not the same thing as being inspired by them.

I took so much from the bands, musicians, footballers and managers of my youth because I didn't have any people in 'real' life who offered any example or guidance apart from one teacher.

Importantly, I had a Form, Maths and Games teacher called Gary Hanrahan who was progressive enough to take a bunch of us to see Eric Clapton and Barclay James Harvest at Newcastle City Hall in the school minibus when we were in the fifth year. He was a decent sort. He let us drink beer in the minibus on the way up there, even cracking a few himself while behind the wheel.

Uniquely, he treated me like a young man rather than as a daft kid. A massive bloke, built like a prop forward, he had a physical authority but also, by virtue of his attitude, a moral authority too. He got under your skin by believing in you and so you ended up not wanting to let him down and thus worked harder.

Somehow, I'd got into the rugby side as a winger and Gary, a decent amateur player, was our coach. Once during a match on a snow-strewn pitch on a Saturday morning, I received the ball wide on the left, side-stepped one player and was promptly hammered by an on-rushing forward. I hit the deck and blacked out. The next thing I am conscious of is Gary leaning over me shouting 'Nicholson?! Can you hear me?' I responded that I could. He helped me to my feet and looked in my eyes. 'Can you walk Nic?' I was dazed but managed a few paces. 'Aye, good lad, you're fine, you'll run it off, you've got the beating of their winger,' he said and slapped me hard on the back.

I probably actually had concussion, but what the fuck, there was no harm done. I was young, fit and strong, so I got on with it, keen not to show Gary any weakness. He was like that in class too. I'm sure his forceful personality helped me learn more and at a faster rate because I wanted to please him and show him I had talent. He was the only teacher in all my years that did that; indeed, outside of those vicarious authority figures in football, he was the only person in my life to do so.

From him I learned to be mentally stronger, to not let knock-backs stop you and also, most importantly, self-belief. His approach was to assume you'd be good at whatever challenge you were set. Again no one ever said to me that they thought I could do anything, so this level of belief in me was totally without precedent and I really responded to it. I was never as good as he assumed I would be at maths or rugby, but I was better than I would have been without his encouragement.

Are there teachers who can fill that role today? I hope so.

Football continues to be part of the glue that holds society together. It unites people and provides a universal language to connect with strangers over. As I said earlier, if you get stuck at a party with someone who you have nothing else in common with, if they follow football, you are unlikely ever to lack something to talk about. In an increasingly fractured society, this element has never been more important. We live increasingly isolated lives outside of traditional communities. Football is an echo of the tight-knit society where there were common causes and common problems. In that sense football helps us stay in touch with our more social communal selves.

The trouble is that the Premier League has become so predictable that it's not really a proper competition any more. The 2009–10 season ended up as a battle between Chelsea and Manchester United for the title. It's now fifteen years since anyone other than those two clubs or Arsenal won the league. Fifteen years!

A whole generation of kids has grown up with this being the norm. The same clubs winning the league year after year, the same clubs in contention. By the time I was eighteen, eleven different clubs had won the First Division, as it then was. This year, kids born in 1992 come of age along with the Premier League and have in all that time seen just four teams win it.

In the same period in Germany and France there have been seven winners, in Italy and Spain, five. So clearly, this constriction of potential winners isn't confined to England, but crucially there are some signs that in at least a few countries, it's changing. In Holland, FCTwente, managed brilliantly by Steve McClaren, have won the league this year – that's like Birmingham or maybe Sunderland winning the Premier League. That would never happen here. Last year in Germany unfancied Wolfsburg won the title. In France, Marseille are set to win it for the first time since 1992.

But it's not just the fact that the eventual winners are so predictable – it's that the challengers are too. In the last fifteen years since Blackburn won the title, the top three has comprised just Manchester United, Liverpool, Arsenal, Chelsea and (three times), Newcastle and (one time only), Leeds. That's just six clubs in the top three in fifteen bloody years, man! Forty-five positions filled by just six teams. Call that a competition? It's got less and less like a competition every year and more and more like a cartel.

If it doesn't change I would love to kick United, Chelsea and Arsenal out of the Premier League, put them in to a European super league with all the other teams who choke the competition in their domestic leagues. Overnight we'd get a fantastic European league of the best sides and a vibrant, competitive domestic league where the winners might be different every year. Is that so wrong? People say it would reduce the league's credibility, but what credibility does it have when the same teams win it every year? I'd argue less and less. But football fans are quite reactionary and don't like change. It seems most of them would rather have the traditional set-up judging by the ruthless abuse I receive whenever I mention a European super league. So be it.

All I want out of football is a good time. I want excitement, aggression, skill and laughter. I'm not bothered about watching the biggest or best league, however you might judge that, I just want to have a good time, and seeing Chelsea and Manchester United power their way to titles season after season is becoming tedious. If it doesn't change in the next few seasons, I'm sure something will have to be done about it. I like to think I'm ahead of the curve rather than miles away from it, lying on the floor drunk, which would be probably nearer the truth.

Thankfully, the Premier League is not the only show in town, even though many with a vested interest have brainwashed some into thinking it is. Mind you, I still watch every game and I still enjoy the football, so maybe I'm just being unnecessarily arsy and altruistic about it all. See how even-handed I was there? Very out of character that. I must be mellowing in my old age.

Anyway, as I said in the introduction to this book, moaning about football is one of the very best things about the game as I have just proved.

The bottom line is that the game is still brilliant. It still has the capacity to thrill and amaze. As I started writing this chapter, Wigan were playing Arsenal in the Premier League, and with ten minutes left Wigan were 2–0 down, the game was dull, with little atmosphere and seemed to be a desultory match which Arsenal were bound to win. But then Wigan scored three goals in the last ten minutes and won.

Amazing. The game was transformed in such a short space of time! In such results the endless fascination and hope of the game resides. We all know such things can occasionally happen and that knowledge keeps everyone coming back for more.

Football continues to dominate British culture and it still reflects the nature of the society that it exists in better than any other sport. We continue to crave it in huge numbers, possibly because it somehow informs us about the world we live in while at the same time entertaining us and providing a social and internal structure to our lives.

It is a big-tent philosophy and welcomes in anyone and everyone, no matter who you support or even if you don't support anyone. You can hold any point of view and you are free to love, hate or be indifferent about the players, referees, managers, other fans, the pitch, the ball, the strip, the pies, everything. Unlike almost any other sport, there is no orthodoxy to adhere to if you don't want to.

And at the end of the day, Brian, that's the unique thing about the game: the huge culture and lifestyle that surrounds it is all-encompassing. It got under the British skin like nothing else before or since, and its combination of tribal loyalty and unpredictable action has proved compulsive.

So while football doesn't *really* matter – it is just a game – it somehow has significance for millions of people, and sometimes it matters far too much. Football is many people's whole world; it is their routine, their obsession, their best friend. If it could be their lover it would be. It has filled up lives for over 130 years and will continue to do so, a never-ending story, a world without end.

It is reliable and yet unpredictable and, like all the best relationships, can deliver utter joy and desperate heartache. To the true believers nothing else can do this in quite the same comprehensive, visceral manner. Many have called it a drug, an addiction. It may well be, but it's one we never have to go into cold turkey to kick because there is never a shortage. We have a good dealer who keeps us well supplied. It will continue to keep me and all the other millions of followers hypnotised.

So yes, we all ate all the pies, both literally and metaphorically. We have eaten up as much as football as possible and in return football has consumed us completely. And we love it.

Index

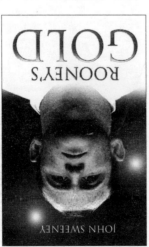